Trading with China
A practical guide

This is a comprehensive and practical guide to all aspects of trading with the People's Republic of China — a country with a population of 1 billion and with a market which is potentially enormous, but about which relatively little is known.

Written by international experts with many years' experience of China, this book fills a large gap in the available literature.

It is a short cut to detailed, practical information on:

* How to research and enter the China market
* How to negotiate deals
* China's legal system
* How China finances trade
* Shipping and insurance
* Joint ventures and compensation trading
* How to receive a Chinese delegation

Enough information is given on problems and unusual features of trade with China to enable you to ask the right questions and get the answers you need.

Enough background detail is provided to allow you to assess the likely value of trade with China to your organization.

Selling to China, always competitive, is likely to become more so in the near future. The more understanding of Chinese practices you bring to your contacts, the more likely you are to pull off a satisfactory deal.

The genesis of this book was a series of missions of top ranking industrialists to China, jointly sponsored by *The Times* and Business Perspectives. It sums up the experience of traders in the UK, Europe, the USA, and Japan. Guidance is given on visiting China and useful names and addresses are provided.

This is a storehouse of professional information that would otherwise be near impossible to come by.

Trading with China

A practical guide

Edited by

Colina MacDougall

McGRAW-HILL Book Company (UK) Limited in
association with BUSINESS PERSPECTIVES Limited

London • New York • St Louis • San Francisco • Auckland • Bogotá
Guatemala • Hamburg • Johannesburg • Lisbon • Madrid • Mexico
Montreal • New Delhi • Panama • Paris • San Juan • São Paulo • Singapore
Sydney • Tokyo • Toronto

Published by
McGraw-Hill Book Company (UK) Limited
MAIDENHEAD • BERKSHIRE • ENGLAND
in association with
BUSINESS PERSPECTIVES Limited
LONDON • ENGLAND

British Library Cataloguing in Publication Data
Trading with China.
1. China – Commerce
2. East-West trade (1945–)
I. MacDougall, Colina
382′.09171′3051   HF3837   79-41272

ISBN 0-07-084531-X

12345 PP 83210

PRINTED IN GREAT BRITAIN AT THE CAMBRIDGE UNIVERSITY PRESS, CAMBRIDGE

Contents

Contributors

Colina MacDougall, who has edited and contributed to this book, has written on China for the *Financial Times* since 1970 and before that spent 10 years in Hongkong as assistant editor of the *Far Eastern Economic Review*. She was educated at Edinburgh University and subsequently worked at the Royal Institute of International Affairs. She has visited China several times.

Stephen Biller is Counsellor in the European Parliament for the Political Affairs Committee and the Committee for Energy and Research, with special responsibilities inter alia for European Community relations with China. He was First Secretary-Commercial at the British Embassy in Bonn. He has also worked for Joseph Lucas Ltd.

A. H. Cave, MBE is President of Biddle Sawyer & Co. Ltd, one of the major international trading companies doing substantial business with China. He has visited China almost annually since 1954 and attended the first Canton Fair in 1956. Mr Cave is a Director of Lewis & Peat Ltd, and commercial adviser to the Guinness Peat Group of Companies.

Michael L. Emmons is Tax Partner of Arthur Andersen & Co. Until early 1979 he was based at their Hongkong office as head of the Tax Division where he worked with clients extensively on China matters. In 1978, he was President of the Hongkong American Chamber of Commerce and in that capacity participated in several Canton Trade Fairs.

Nellie K. M. Fong is Senior Tax Partner of the Hongkong office of Arthur Andersen & Co., and has had considerable experience working with clients involved in trade with China. She is a chartered accountant.

Margaret van Hattem is currently Brussels Correspondent of the *Financial Times* specializing in third world development and the EEC agricultural policy. Before this, she specialized in Asian economic affairs and travelled extensively in South and South-East Asia.

Christopher Howe is reader in economics with reference to Asia at London University. After working for the CBI he joined the School of Oriental and African Studies to study Chinese, and later Japanese, economic affairs. He was Head of the Contemporary China Institute from 1972 to 1978 and has visited China several times. He is the author of various articles and four books, of which the most recent is *China's Economy: A Basic Guide* (Elek, London, 1978).

A. Lagopus is an insurance expert with a well-known company who has specialized in the China field.

Stanley B. Lubman is a member of the law firm Heller, Ehrman, White & McAuliffe of San Francisco and Hongkong. He specialized in Chinese affairs and from 1967 to 1972 was a professor at the School of Law of the University of California, Berkeley. He has also taught as Visiting Lecturer at the Yale Law School. Since 1972 he has been advising clients on trade with the People's Republic of China, which he has visited frequently.

Nicholas H. Ludlow, a specialist in Asian business affairs, joined the National Council for US-China Trade in the autumn of 1973, and established the Council's magazine, the *China Business Review*, which he continues to edit. He organized and escorted the Council's first industrial delegation to China in 1976, and, more recently, organized and accompanied the National Council's Construction Equipment Delegation to China.

C. M. O'Connor was Managing Director of the Blue Funnel and Glen Lines of Ocean Transport & Trading Limited and, following his retirement, is now a shipping consultant. He has had 30 years of experience in Chinese maritime affairs and has visited China. These shipping companies have been associated with the China trade for many years.

Ian Rae is Managing Director, China Translation and Printing Services Ltd, Hongkong. This company specializes in the translation into Chinese and full production of literature aimed at China, including advice on how to approach the market. He holds first-class interpreterships in both Mandarin and Cantonese and a BA Honours degree in Chinese from London University. He has been involved in China trade since 1961 and has travelled widely in China. He also advises on foreign exhibitions in Peking.

Charles Smith is currently Far East Editor of the *Financial Times*, based in Tokyo. He writes extensively on the Japan–China trade for his newspaper and has also written many articles on China's foreign trade and foreign relations. He has visited China about eight times over the past 12 years.

Philip Snow graduated from Oxford with a first-class degree in Chinese in 1975. From 1976 to 1979 he worked for the Sino-British Trade Council in London. He helped to organize the visits to Britain of many technical and commercial delegations from China and accompanied them during their tours. He has visited China five times, mainly with UK trade missions and exhibitions. In November 1979 he joined The First National Bank of Chicago.

Nicolas Wolfers is an Assistant Director in the International Banking and Finance Division of merchant bankers Samuel Montagu & Co. Ltd, a subsidiary of the Midland Bank group. He is a member of various CBI committees and of the Monetary Commission of the International Chamber of Commerce.

Introduction

COLINA MacDOUGALL

Trading with the Chinese is difficult, even for the initiated. Not only is there the difference in organization of trade that exists between a planned and a market economy, but also there is a host of other dissimilarities which arise from the gulf between the cultures of east and west. On top of that there are the unique practices evolved by the Chinese since 1949.

For the foreign businessman, accustomed to western commercial practices and confronted with the problems of making his product known to the Chinese, meeting potential end-users, discussing prices, making contracts, arranging shipping and payment, all in the teeth of competition, selling to the Chinese is hard work. Even buying from them can be difficult, since their economic ups and downs and limited knowledge of the outside world often mean commodity shortages and products unsuited to a western market.

The idea for this book sprang from the lack of easily available practical information which became evident during a series of missions to Peking and conferences on China jointly sponsored by Business Perspectives with *The Times*. It should help to illuminate some of the problems confronted by even the very experienced China hand.

The chapters on the practical aspects of trade have been contributed by highly professional people, well established in their fields and with scores of years of experience between them, while the historical background and regional surveys have been written by longstanding observers of the political, economic, and trade scene. I am extremely grateful to the contributors for putting other work aside at what was a very busy time to enable this book to be completed.

Thorough briefing for the would-be China trader is even more important now because selling to China, always competitive, is likely to become more so in the near future. Constraints on China's trade will be tight. The most obvious of these is the scarcity of foreign exchange with which to pay for imports. Although reconciled to the idea of credit, once ideologically suspect, the Chinese are unwilling to shoulder any debts they feel they cannot easily pay off.

As important as the question of foreign exchange are the problems of inadequate infrastructure and shortage of trained manpower. At present the Chinese harbour and transport system can hardly handle its current load. Its capacity can be raised, but at a steady rate rather than a leap. As for manpower, the political intervention in education since the Cultural Revolution has meant a serious shortage of educated technocrats.

But although these are real problems, they are not insoluble. With careful planning, judicious expenditure and good administration, the Chinese should be able to bring them under control. As they build up their own industries, their productivity will rise and along with it their ability to earn foreign exchange. There may be ups and downs in their trade but the trend will be one of significant growth.

Thus China will become an important market for sophisticated industrial goods and technology. The market will be a competitive one, but it will be there. It is hoped that this book will help to alert would-be suppliers to the potential and eliminate some of the initial worries.

Notes

The word 'billion' as used in this book means one thousand million.

The word 'dollars' in this book means US dollars unless otherwise stated.

On 1 January 1979 the New China News Agency (NCNA—Xinhua), began using the Chinese phonetic alphabet (*pinyin*) for the romanization of Chinese personal and place names. Wherever possible this book has followed suit except in the case of the traditional English forms Peking and Canton. New and old spellings of some of the names more frequently encountered are given in Appendix II.

1. Why China needs trade

CHRISTOPHER HOWE

The new strategy

The death of Mao Zedong in September 1976 was the starting point for a surge forward in China's political and economic policies; in particular, there was an acceleration of industrialization, linked to a dramatic widening and deepening of China's economic contacts with the outside world. The Chinese made this plain in a series of speeches by important leaders, in an ever-growing tide of Chinese economic missions abroad, matched by an even greater flow of foreigners invited to Peking, and finally, through soaring foreign trade. Two-way exchanges jumped from around 11–12 per cent per annum in 1973–77, to 28 per cent in 1978, with a further sharp increase in 1979. The pace of change was illustrated by the point that the level of trade widely forecast (in 1978) for 1980, was almost achieved in 1978!

A comprehensive programme

The programme, nicknamed the 'Four Modernizations' (of agriculture, industry, science and technology, and defence) now unfolding in China, in an effort to find a way forward from the difficulties and errors of the past, has two outstanding characteristics: urgency and comprehensiveness. The tone of the press, and even more of officials in touch with foreigners, confirms that the Chinese view their present predicament as serious, even desperate. The improved production of 1976–78 (Table 1.1) gives no ground for confidence, for as the Chinese leader, Chairman Hua Guofeng has pointed out, 'the present progress, we should note, is in the nature of a recovery.'

In spite of this urgency, the behaviour of the Chinese suggests that, as far as possible they intend to avoid the errors of leaping forward too rapidly, or of seeking over-simple solutions to complex problems, problems that have

1

Table 1.1 Rates of growth of key economic indicators 1952–78 and 1978 plan targets for 1985 (per cent per annum)

	I 1952–70	II 1952–60	III 1958/60–70	IV 1970–75	1976	1977	1978	1978–85 (Plan)
Industrial output	11.56	18.34	6.59	9.11	2	14	14	10+
Steel	15.65	22.02	1.43	7.87	−12	4	25	12.14
Crude oil	26.67	37.28	23.39	21.38	13	8	11	unknown
Coal	8.93	19.69	2.52	6.61	5	10	21	7.18
Cotton cloth	4.57	5.85	3.70	2.39	−7	13	unknown	9
Grain	2.31	4.44	1.39	3.17	0	−2	0	4.33

Sources: As cited in Christopher Howe, *China's Economy: A Basic Guide*, Elek, London and Basic Books, New York, 1978, and reports from the National Foreign Assessment Center, Washington. Targets from Hua Guofeng's speech to the Fifth National People's Congress and other contemporary reports.

Notes

1. Data in Column III has been selected to show performance subsequent to the previous *peak* performance, i.e., for steel the peak was 1960, for grain 1958.
2. The 1978–85 Plan refers to targets set in spring 1978. The fulfillment of most of these has been postponed, but it has been affirmed that all the large-scale projects in these targets will at least be *started* before 1985.

congealed in the system over many years. This has been reflected in the 'readjustment' of priorities they embarked on in the spring of 1979.

The new strategy has been spelt out in a series of speeches and articles in the press. The most important clues to the evolution of current thinking are in the following documents:

Chairman Hua's speeches to the Fifth National People's Congress (March 1978 and June 1979), his speech to the National Conference on Finance and Trade (August 1978),
Vice-Premier Yu Qiuli's speech to the Fifth National People's Congress (June 1979),
Vice-Premier Li Xiannian's speech to the National Conference on Capital Construction in Agriculture (August 1978),
Vice-Premier Fang Yi's speech to the National Science Conference (March 1978), and
senior economist Hu Muqiao's article in the *People's Daily* (October 1978).

The article by Hu Muqiao is particularly interesting since it deals with the problems from a very general point of view. In it, Hu argues that comprehensive control planning makes the socialist economic system *potentially superior to capitalism*. But he points out that, in practice, if leadership is incorrect or corrupt, socialism's centralized power becomes a liability since it can lead to chaos. Hu also argues that at the level of the *individual* unit of production, the evidence is that capitalist managerial experience and theory have produced levels of productivity far higher than those achieved in socialist economies. This judgement reflects a complete re-evaluation of the relative merits of socialism and capitalism and since, as Hu argues, the conclusion is that the key to China's economic future lies in correct economic policies, the evolution of a socialist system appropriate to the Chinese situation, and the scrupulous study and application of the most advanced foreign technology and managerial practice, it is clear that the new opening to the West and Japan is a passage for goods and, especially, for the entire culture of modern industrialization. An implication of this is that countries and firms that look most likely to contribute to *the whole package*, will be the more successful in the China market.

Together with Hu, the other statements and plans add up to a programme as radical and far reaching as the policies of the first phase of China's communist development, in which the slogan was 'follow the Soviet example', and, in some senses, as radical as the 'Great Leap Forward' of 1958 during which Mao attempted to find a utopian solution to the contradictions of those early years.

At the general level, an impressive aspect of all these plans is the emphasis on material goals and on pragmatism and science as means of achieving them. Indeed, the central political tasks of socialism have been redefined in these terms.

In March 1977, Chairman Hua stated that in opposing the 'Gang of Four', the Shanghai radicals who fell soon after Mao's death: 'The crux of the struggle was [is] whether to make China a prosperous, modern and powerful country or to reduce it to its former semi-colonial and semi-feudal status,'

Hua went on from this argument to set public targets for 1985—the first such targets for eighteen years. These comprised growth rates for agriculture and industry as sectors, and for grain and steel as commodities (Table 1.1). These targets were modified in the spring of 1979 but the long-term shape of the economy envisaged in current plans has not altered significantly—only the date of realization is postponed.

The Chinese leadership has emphasized that attainment of current targets will require:

1. increased investment and imports of foreign plant,
2. provision of large incentives,
3. establishment of new, vocationally oriented, élitist educational and training programmes, and
4. radical improvements in planning and organization.

Economic plans and priorities
The original investment envisaged by the current, medium-term plan, (i.e., 1978–85), was reported to be 1000 billion yuan (approximately $640 billion). The scale of this may be appreciated by comparing the annual rate implied by this figure—125 billion yuan—with the annual rate achieved during the first Five Year Plan, which was 8.6 billion yuan. Although the spring 1979 retrenchment may have meant a cut in investment, it probably still remains substantial compared with earlier rates.

What are the priorities of the Chinese within the economy? Interestingly enough, there has throughout been widespread recognition that agriculture is still the key. 'If agriculture does not develop faster', stated Chairman Hua, 'there will be no upswing in industry and the economy as a whole, and even if there is a temporary upswing, a decline will follow . . . .' An article in the press described the plans for steel and grain as 'arduous, especially that for agriculture which is considered the more difficult of the two.'

This must, indeed, be true. Since 1974, growth of grain output has at best been erratic. To some extent, this may have reflected truly exceptional weather conditions. It must, however, also reflect technical and agronomic conditions and (emphasized by the Chinese) lack of incentives. To remedy this, the Chinese are proposing, not merely to raise investment in agriculture, but to raise the sector's share of total investment. These funds will partly be used in a new plan for land reclamation—mainly in the north-eastern province of Heilongjiang—and partly for the further mechanization of agriculture, much of which is to be concentrated on state farms, located in a series of strategic grain exporting 'bases'. Hua and other leaders emphasize that none of this will be effective unless incentives are increased, and, accordingly, state purchase prices for grain and other agricultural commodities have been increased.

The official industrial priorities have also been described in outline. The list is predictable, and from Japanese, European, and American sources, we are beginning to get some idea of the details as well. Sectorally, the order is electrical power and basic fuels, raw and semi-finished materials, and the transportation industries. For steel, the original target of 60 million tons published in 1978 has been revised and the focus of effort will be on improving efficiency.

Fuel investment will include a programme to modernize existing coal mines and develop new ones; to continue on and off-shore oil exploration, production development, and transportation; and to build new generating stations with emphasis on hydro and nuclear technology. Transport plans have already got under way with purchases of trucks, and current and future purchases include planes and aero engines.

The foreign role will be crucial and Chinese policy appears to be to allocate specific *sectors* to carefully pre-selected trading partners: steel, mainly to Japan and West Germany; petro-chemicals, to Italy and Japan; transport and nuclear plant, to France; coal mining, to Britain and Germany; and, probably, off-shore oil extractive industries and electronics, to America.

By early 1979, the foreign exchange cost of this package for the period 1978–85 appeared likely to be about $60 billion to $70 billion (at current prices). Of this, over half seems likely to go to Germany and Japan, with shares of the remainder going to France, Italy, and Britain. The scale of future American sales is an interesting question. It is possible that the main areas of success will be agricultural products and certain types of industrial plant. It is rather too late for the Americans to make a major impact in the whole range of basic industries, and in fact, had the Chinese wished for a larger American role, the evidence is that, even without diplomatic relations, they would have been given it.

Tables 1.2 and 1.3 show the present size and distribution of China's trade, and from these one can obtain some conception of what these proposals may mean in future. It seems unlikely that the Chinese will succeed in radically re-structuring their trade—particularly imports—and we may therefore estimate that, if machinery and plant imports are to be $60 billion to $70 billion, *total* imports will have to be at least $120 billion to $140 billion. To achieve this would require a growth of exports of about 11 per cent per annum.

Does the plan make sense?
There are four obstacles that could, potentially, frustrate these plans. These

are:

1. an inability to earn adequate foreign exchange to pay for imports,
2. a lack of domestic capacity to invest on the planned scale, or to absorb new technology of the proposed sophistication,
3. the appearance of inconsistencies in the overall plan, and
4. political instability.

On each of these scores there is ground for some pessimism. It must certainly be borne in mind that the major plans for economic and technical

Table 1.2 The main commodities in China's trade (1977) (percentage shares)

Imports		Exports	
Foodstuffs	17	Agricultural	36
(grain)	(10)	(grain)	(6)
Industrial supplies	65	Extractive	13
Chemicals	12	(oil)	(10)
(Iron and Steel)	22	(minerals and metals)	(2)
Capital goods	18	Manufactures	51
Non-electric	(6)	(textiles, clothing)	(24)
machinery		(chemicals)	(5)
Transport equipment	(9)	Other light	12
		manufactures	
TOTAL VALUE $7 100 million		TOTAL VALUE $7 955 million	

Source
China: Economic Indicators, National Foreign Assessment Center, Washington, December 1978.

Table 1.3 China's top trading partners (1978 percentage shares)

Japan[1]	22
Hongkong[1]	10
West Germany[1]	7
Romania[1]	3
United States[1]	5
VALUE TOTAL TRADE[2]	$20.8 billion

Sources

1. Estimates quoted in *China Business Review*, September/October 1978.
2. *China: Economic Indicators*, NFAC, Washington, 1978.

advance have, in the past, had short lives. Nonetheless, I believe that it may still prove possible to come fairly close to the new targets for 1985.

The foreign exchange problem is one that is exercising a number of the countries selling large-scale plant on deferred payments, and the Chinese themselves have mentioned it. But from 1952 to 1960, for example, China's exports grew at 10.6 per cent compound—a figure only slightly lower than what appears necessary for the next seven years. It is true that China will have problems selling in competitive markets where the importer and the government demand high standards. (The Soviet plant provided in the 1950s was paid for by exports of agricultural products, which the Chinese now need for themselves, and with cotton goods that would be largely unsaleable in world markets today.) The Chinese show every indication that they are aware of this situation, and are making unprecedented efforts to sell manufactured goods in Europe and the United States. Moreover, exports are not the only means the Chinese have to acquire foreign exchange. They are actively developing invisibles (banking, insurance, and tourism) and even direct investment in China by Chinese abroad and others.

The problem of absorptive capacity is more serious. There are likely to be both inter-industry and transport bottlenecks, and also shortages of skilled staff at every stage of the investment process, i.e., from design work to the shop floor. It is true that to meet the latter, the Chinese have taken drastic steps to overhaul their educational and training work, have plans to send about 10 000 students abroad, and have included a training element in many of their foreign contracts. There is, however, a limit to the speed with which the errors of recent years can be corrected, and it is likely that the full benefits of current investment programmes will not, in fact, become available, even at the speed at present envisaged. This is the problem currently referred to as the 'over-extended battle line'.

The consistency of the overall strategy perhaps raises the greatest question mark of all. And here there are two linked problems. First, as in the thirties and the fifties, agriculture may fail to perform adequately. The leadership has said that this sector has priority, but this has yet to be translated into action and the blinding glamour of machines and computers could prove too powerful. It is true that provision already is being made for imports of grain on an unprecedented scale, but unless agriculture picks up its rate of growth, this will not be enough.

This possibility leads us to the second problem: the relationship between investment and consumption. At present, the leadership is promising:

1. a tremendous increase in investment,
2. an increase in consumption, and
3. greater incentives in agriculture and industry.

Reconciling these is likely to prove formidably difficult and to judge by present trends the outcome is likely to be greater inequality around an average income that, at best, will grow slowly. This pattern could generate widespread frustration and social dislocation, since the most obvious bene-ficiaries of the new policies (graduates, cadres, and labour-rich peasant families) are a minority of the population. (A minority, incidentally, from whom most foreigners derive *all* their impressions of the Chinese scene.)

We are thus led to the final question: is China likely to be more stable in the future? One could argue that the disappearance of Mao from the scene has removed the most destabilizing factor in China's modern history. How-ever, it must be remembered that Mao has left behind a factionalism based, not only upon 20 years of bitter, violent conflict, but also on genuinely different perceptions of how China is best developed.

Any setback to the present, ambitious plans could initiate internal struggles in which the radical version of Mao's thinking would be used to rally dissent against current thinking.

The problems of the seventies
The economic problems of the seventies are suggested most dramatically by comparing columns II and III in Table 1.2. Here we can see that looked at from 1970, the growth of industry (exclusive of oil), and agriculture since the peaks of 1959–60 was totally inadequate. Steel and grain, long described by Mao as *the* key commodities, grew at rates lower than the population increase; and coal, which accounted for 76 per cent of total energy con-sumption, grew only slightly faster. Oil and the related chemical fertilizer industry had done much better, reflecting the priority given to them during the sixties. Clearly, however, with population growth still in excess of 2 per cent, this was inadequate. The seriousness of these trends was in the early seventies compounded by two factors. First, the collapse of the Bretton Woods monetary system and the 1973 oil crisis initiated an inflation which, on balance, raised the prices of China's imports above those of her exports. At the same time, there were signs of a shift in the global food balance, which must for the Chinese have raised serious questions as to their ability to remain indefinitely as food importers. Either they had to step up food production to become genuinely self-sufficient, or they had to produce an industrial transformation that would ensure that, if China needed to import food, it could afford to pay the high prices likely to be demanded in the eighties and nineties.

The second development was the crystallization of China's belief that a third world war in which China and the Soviet Union would be on opposing sides was inevitable. Avid students of history, the Chinese began to see their position as analogous to that of the Soviets in the years before the Nazi invasion. Thus, the four modernizations became, more than ever, not merely a question of economic improvement, but one of national survival.

The reasons for China's inability to maintain the rates of growth achieved in the fifties were complex, and accordingly, the remedies which are still being devised are equally so. Western and Chinese analyses, however, have agreed on five problems that can between them account for much of the economic situation between 1970 and 1977:

1. The level of investment has been too low. The central planners rely on local authorities to collect and remit taxes, which are then redistributed according to plan. A statement in 1978 revealed that budgetary income had failed to meet plan targets 'for several years running'.
2. Lack of financial incentives has deadened individual and collective initiative and willingness to work hard. In agriculture, it is reported that in some areas physical intimidation has been common, and the leadership admit that the peasantry have been suffering under the 'eight excess burdens'—notably in the form of compulsory procurement at low prices and forced labour services. As the *People's Daily* put it: 'The heavy and unreasonable burdens on the peasants are, at present, a key problem that should be solved to ensure our high speed development of agriculture.'

   In some senses the industrial situation has been worse. all estimates agree that real incomes in agriculture have risen since 1957, but in industry, overall real wages were held virtually constant from 1957 to 1977, with only minor improvements for the lower paid in 1963 and 1971. This stringency on individual incomes has, it is said, been tempered by incomes from collective funds being potentially available for expenditure on welfare—notably on housing.
3. Lack of incentives has weighed particularly heavily on the higher skilled. Indeed, we know that those in the upper income brackets have in many cases suffered reductions. Only in a few instances have these been direct, but the freezing of promotions to save money has meant that many have been denied the advancement they expected. The financial demoralization of the skilled was compounded for a decade (1966–76) by harassment during and after the Cultural Revolution and irrational and vindictive placement in unsuitable jobs. Finally, not only have the skilled suffered, but their numbers have diminished as a result of the educational changes that came in with the Cultural Revolution. Vice-Premier Deng Xiaoping has described the results of all these trends as 'the greatest crisis' in the contemporary Chinese situation.
4. Owing to the political disruption, the planning system has been in a state of disorder for years. Throughout the seventies, the then Premier Zhou Enlai and Vice-Premier Deng attempted to re-impose on the economy a degree of planning and administrative rationality. They emphasized the role of the centre, reinstated professional administration, and called for the re-introduction of planning norms.... Chinese reports of the past two to three years, however, speak of 'anarchy', 'disorder', and 'chaos', and there is specific evidence that confirms that these words are not mere rhetoric. For example, a purge in the Seventh Ministry of Machine Building revealed a history of 'frameups', 'torture in private prisons', and

a leadership group of whom 80 per cent were 'thugs who intimidated good workers.' The picture that is now emerging of the seventies is worse than even the most pessimistic believed likely at the time.

5. Finally, for many, the most important problem of all has been the lack of contact between China and the outside world. Seven years of self reliance preceded by four of the Cultural Revolution, reduced not only physical contacts and imports of foreign equipment, but led to a situation where, as Chairman Hua put it, 'Many of our colleagues are scarcely aware of what is going on abroad.'

Industrialization and trade: following the Soviet example
The progressive slow down in growth during the sixties and seventies was all the more striking because China made rapid progress when the communists first came to power in 1949. This was stimulated by huge and successful imports of technology from the USSR. Later in the middle sixties, China tentatively began again to import technology (this time from the West).

Both these programmes were cut short by devastating semi-political movements (the Great Leap and the Cultural Revolution). Their economic success (particularly that of the much wider and more prolonged Sino-Soviet relationship) is probably the spur behind present Chinese thinking that foreign technology offers a short cut to modernization. Hence, both are worth a look to see how far they succeeded and why they were cut short.

In the fifties there was widespread confidence, both in China and among outside observers, that it would be possible for Chinese development to emulate the forced industrialization imposed upon the Soviet Union by Stalin, starting in the late twenties, and continuing until his death in 1953. It was believed that, by the establishment of socialist and transitional institutions, China would be able to mobilize resources to initiate a fundamental economic transformation. By socialist institutions, the Chinese at this time meant public ownership, and the administrative machinery necessary to ensure central control of industry, finance, foreign and domestic trade.

This strategy found its fullest expression in China's *first Five Year Plan* (1953–57), which was prepared in 1953 and 1954 under Soviet guidance. The early drafts were extremely ambitious, calling for industrial growth of over 20 per cent per annum. Even the final version, published in 1955, called for 18 per cent per annum. This plan was largely fulfilled by the target date of 1957, and that year marked the end of the first of the three major phases of China's trade policy.

In the Plan, foreign trade and contacts played an extremely important role. Capital equipment imported from the Soviet Union and east European countries was used, both to develop existing industries (iron and steel and mining) and to establish new ones (vehicle manufacture and oil production). The original plans were for a programme costing over $3 billion, to extend for three Five Year Plans, i.e., to 1967. In the early stages (1950–55), short-term credit was given to an estimated value of $430 million. When the break with the Soviet Union came in 1959, the programme was scrapped. By that time deliveries worth $1.3 billion had been made, but all the debts incurred were paid off by 1965.

The Sino–Soviet relationship, however, was not simply a question of capital equipment and credits. Soviet assistance included a complete package of skill transfer aimed, in the first place, at training the Chinese to install, manage, and maintain their new equipment, and in the second, at enabling them to undertake theoretical research and to establish a series of institutions for developing the application of scientific work to the economy. Taken together, the scale of trade and the attempt to provide a complete institutional and intellectual framework for the Chinese, constituted a programme which, at the time, had no parallel. There are some analogies with the Marshall Plan in Europe, but the size and imagination of the Sino–Soviet link made it unique.

It has been estimated that the Sino–Soviet programme was responsible for half the growth of China's national product between 1953 and 1957. In the case of modern industry, if we extend the period to 1960, its significance was much greater. In Table 1.2, we may compare the behaviour of key indicators of the economy in the 'Soviet phase' (1952–60) and subsequently. It will be seen that in these years, the Chinese achieved rates of industrial growth far above the average for the whole period from 1952 to the present. Why then did they cut away from the Soviets, and abandon a long-term plan of trade-based industrialization that appeared to be bearing such brilliant fruits? In the *present* context, this is a question which anyone concerned with China's future policies has to ask.

Part of the explanation lay in Mao's personality, and in the unfolding of strategic, ideological, and even cultural differences between the partners in the enterprise. Mao's role was particularly important for, not only did he despise the post-Stalin Soviet leadership, but he combined a brilliant long-term vision of China's potential with a preference for speed at all costs, and a disastrous belief in the efficacy of institutional reform and intellectual re-moulding (to be conducted by himself) as solutions for almost any problem. This philosophy largely determined the character of the Great Leap Forward in 1958.

The other reasons lay in serious economic difficulties. The flaw in the strategy of the 'Soviet phase' was that it overestimated the ability of agriculture to absorb labour and increase output *without* major investment. The agricultural economy inherited by the communists was complex, labour-intensive, unstable, and poor. Two centuries of relatively rapid population growth had created widespread underemployment and poverty, and over twenty years of civil and anti-Japanese war had disrupted the delicate patterns of work and trade upon which the maintenance and growth of output depended. Between 1949 and 1952, peace and the Land Reform provided incentives and a framework that encouraged the sector to reach the best pre-war levels of performance.

The planners believed that gradual collectivization, and some investment in water control, would enable output of grain and other key crops to achieve rates of growth that by historical standards were high. This proved not to be the case, and the combination of natural disasters and abortive collectivization campaigns—particularly in 1954—led Mao, in 1955, to the view that only an ambitious collectivization drive would solve the problem. This was undertaken during the winter of 1955 but did not have any favourable effects.

The implications of this were far reaching, since the overall economic strategy called for agriculture to provide large export surpluses every year to balance the imports of machinery and equipment. Since the import plan was linked to the *Five Year Plan*, this meant that the impace of any *year-to-year* shortfalls had to fall on consumption. In practice it was the peasants who suffered, not the urban dwellers whose consumption was still governed by relatively generous ratio standards. Further, by 1957 the *trends* of output were so inadequate that procurements for export were becoming progressively under-fulfilled and export contracts were being broken.

In his Great Leap Forward, Mao attempted to break out of the encircling problems created by overambitious plans by setting even more ambitious ones. These, he thought, could be fulfilled if China could only find a strategy—'a way'—uniquely its own, and appropriate to its particular configuration of resources, history, and personality. Domestically, this new strategy involved the mobilization of the population through political education and the creation of new, large, and highly socialized institutions—the People's Communes. Externally, while the Leap could not shatter the patterns of foreign dependence immediately, Mao began to emphasize the need for a form of growth that minimized such dependence, and official policy stated that, in future, the level of imports of industrial goods would be determined by the foreign exchange available *in that year*. No longer, in other words, were imports to be determined by long-term, inflexible industrialization plans.

Although the Great Leap officially ended in 1960–61 (in disaster), the doctrines of self-reliance and the practice of annual planning remained operational throughout the sixties, and were influential up to 1976. Indeed, although the Leap officially ended nearly 20 years ago, as long as Mao was alive its ideas remained important, and the present phase of economic strategy can only be properly understood if it is seen as marking the final extinction of the Leap and of the philosophy that underlay it.

From the end of the Leap to the death of Mao
After the collapse of the Leap, the moderates in the leadership took control and began to rebuild the economy. In the mid-sixties they started to buy plant on a small scale from the West to replace the technology that had previously been available from the Soviet Union. But first they had to feed

the hungry millions whose normal grain supplies had been devastated by the Leap. In the first years of the decade China became a massive food importer (from nil in 1959 to 39 per cent of total imports in 1962), while industrial purchases fell away to almost nothing.

From the aftermath of the Great Leap to the end of the Cultural Revolution

Agriculture gradually recovered and plants abandoned by the Soviets in 1960 were slowly completed. This led to a general economic recovery, which in turn affected trade. By the mid-sixties this was beginning to alter the economic factors that made annual planning and 'self-reliance' rational. At the same time, Liu Shaoqi and Zhou Enlai were aware that, in the world economy, technical progress in chemicals, metallurgy, and electronics was accelerating and that the main beneficiaries of this were countries and organizations engaged in international trade. Liu, in particular, recognized the significance of electronics, and argued that China, having missed the first, could not afford to miss what he was reported as describing as the 'second industrial revolution'.

Thus, between 1963 and 1965, China began to show interest in importing foreign technology from European and Japanese suppliers. The link with Japan was very significant. For, although Europe at this time clearly led the way in whole plant sales, it appears that after the Soviet break, Zhou turned directly to Japan for other goods. Throughout the sixties trade grew exceptionally fast, paving the way for Japan's domination of trade with China after the resumption of full diplomatic relations in 1972.

At the Third National People's Congress in December 1964, Zhou summed up his programme for China in a speech in which he argued that China must achieve 'Four Modernizations' (of agriculture, industry, defence, science and technology). Zhou's programme emphasized that foreign technology was indispensable, and during the first half of 1965 the planners continued to work on a third Five Year Plan (1965–70) in which imported plant was to play a role.

The beneficial effects of this policy fostered the economy. But, for political reasons, Mao, who had virtually been shelved by the rest of the leadership at the end of the Leap, began to build up opposition to the new pragmatism. This culminated in the 1966–69 outburst against party, administrative, economic, and cultural authority—the Cultural Revolution. It overwhelmed industry, agriculture, government, and education and banished from view almost all China's economists and planners.

Trade suffered badly. Japanese and European businessmen were physically assaulted, framed, and gaoled; disruption in factories led to the suspension of export production; and the creation of diplomatic disputes with 32 countries by autumn 1967 put the clock back on economic diplomacy by several years. It is a tribute to Chinese resilience and flexibility that, by 1970, Zhou was ready to re-launch China on the path of development he had mapped out in the sixties. The difference, however, was that whereas in 1964 Zhou had hoped for a smooth transition to the new policy, by 1970 the need for change had become urgent.

But it was not until both he and Mao were dead that moderate Chinese leaders were able to reduce radical influence by arresting the 'Gang of Four' and restoring the technocrats. They were then able to revert to contemplating the import of sophisticated technology on a large scale.

The economic and political problems in Peking's new departure have caused some anxiety in the West about China's reliability as a trading partner. But as trading partners looking at China, it is all too easy to forget the instability in the non-Chinese world which the Chinese must view with some apprehension. Europe and Japan both have problems, but above all the United States, with its decaying basic industries, depreciating currency, and weak central government, cannot look too attractive as a long-term trading partner.

Conclusion

The best approach to Peking's present policies is, probably, to ignore precise Chinese figures and to regard current plans for China's economic future as statements of general intent: to accelerate industrialization and to bring China into a world-wide framework of trading, scientific, and political relationships. This venture, if pursued, will be without parallel in Chinese history, and western reactions to it should be positive in every way. Although in early 1979 Peking became relatively cautious in its planning we should still be prepared for a more difficult passage to the year 2000 than anything envisaged in contemporary Chinese statements.

2. A guide to market information on China

NICHOLAS H. LUDLOW

The needs of the Chinese have always fascinated western entrepreneurs, even in the days when the Chinese population was 400 million or less. The inch to the hem of every Chinese shirt, the kerosene lamp in every home, the pack of cigarettes in every pocket were dreams western salesmen once peddled daily in Shanghai.

Things have changed. In 1979, with China's population probably around one billion,[1] the emphasis has swung, not so much to the idea of a billion non-returnable Coca-Cola bottles a day or an aspirin for each Chinese, but to a logistical problem: with a population almost five times that of the United States and almost twenty times that of Britain, what potential gains in technology systems development does China represent?

The Chinese market is primarily one for heavy industrial goods, plant and technology, grain and commodities. While Coca-Cola, Kent and Marlborough cigarettes, Seagram's whisky and other foreign consumer goods have been bought by the People's Republic, these purchases have been mainly for foreign tourists, 100 000 of whom visited China in 1978. As China's Minister of Science and Technology, Fang Yi, stated on his visit to the United States in February 1979: 'We Chinese prefer to drink tea'.

The least romantic aspect of the China trade is its size. With 25 per cent of the world's population, China only has about 1 per cent of the world's trade. In 1978, Peking imported just over $10 billion worth of goods from everywhere including the Soviet Union and eastern Europe. At $20 billion, China's total trade in 1978 was less than Norway's or Denmark's. By contrast, in the same year the US imported $183 billion worth of goods.

1. At the National People's Congress in June 1979 a new population figure of 970 million (including Taiwan) was announced.

But China is definitely a worthwhile and profitable market, characterized by a system that centralizes its large purchases far more than does the Soviet Union. One organization is responsible for most plant purchases, another for agricultural purchases—so that when China buys, the individual contracts are often sizeable.

Some of the bigger contracts that have been signed by the Chinese with foreign firms in the seventies include a $250 million steel processing complex from Germany's Demag-Schloemann, a $282 million petrochemical complex from Technip-Speichim in France, $125 million worth of Boeing 707s and $156 million worth of 747s, a $190 million licensing pact with Rolls-Royce, eight ammonia plants costing $205 million from Pullman Kellogg in the USA and more recently a $2 billion steel works near Shanghai sold by Japan's Nippon Steel. In the 1971–75 period China bought almost $3 billion worth of foreign plant and equipment. In 1978 alone it contracted for $7 billion worth.

More research on China has been done in the US than anywhere else, probably more than in the Soviet Union. Even before trade became a factor, the political importance of China as a major communist and Pacific power meant that considerable resources of talent, time, and money were devoted to the study of its politics and economics. As a result, US government departments and universities have a long history of research on China and excellent collections of Chinese materials. This explains why much of the reading matter recommended here is American in origin.

Why seek market information on China?
The reasons for seeking market information on the People's Republic of China (PRC) are becoming more compelling:

–The Chinese market is growing. In the fourth Five-Year Plan period (1971–75) China's trade rose over 250 per cent in current terms. It shot up from a mere $4.3 billion in 1970 to $21.3 billion in 1978, and promises to continue to rise substantially up to 1985.

–In a purely commercial sense, a company should prepare as thoroughly for doing business with China as it would for any other major foreign market such as Japan or West Germany. In establishing one's commercial strategy one should not be captivated by the romance of a trip to Peking, the Great Wall and the Forbidden City, or by the mysteries of doing business with the Chinese.

–The China market is intensifying. Normalization of American relations with the PRC has tended to increase the competition between China's trading partners. While, as indicated by the list of purchases above, China likes to spread its buying over different suppliers, political considerations may not be as important in the future. The practice of open bidding is tending to increase.

–The Chinese themselves are better informed, and more selective in choosing suppliers. In their urge to modernize, they set increased store by the thoroughness of a company's response, the seriousness of approach, and the first impression a company makes.

–With increased flexibility in ways of doing business with the Chinese, and a fast-changing economic system in China, those companies able to assess changes and respond to them may have a definite edge over their rivals when it comes to winning or losing a contract.

–If market research establishes 'needs', then it can identify needs that China itself does not realize exist at present, as several US firms have already discovered. In a sense, China is an open book: it requires almost every kind of available modern technology, or probably will require it between now and the year 2000 in its 'Four Modernizations' programme (see Chapter 1 for an outline of the programme).

–The Chinese market is a long-term proposition, involving a relationship that will be built up over five, ten, and twenty years. A commitment in time, research efforts, resources, and budget should be made in those terms.

–Perhaps the most important reason for investigating China and the characteristics of its market fully is the need to understand the realities of doing business with the Chinese from every standpoint—financial, technical, managerial, legal, cultural— with a contract's bottom line firmly in view. This need cannot be overemphasized. The pitfalls and difficulties in Chinese business are many.

On the other hand, some companies say: 'Let the Chinese come to us. When Peking wants to buy something, we'll be happy to review our capabilities and technologies with them. Why bother with research?'

While this approach may work, a company can hardly afford such a lackadaisical attitude if it wants to reach a mutually profitable business relationship with the Chinese over the long term.

Objectives of market research in China
The objectives of market research for the PRC are:

Market conditions in China. What are the characteristics of China's development plans, economy, industries, technology programmes, and economic and trade organizations? How do politics affect these plans?

Statistically, what is the present import market? Where is that market headed? What countries share the market, and how are their shares changing?

What has China bought? Who has sold what to China? What contracts have been signed? Who are your competitors, and how much exposure have they had in the market? What are they doing in China now?

Business conditions in China. What are the legal, financial, technical, practical, and cultural aspects of doing business with China? How much technology can China absorb? Can China afford everything it is buying?

Finally, how do you business with China? What should be your business strategy? How do you educate the Chinese about your company and its products? How do you get to China? When you get there, how do you negotiate? What is the best approach for your company?

Armed with this information, any company should be well prepared for all segments of its China strategy.

Market conditions in China—the data base and its problems
Researching into the Chinese market has formidable obstacles to overcome. For 20 years, until June this year, the People's Republic had not published production data, national accounts or balance of payments figures, transportation data, import and export figures, economic plans, prices or wages figures and indices, capital formation statistics, or anything else on a regular basis. It had not published any statistical series since 1959, the end of its second Five Year Plan. Fortunately, all the statistics available publicly to that point were collected in a volume, *Ten Great Years*, now issued by AMS Press in New York. This is a key reference book for the Chinese economy. Peking has now published fairly complete figures for 1977–78, and targets for 1979. While these are generally believed to be quite accurate, much analysis remains to be done on them. In recent years, with a certain economic liberalization, more solid figures have been released by Peking than before, but these usually need interpretation. Often they have been buried deep in articles in China's press or radio broadcasts.

To give an idea of the difficulty faced up till now by the ardent daily analyst of China's economy, a typical passage is quoted below from a March 1979 Chinese broadcast on fisheries:

> According to statistics, since 1949 more than 20 million mou of farmland have been reclaimed from lakes throughout the country. In addition, from 1959 to 1978 the proportion of freshwater fish output to the total output of aquatic products declined from 40 per cent to 23 per cent. At present, our country's output of freshwater fish products has still not yet reached the peak record set some 20 years ago . . .
>
> In Hubei Province there are many lakes rich in aquatic resources. There used to be 1065 lakes in the province, each with a water surface of more than 1000 mou (1 mou = 0.1647 acres) but because of the large-scale reclamation undertaken in the past several years, there are now fewer than 500 lakes in the province and the water surface has been reduced by some 75 per cent. Dongting Lake's water surface was as much as 6.53 million mou in the early years after China's liberation, but over the past several years some 2.3 million mou of land were reclaimed from the lake and now its water surface is only 4.23 million mou. In Zhejiang Province approximately 50 000 mou of fish ponds were reclaimed to grow crops. There used to be more than 280 000 mou of water surface for fish breeding in the outskirts of Shanghai Municipality, but there are now

Table 2.1 Total population figures, alternate models, selected years: 1953–2000 (in thousands)

| | Jan. 1 | | |
Year	Low model	Intermediate model	High model
1953	576 049	576 049	576 049
1954	589 150	589 150	589 150
1955	602 879	602 920	602 970
1956	617 133	617 519	617 909
1957	631 985	630 704	633 428
1958	646 530	647 790	649 050
1959	660 469	662 577	664 680
1960	673 659	676 876	680 090
1961	686 378	689 274	691 947
1962	698 493	699 906	700 591
1963	712 316	714 115	715 180
1964	726 704	729 444	731 438
1965	741 362	745 479	748 839
1966	757 257	762 554	767 026
1967	773 122	779 647	785 270
1968	789 698	797 752	804 823
1969	807 095	816 750	825 332
1970	825 109	836 510	846 703
1971	843 360	856 649	868 550
1972	860 868	876 652	890 783
1973	877 311	896 168	913 086
1974	892 787	915 188	935 300
1975	907 322	933 709	957 408
1976	922 002	952 364	979 564
1977	937 388	971 427	1 001 736
1978	956 043	993 635	1 026 889
1979	972 457	1 014 074	1 050 699
1980	987 387	1 033 142	1 073 218
1985	1 051 754	1 114 482	1 168 128
1990	1 113 034	1 190 233	1 255 403
1995	1 179 453	1 275 546	1 357 115
2000	1 248 125	1 369 858	1 475 174

Source: Chinese Economy Post-Mao, US Government Printing Office, page 465, November 1978.

fewer than 200 000 mou of water surface. (*Foreign Broadcast Information Service*, pp. L14, L15, 20 March 1979.)

The two best sources for available figures from China's daily media are known as FBIS and SWB. FBIS is the Foreign Broadcast Information Service: People's Republic of China, issued daily by the US Government's National Technical Information Service (NTIS), Springfield, Virginia 22151. The SWB is the BBC's Survey of World Broadcasts, Part 3: The Far East, available daily or weekly from the BBC, Caversham Park, Reading, Berkshire RG4 8T7, England.

With no handy bulletin of monthly statistics available from China, the job of market assessment is labour-intensive. While easier to carry out than it was a few years ago because of the newly issued figures, an accurate study must, in part, depend on compiling data from China's own media as typified above. The modern researcher on China is nowadays aided by a number of studies on individual sectors that have already done the job of compiling available figures, plus trip reports of specialists visiting China.

Statistics issued by the Chinese themselves should not always be taken at face value. For example, the Chinese population was officially 700 million from 1966 to 1974, when it was revised to 800 million—until March 1978. During that month the Chinese began using 900 million as a figure. Then, in mid-1979 they revised it to 970 million. Compilation of provincial data tells us that the actual number, as of 1 February 1979, was probably just over one billion, according to the American demographic expert John Aird.[1]

The Table 2.1 showing Aird's population projections through the year 2000 is based on an analysis of current provincial population totals and assumed annual growth rates since the late fifties.

Guides to the state of China's economy

The following titles are recommended as guides to the state of China's economy since the fifties. A basic text is *Chinese Economy Post-Mao*, edited by John Hardt and published by the Joint Economic Committee of the US Congress in 1978 (Volume I, over 800 pages) and 1979 (Volume II), available from the US Government Printing Office, Washington, DC. These volumes form part of a series of which one is compiled every few years. They include comprehensive chapters by world experts on almost every facet of China's economy, including general policy perspectives and articles on manufacturing and mining industries, population and labour utilization, agriculture, and foreign economic relations. Another starting point, less detailed but more readable is *China's Economy: A Basic Guide* by Christopher Howe, published by Basic Books of New York and Paul Elek of London in 1978.

A general guide to China, published by Harper & Row in 1978, is good introductory reading; this is the *Encyclopedia of China Today* by Frederic M. Kaplan, Julian Sobin and Stephen Andors.

A forthcoming book edited by the late Professor Alexander Eckstein, *Quantitative Measures of China's Economic Output*, was to be published by the University of Michigan Press in 1979.

For researchers interested in more depth reading, good studies of the

1. Aird, John S., 'Population Growth in the People's Republic of China', a compendium of papers submitted to the Joint Economic Committee of the Congress of the United States, *Chinese Economy Post-Mao*, Volume I, 9 November 1978.

Chinese economy are Eckstein's *China's Economic Revolution*, Cambridge University Press, 1977 and Dwight Perkins' *China's Modern Economy in Historical Perspective*, Stanford University Press, 1975. *China's Economic System*, Praeger, New York, 1967 by Audrey Donnithorne, being updated, Stephen Andors' *China's Industrial Revolution: Policy, Planning and Management*, Pantheon Books of New York, 1977, and Dwight Perkin's *Market Control and Planning in Communist China*. Harvard University Press, 1966, are also useful aids to understanding the complex organizational structure and nature of China's economy.

Because figures issued by the Chinese need interpretation, conclusions drawn are normally estimates and projections based on the best judgement of the analyst. Several people may take the same figures and derive different conclusions, each equally valid. Always check sources, methods and conclusions.

The first questions a market analyst usually wants answered are: What is China's gross national product (GNP) or domestic product (GDP), and how fast is economic growth? Beyond the books noted above, almost the only regularly available source is the National Foreign Assessment Center (NFAC) of the United States Central Intelligence Agency which publishes estimates of China's GNP and other economic indicators yearly in its Reference Aid series entitled *China: Economic Indicators*. This unclassified report may be obtained, along with other CIA publications series on China, from the Document Expediting Center (DOCEX), Exchange and Gift Division, Library of Congress, Washington, DC 20540, USA.

In 1978 the CIA's preliminary estimates placed China's gross national product in 1977 at $407 billion, its population at 1004 billion, and its per capita GNP at $405. The figures are given as a series from 1952 on. Other statistical series in this report cover agricultural production, industrial production, machinery and other producer goods, consumer goods, and foreign trade. The figures are revised yearly. Generally speaking the estimate for a year's GNP is not issued until at least nine months into the following year, though preliminary figures are available much earlier.

The summary table of the CIA's 1978 publication on economic indicators for China is reproduced in Table 2.2.

Others studying the same figures may draw different conclusions. Economists such as Dwight Perkins of Harvard, Robert Dernberger of Michigan, Nicholas Lardy from Yale, or Christopher Howe of London University may decide upon different indices with different sets of assumptions and thus different projections. Even within the US government there are differences of opinion, for instance between the CIA and the US Department of Agriculture on China's grain output figures, or between the Bureau of Mines and the CIA for the PRC's oil production. One point of agreement, however, is that most economic figures officially released by the Chinese usually reflect the truth in some way.

The CIA's 1978 46-page report on China's economic indicators contains a

Table 2.2 China: selected economic indicators

	1952	1957	1965	1970	1971	1972	1973	1974	1975	1976	1977	1978
GNP (billion 1977 US $)	92	128	172	244	261	273	308	320	342	342	370	407
Population, mid-year (million persons)	570	640	754	847	867	886	906	924	943	962	983	1004
Per Capita GNP (1977 US $)	162	201	228	288	301	308	341	346	363	355	377	405
Agricultural production index (1957 = 100)	84	100	101	126	130	126	142	146	148	148	146	151
Total grain (million metric tons)	161	191	194	243	246	240	266	275	284	285	286	295
Cotton (million metric tons)	1.3	1.6	1.6	2.0	2.2	2.1	2.6	2.5	2.4	2.3	2.0	2.2
Hogs (million head)	90	115	168	226	251	261	—	287	—	—	290	—
Industrial production index (1957 = 100)	48	100	199	316	349	385	436	455	502	502	572	646
Producer goods index (1957 = 100)	39	100	211	350	407	452	513	536	602	—	—	—
Machinery index (1957 = 100)	33	100	257	586	711	795	930	992	1156	—	—	—
Electric generators (million kW)	Negl.	0.3	0.8	2.3	2.9	3.6	4.3	5.1	6.0	6.6	—	—
Machine tools (thousand units)	13.7	28.3	45.0	70.0	75.0	75.0	80.0	85.0	90.0	85.0	—	—
Tractors (thousand 15-hp units)	0	0	23.9	79.0	114.6	136.0	166.0	150.0	180.0	190.9	221.8	271.0
Trucks (thousand units)	0	7.5	30.0	70.0	86.0	100.0	110.0	121.0	133.0	135.0	150.0	181.0
Locomotives (units)	20	167	50	435	455	475	495	505	530	530	555	—
Freight cars (thousand units)	5.8	7.3	6.6	12.0	14.0	15.0	16.0	16.8	18.5	19.0	21.0	—
Merchant ships (thousand metric tons)	6.1	46.4	50.6	121.5	148.0	164.6	209.4	288.4	313.6	318.8	—	—

Other producer goods index (1957 = 100)	41	100	200	294	336	371	415	429	472	—	—	—
Electric power (billion kWh)	7.3	19.3	42.0	72.0	86.0	93.0	101.0	108.0	121.0	128.0	141.0	162
Coal (million metric tons)	66.5	130.7	232.2	327.4	353.6	376.5	398.1	410.6	479.6	488.0	546.6	605
Crude oil (million metric tons)	0.4	1.5	11.0	28.2	36.7	43.1	54.8	65.8	74.3	83.6	90.3	100.3
Crude steel (million metric tons)	1.3	5.4	12.2	17.8	21.0	23.0	25.0	21.0	24.0	21.0	24.0	31.7
Chemical fertilizer (million metric tons)	0.2	0.8	7.6	14.0	16.8	19.8	24.8	24.9	28.8	24.3	38.0	48
Cement (million metric tons)	2.9	6.9	16.3	26.6	31.0	38.1	41.0	37.3	47.1	49.3	56.2	67.8
Timber (million cubic meters)	11.2	27.9	27.2	29.9	30.7	33.2	34.2	35.2	36.2	36.7	37.2	39.2
Paper (million metric tons)	0.6	1.2	3.6	5.0	5.1	5.6	6.0	6.5	6.9	7.0	7.1	—
Consumer goods index (1957 = 100)	60	100	183	272	272	295	334	347	368	—	—	—
Cotton cloth (billion linear meters)	3.8	5.0	5.7	8.5	—	—	—	—	9.6	8.9	10.0	11.1
Wool cloth (million linear meters)	4.2	18.2	—	—	—	—	—	65.2	—	—	—	—
Processed sugar (million metric tons)	0.5	0.9	1.5	1.8	1.9	1.9	2.2	2.2	2.3	—	—	—
Bicycles (million units)	0.1	0.8	1.8	3.6	4.0	4.3	4.9	5.2	5.5	—	—	—
Foreign trade (billion current US $)	1.9	3.1	3.9	4.3	4.8	6.0	10.3	14.1	14.6	13.3	15.1	20.8
Exports, f.o.b.	0.9	1.6	2.0	2.1	2.5	2.5	5.1	6.7	7.2	7.3	8.0	10.2
Imports, c.i.f.	1.0	1.4	1.8	2.2	2.3	2.8	5.2	7.4	7.4	6.0	7.1	10.6

1. Preliminary. *Source:* NFAC ER 78—10750, December 1978.

host of tables and maps with output estimates of everything from tractors to locomotives. Individual CIA reports cover individual topics such as mineral production, forestry, oil, or coal, as well as international trade in statistical analyses.

One way to keep up with the figures developed by various experts on China, in and out of government, is to read the *China Business Review*, published by the National Council for US-China Trade (NCUSCT), 1050 17th Street, Washington, DC 20036, USA. The magazine reports all significant market research material as it becomes available.

But market conditions do not consist merely of figures. While there is no doubt that they are one of the best starting points for study, US Government reports have been criticized in the past as written too much for economists by economists.

The Soviets incidentally also publish estimates of the Chinese economy, usually in the magazine, *Far Eastern Affairs*. Typically, the USSR estimates are at least 5–25 per cent below those of the CIA's corresponding estimates. For example, the Russian estimate of Chinese output for 1976 at 221 billion yuan was less than half the American estimate of 580 billion yuan.

Beyond statistics—keeping up with China's plans, politics, and science

How does one keep up-to-date with market conditions in China qualitatively? How can one interpret what is happening to the Chinese economy and to China's economic priorities? The easiest way, if one has time, besides reading FBIS and SWB, is to check Chinese newspapers and periodicals, of which the best are the *People's Daily* (available only in Chinese as the *Renmin Ribao*) and the *Guangming Ribao*, obtainable through China Books and Periodicals at 125 Fifth Avenue, New York, NY 10003, USA, and other outlets. The Xinhua News Agency or New China News Agency (NCNA) publishes an official news service daily and weekly in English, available from Peking, London, and other European capitals. Eventually it will be published in the US.

The Chinese media are the first to make China's economic development programme known in broad terms. What to look for are keynote speeches by China's economic leaders. Speeches at national conferences on agriculture, industry, science and technology, and other sectors in the years 1976–78 detailed the broad scope of China's planned developments in each of these areas, following a major economic policy speech by the late Premier Zhou Enlai in early 1975. Later statements elaborated on the general programme for China's so-called 'Four Modernizations', which Premier Zhou had summarized.

Better still, in rare pronouncements of solid figures, actual targets for particular industries may be stated. For example, in a speech on 26 February 1978, Chairman Hua Guofeng said (though these targets have now been retracted as overambitious) that China intended to produce 60 million tons of steel and 400 million tons of grain, and to have 85 per cent agricultural mechanization, all by 1985.

Other Chinese publications are helpful. Recommended reading are the *Beijing(Peking)Review*, *China Reconstructs*, *China Pictorial* and *China's Foreign Trade*, all of which are in English, available from Guozi Shudian, China's publications export company, at Box 339, Beijing (Peking), People's Republic of China. Nuggets in the March 1979 issues of *Beijing Review* and *China Reconstructs* included hard data on China's 1978 steel production (31.7 million tons) and details of major projects under construction. All these magazines normally publish regional, economic and technology-oriented articles. Indeed, it may only be through these publications that one gets to know that such-and-such a factory exists, or that a certain type of machine is under production in China.

Clearly Peking's politics and economics are closely intertwined and may seriously affect business negatively or positively. It is good, sometimes essential, for the market analyst to keep a close eye on what is going on in the top echelons. Historically, there have always been disputes between China's hard-line ideologues, with their slogans of self-reliance, egalitarianism, and committee-oriented management, and economic pragmatists interested in individual accountability, productivity, and raising the general standard of living. The lattter group of leaders is now in power, trying to modernize China's economy as fast as possible.

But where, in the early seventies, a foreign company was affected by the activities of the 'Gang of Four' (the late Chairman Mao Zedong's wife and her colleagues)—sabotaging or delaying textile shipments, diverting oil tankers, and so on—in the late seventies the question is more a matter of judging how far and fast China can go technically, managerially, and financially in absorbing the immense amounts of foreign technology that it wants to buy. A researcher with his finger on the pulse of Chinese matters, interested in the realities of the People's Republic's activities, might have detected the signs of trouble in Peking's purchasing plan in late 1978. This was well before the spring 1979 reassessment of the economy, when Peking suddenly began postponing major contracts.

He or she would also be noting the early 1979 shift in China's priorities, away from heavy industry, with the pendulum swinging back towards agriculture and light industry as it has several times before in China's history.

If one cannot scan China's press reports, the next best thing is to read the weekly, *Far Eastern Economic Review*, available from PO Box 47 in Hongkong and the daily, *Asian Wall Street Journal*, as well as most of the major dailies such as the *New York Times*, *The Washington Post*, and *Financial Times* (published in London and Frankfurt), which have good ongoing China political and economic coverage.

The China Quarterly, available from the Contemporary China Institute, School of Oriental and African Studies, Malet Street, London WC1E 7HP,

England, is the leading scholarly journal on China. Each issue contains over 250 pages. It often has up-to-date economy-oriented articles, on, for instance, China's energy or oil. In addition, it carries pieces providing insight into China's politics, personalities, and ground-level socio-economic life, such as surveys of villages, factories, or communes.

Another important aspect of China's science and technology programmes may also be covered by reviewing China's publications for important conferences in China, policy speeches, announcements of reorganization and other indicators of where China's science is headed. Peking's technology development holds great interest for foreign equipment suppliers, in everything from computers to analytical instruments and data networks, planned to grow substantially in China's future.

Important sources of information are the *China Exchange Newsletter* published by the Committee on Scholarly Communications with the People's Republic at 2100 Pennsylvania Avenue, Washington, DC 20418, USA; *Developments in PRC Science and Technology Policy*, published quarterly by the Stanford University US–China Relations Program; and *Chinese Science and Technology*, translations of Chinese technology-related articles published by M. E. Sharpe Inc. of New York. These publications also carry details of reports published by the numerous scientific interest groups now visiting the PRC. China itself of course produces many scientific publications, some with articles or abstracts in English.

Focusing on China's trade
Going from the general to the particular, how does one focus on what China has bought and sold in terms of product categories, value and quantity? Peking does not publish detailed import and export statistics. Until now this has been a matter of policy: questions about it receive the answer: 'That is not our system', or 'Our way is different'.

The first general market research tool for detailed trade data is the CIA's annual research paper, *China's International Trade*. The latest was published in December 1978 for 1977–78 (ER 78-10721), available from

Table 2.3 China: balance of trade (billion US $)

	Exports	Imports	Balance
1970	2.1	2.2	−0.2
1971	2.5	2.3	0.2
1972	3.2	2.8	0.3
1973	5.1	5.2	−0.2
1974	6.7	7.4	−0.8
1975	7.2	7.4	−0.2
1976	7.3	6.0	1.3
1977	8.0	7.1	0.9

Table 2.4 China: top 10 trading partners

	Total Trade (million US $)		Rank	
	1976	1977	1976	1977
Japan	3052	3509	1	1
Hongkong	1620	1779	2	2
West Germany	952	826	3	3
Australia	380	631	7	4
Romania	451	600	5	5
Canada	309	459	9	6
United States	351	391	8	7
USSR	417	338	6	8
Singapore	295	324	10	9
United Kingdom	277	284	12	10

DOCEX (noted above). In this report the agency works backwards, by pooling the official statistics of China's trading partners, including some fragmentary data from less developed countries, to form a reasonably complete picture of China's total trade by country and category, adjusted to place Chinese exports on an f.o.b. basis and imports c.i.f. However, one must wait almost 12 months for the complete figures of the previous year. In addition, the report lists contracts for whole plant sales to China.

Tables 2.3 to 2.5 are reproduced from the CIA's 1977–78 report.

To trace individual products purchased by China from industrialized nations, consult a printout of OECD figures available from the OECD or the Bureau of East–West Trade at the US Department of Commerce. These figures show, at five digit Standard International Tariff Classification (SITC) categories, market shares by dollar volume and percentages over a series of years. A typical entry is reproduced in Table 2.6.

The trade statistics of individual countries can be easily monitored. The *China Trade Report* at P.O. Box 47 in Hongkong prints Chinese exports and imports for various trading partner countries such as the United Kingdom, Switzerland, and Belgium every month in each issue.

In the US, the NCUSCT publishes *Sino–US Trade Statistics* every year giving a seven-digit breakdown of exports to and imports from the People's Republic. In this book, the categories are enumerated both by volume and by reference numbers so that you can look up any category of product, by the most specific description available, and find out where it ranks in Sino–US trade. Table 2.7 is a page from the 1977 volume.

The Japanese External Trade Organization (JETRO) publishes a quarterly newsletter on trade with China in English, the *JETRO China Newsletter*, which has analyses of Sino–Japanese trade as well as dollar volume by specific categories. Subscriptions to this worthwhile newsletter can be obtained from 2 Akasaka Aoi-cho, Minato-Ku, Tokyo, Japan.

Table 2.5   China: commodity composition of trade[1] 1977

	Million US $	% of Total
Exports (f.o.b.)	7955	100
Agricultural	2840	36
Animals, meat, and fish	650	8
Grain	455	6
Fruit and vegetables	490	6
Oilseeds	90	1
Textile fibers	290	4
Crude animal materials	330	4
Other	535	7
Extractive	1000	13
Crude minerals and metals	120	2
Crude oil	785	10
Coal	95	1
Manufacturing	4115	51
Petroleum products	230	3
Chemicals	380	5
Metals and metal products	355	4
Machinery and equipment	270	3
Textile yarn and fabric	1300	16
Clothing and footwear	625	8
Other light manufacturers	955	12
Imports (c.i.f.)	7100	100
Foodstuffs	1230	17
Grain	745	10
Sugar	320	5
Others	165	2
Industrial supplies	4545	65
Rubber	225	3
Textile fibers	500	7
Chemicals	885	12
Iron and steel	1570	22
Non-ferrous metals	265	4
Metal products	55	1
Other	1045	15
Capital goods	1290	18
Non-electric machinery	455	6
Electric machinery	105	1
Transport equipment	640	9
Other	90	1
Consumer goods	35	Negl.

1. The sectors of origin and end-use categories in this table differ somewhat from the categories found in the appendix. For example, the foodstuffs series includes oilseeds but excludes tobacco; capital goods cover hand tools and precision instruments in addition to machinery and transport equipment. The manufacturing sector includes chemicals, petroleum products, synthetic textile fibers, and other processed goods not included under SITC sections 6, 7, and 8. For a detailed description of procedures see ER 77-10477, *China: Trends in Trade with Non-Communist Countries since 1970*, October 1977.

What has China bought?
While the statistics of trade shipments to and from China give a general indication of trends in China's commerce, they cannot reveal the names of the products or the companies selling them. A company's first interest usually is in knowing what its competitors have sold. How can one find out?

Undoubtedly, the best single source is a book called *Doing Business with the People's Republic of China: Industries and Markets* by Bohdan and Maria Szuprowicz, published in 1978 by John Wiley and Sons, New York. Though now somewhat out of date, this unique guide to every major industry in China includes details of industrial organization, economic priorities, and technology needs. Compilations of both imports and actual contracts over a period give a fairly good picture of both trends and what companies have been successful in selling to China.

Another major guide, though more expensive, is the *Directory of Foreign Trade Exhibitions in the People's Republic of China*, a comprehensive list of over 10 000 products, most with model numbers, exhibited in China by foreign companies during the seventies. This 540-page guide to both companies and products, cross-referenced and carrying details of over 50 exhibitions in China (including floor plans), is available from the NCUSCT. Since these exhibitions are almost the only shop window a foreign company has to display its wares in China, and as most items displayed are bought by the Chinese—some at substantial discounts—this volume provides a unique source of information as to which companies have entered the Chinese market, and sold products to China's trading organizations.

Several magazines and newsletters are recommended reading to keep abreast of what is going on. *Business China*, published by Business International in Hongkong, is a fortnightly eight-page newsletter that notes developments and deals in the China trade. This newsletter has some details of contracts, plus individual company experience and developments in China's industry. The *China Trade Report*, also from Hongkong, noted above, gives trade developments but more on a country than a company basis.

In England, *Sino-British Trade* from the Sino-British Trade Council, 55 Queen Anne's Gate, London SW1, and the *China Trade and Economic Newsletter* published by Monitor Consultants, 25 Bedford Row, London WC1R 4HE, are monthly bulletins featuring mainly European trade contracts and developments with China. Both include news of delegations to and from China, important clues as to what China is thinking of buying, if one can track down the companies and technologies involved.

The most comprehensive basic source of information on China's trade with the United States is the *China Business Review*, published by the NCUSCT. This bi-monthly carries several sections of essential interest to the market researcher. One is 'Exporters' Notes', in which American negotiations, sales and selling experience are described, as well as details of technology of potential interest to the Chinese. Another is the 'International Notes' section, which covers most major industrial categories such as energy,

Table 2.6 Printout showing exports from industrialized nations to China

IW Exports to the PRC

	1972 (000$)	1972 (%)	1973 (000$)	1973 (%)	1974 (000$)	1974 (%)	1975 (000$)	1975 (%)	1976 (000$)	1976 (%)	1977 (000$)	1977 (%)
France	22	10.9	62	13.9	26	3.1	756	23.2	748	57.7	122	15.2
Italy	10	5.0	34	7.6	15	1.8	37	1.1	95	7.3	67	8.4
Japan	26	12.9	23	5.1	227	27.4	1575	48.4	69	5.3	252	31.4
Netherlands	0	0.0	3	0.7	0	0.0	13	0.4	4	0.3	0	0.0
Sweden	0	0.0	12	2.7	1	0.1	48	1.5	0	0.0	3	0.4
Switzerland	47	23.4	104	23.3	61	7.4	99	3.0	83	6.4	154	19.2
United Kingdom	12	6.0	122	27.3	216	26.1	436	13.4	94	7.3	93	11.6
United States	0	0.0	0	0.0	145	17.5	0	0.0	1	0.1	0	0.0

SITC: 71714 Felt MF, finishing machs

IW Exports to the PRC

	1972 (000$)	1972 (%)	1973 (000$)	1973 (%)	1974 (000$)	1974 (%)	1975 (000$)	1975 (%)	1976 (000$)	1976 (%)	1977 (000$)	1977 (%)
IW Total	0	100.0	35	100.0	7	100.0	0	100.0	0	100.0	0	100.0
Austria	0	0.0	35	100.0	0	0.0	0	0.0	0	0.0	0	0.0
F R Germany	0	0.0	0	0.0	1	14.3	0	0.0	0	0.0	0	0.0
Italy	0	0.0	0	0.0	6	85.7	0	0.0	0	0.0	0	0.0
Japan	0	0.0	0	0.0	0	0.0	0	0.0	0	0.0	0	0.0

SITC: 71715 Textile machinery nes

	1972 (000$)	1972 (%)	1973 (000$)	1973 (%)	1974 (000$)	1974 (%)	1975 (000$)	1975 (%)	1976 (000$)	1976 (%)	1977 (000$)	1977 (%)
IW Total	925	100.0	5594	100.0	10083	100.0	10737	100.0	5926	100.0	4441	100.0
Belg–Lux	0	0.0	0	0.0	0	0.0	0	0.0	0	0.0	0	0.0
Denmark	0	0.0	0	0.0	0	0.0	105	1.0	2	0.0	0	0.0

IW Exports by the PRC

SITC: 7172   Skin, leather working mach

	1972 (000$)	(%)	1973 (000$)	(%)	1974 (000$)	(%)	1975 (000$)	(%)	1976 (000$)	(%)	1977 (000$)	(%)
F R Germany	6	0.6	657	11.7	820	8.1	255	2.4	260	4.4	27	0.6
France	39	4.2	46	0.8	97	1.0	36	0.3	58	1.0	43	1.0
Italy	0	0.0	31	0.6	218	2.2	225	2.1	332	5.6	3	0.1
Japan	513	55.5	3942	70.5	7756	76.9	8257	76.9	4325	73.0	3569	80.4
Netherlands	366	39.6	823	14.7	858	8.5	818	7.6	5	0.1	574	12.9
Switzerland	0	0.0	57	1.0	147	1.5	34	0.3	938	15.8	134	3.0
United Kingdom	1	0.1	38	0.7	187	1.9	1007	9.4	6	0.1	91	2.0

IW Exports to the PRC

SITC: 7173   Sewing machines

	1972 (000$)	(%)	1973 (000$)	(%)	1974 (000$)	(%)	1975 (000$)	(%)	1976 (000$)	(%)	1977 (000$)	(%)
IW Total	10	100.0	2689	100.0	3773	100.0	1808	100.0	1039	100.0	537	100.0
Belg–Lux	0	0.0	77	2.9	222	5.9	0	0.0	39	3.8	40	7.4
Denmark	0	0.0	0	0.0	6	0.2	1	0.1	0	0.0	0	0.0
F R Germany	10	100.0	2284	84.9	1914	50.7	947	52.4	605	58.2	378	70.4
France	0	0.0	0	0.0	62	1.6	136	7.5	23	2.2	0	0.0
Italy	0	0.0	14	0.5	198	5.2	25	1.4	98	9.4	107	19.9
Japan	0	0.0	0	0.0	787	20.9	6	0.3	0	0.0	7	1.3
United Kingdom	0	0.0	314	11.7	584	15.5	693	38.3	274	26.4	5	0.9

Table 2.7 US Exports to China by Schedule B seven-digit and SITC numbers (numerical order)

SCHED B	SITC	COMMODITY	YR TO DATE
0311075	03110	GOLD AND TROPICAL FISH, LIVE	9 690
0819940	08199	LIVESTCK FEED, PREPARED, NEC	5 500
0819980	08199	PREPARED ANIMAL FEEDS, NEC	11 888
1110010	11102	SOFT DRINKS & MINERAL WATERS	4 816
2111010	21110	CATTLE HIDES, WHOLE	12 000
2214000	22140	SOYBEANS	14 385 752
2518220	25182	PULP SULFITE SFTWD BLEACHED	1 294 211
2631021	26310	COTTON, UPLND, 1-1/8 IN & OV	3 017 378
2631031	26310	COTTON, UPLND, 1 IN TO 1-1/8	14 501 671
2662120	26621	STAPLE, POLYESTR, NT CRD ETC	18 967 288
2769800	27690	NONMETALLIC MINERALS NEC	8 172
2820078	28200	STEEL SCRAP, NEC	101 955
2925075	29250	VEGETABLE SEEDS, NEC	7 744
2928030	29240	PLANTS, ETC, FOR PREMRY, ETC	52 500
3325050	33250	LUBRICATING OILS, NEC	58 917
3325055	33250	LUBRICATING GREASES	5 399
4113220	41132	TALLOW, INEDIBLE	3 689 785
4212010	42120	SOYBEAN OIL. CRUDE, DEGUMMED	28 297 313
5120219	51200	CYCLIC INTRMEDTE ACIDS, NEC	31 620
5120290	51200	CYCLIC CHEM INTRMDTES, NEC	3 102 932
5120420	51200	RUBBER ACCELERATORS, CYCLIC	438 598
5120430	51200	RUBBER ANTIOXIDANTS, CYCLIC	223 996
5120720	51200	CHEMCLS, ANTIKNOCK, EX PREPS	1 260
5120820	51200	MISC CYCLIC CHEMCL PROD, NEC	34 514
5120915	51200	POLYPROPYLENE GLYCOL	770
5120940	51200	ETHANOLAMINES	28 060
5120969	51200	ACIDS AND ANHYDRIDES, NEC	248 620
5120983	51200	CITRIC ACID	22 348
5120993	51200	MISC ORG CHEMS, EX CYC, NEC	743 000
5136510	51365	ALUMINUM OXIDE	2 240
5136932	51369	INORG BASES, ETC, NEC	77 147
5146040	51400	SODIUM BICHROMATE & CHROMATE	2 080 215
5146070	51400	SODIUM BORATES, REFINED	168 000
5147010	51400	ALKALIES, NEC	203 762
5147020	51400	AMMONIUM COMPOUNDS, NEC	3 262
5151046	51510	R-ACTIV ISOTPS & ELMNTS, NEC	273 334
5333280	53332	IND PROD FINISHES, EX LACQRS	3 358
5419933	54199	X-RAY CONTRAST MEDIA	4 116
5419940	54199	PHARMACEUTICAL GOODS, NEC	11 435
5542010	55420	DETERGENTS, ALKALINE	14 400
5611005	56110	UREA, FERTILIZER MATERIAL	8 075 997
5711220	57112	EXPLOSVS A BLSTNG AGNTS, NEC	116 327
5712100	57121	MNNG, BLASTNG & SAFETY FUSE	5 475
5712200	57122	PERCUSSION & DETONATING CAPS	45 330
5811010	58110	OTHER THERMOPLASTIC RESINS	391 050
5811031	58110	PHENOLIC MOLDING COMPOUNDS	2 564
5811055	58110	SYN RESINS FOR PROTECTIVE CT	12 747
5812006	58120	POLYETH RESIN, HIGH DENSITY	1 223 376
5812034	58120	STYRENE ION EXCHANGE RESINS	3 500
5812035	58120	POLYPROPYLENE RESINS, UNFIN	20 010
5812040	58120	OTHER THERMOPLASTIC RESINS	14 350

Table 2.7 US Exports to China by Schedule B seven-digit and SITC numbers (numerical order)

SCHED B	SITC	COMMODITY	YR TO DATE
5997515	57975	ADDITIVES FOR LUBRCTNG OILS	9 377
5999210	59992	ACTIVATED CARBON	8 650
5999910	59999	NICKEL COMPOUND CATALYSTS	417 997
5999920	59999	CMPND CATALYSTS, EXC NICKEL	1 493 035
5999970	59999	OTHER CHEM PRODUCTS OR PREP	38 574
6210250	62102	UNV RBR ST & FM EX VEH & BAC	980
6210430	62104	PLTS, SHTS, ETC & PREL SHPS	2 500
6291020	62910	TRUCK & BUS TIRES, PNEUMATIC	1 400
6413025	64130	KRET CNTNR BD LINER UNBLESCH	3 397 364
6514030	65140	COTTON SEWING THREAD	1 812
6516636	65161	POLYEST CONT FIL YRN, TEXT	1 294
6516639	65161	P-EST FIL YRN NT TXT	464 859
6535141	65351	WV FAB BL NEC NYLON FIL YRN	35 484
6535151	65351	WV FAB BL NEC P-ESTER FIL	1 880
6535311	65353	NYLON PILE WVN FAR UNBLCHD	7 265
6540220	65402	WVN LABELS, ETC, TEX FIB NEC	3 388
6540330	65403	TRM O D NONELAS M-M-FIB X GL	1 981
6554356	65543	TEX FAB NEC RES-CTD EX VINYL	2 831
6556160	65561	CORDAGE NEC TEXT FIB NEC	1 987
6561025	65610	BAGS OR SACKS NEW PACK TMNEC	84 159
6623205	66232	FIRECLAY BRICK & SIM SHAPES	712
6624620	66241	N-REFRACT CFRAM CO MAT, NEC	11 132
6631130	66311	GRIND POL WHL STN NEC MACH	8 821
6638105	66381	ASBESTOS GASKETS	13 962
6647040	66470	LAMINATED SAFETY GLASS	4 476
6744460	67411	IR & ST PLATES UNCOATED NEC	15 000
6748050	67480	STL PLATE & SHEET COATED NEC	650
6770320	67703	STAINLESS ST WIRE CTD OR NCT	1 522
6782025	67820	CARB ST OIL CTRY GOODS SMLSS	299 460
6782065	67820	AL ST TB & PIP SM FX STL NEC	43 559
6782075	67820	STLS ST PR TUB SMLS NEC	612
6782080	67820	STAINLESS ST MECH TUB SMLS	1 820
6783015	67830	CARBON STEEL LINE PIPE WELD	16 240
6785032	67850	ST TB A PIPE FLANGES FORGED	16 561
6785034	67850	ST TB A PIPE FIT FORG WLD TP	10 000
6785036	67850	ST TB PIP FT UN FORG WLD TP	11 446
6785060	67850	IRN TUBE & PIPE FITTINGS NEC	5 680
6822220	68222	COPPER AL PLTS, SHTS & STR	1 270
6840120	68410	ALUM & ALUM AL. UNWR, NEC	5 311 341
6842220	68422	ALUM & ALUM ALLOY PLATES	19 310
6911045	69110	SHT MT CNS MAT OF I OR S NEC	2 690
6922110	69221	CANS TO TRAN GDS, OF 1 OR S	45 000
6933320	69333	WR CLOTH & OTH WOV PR, OF AL	4 570
6942110	69421	BOLTS, TH RDS & STDS, I OR S	3 276
6952308	69523	MECH HAND SERV TOOLS, NEC	74 178
6952350	69523	HAND TOOLS, AND PARTS NEC	1 790
6952465	69524	DRIL & CORE BIT & RMRS NEC	837 903
6952470	69524	PTS, NEC, FOR DRILL BIT, ETC	28 906
6988710	69887	WELDING ROD, AND WIRE ETC	5 312
6989180	69891	ARTICLES, IRON OR STEEL, NEC	10 498
6989940	69894	BOLT NUT ETC BASE METAL NEC	20 477

Table 2.8 China: January-February 1979 sales and negotiations

Company	Product/plant/technology	Value millions of US $ (local currency if known)	Sale (S) or negotiation (N), date announced
Petrochemical plants and equipment			
Toyo Engineering Corp. (Japan)	4 ethylene plants, nitric acid plant, nitrophosphate plant	$537 (¥102 billion)	S: 1/79
Mitsubishi HI, Nissho-Iwai, Shokubai Kogaku Kogyo (Japan)	Acrylic acid ester plant	$537 (¥102 billion)	S: 1/79
Lurgi Kohle und Mineraloel-technik (W. Germany)	6 chemical plants: coal-based ammonia synthesis plant, methanol synthesis plant, 2 aromatic complexes (benzine and paraxylene), 2 terephthalic acid plants (using US process technology)	$850	S: 1/10/79
Mitsubishi HI (Japan)	Styrene butadiene rubber plant at Shengli Petrochemical works	$33.3	S: 1/79
Toyo Engineering, Mitsui and Co, Sauko Trading (Japan)	2 vinyl chloride monomer manufacturing plants	$57	S: 1/79
C-E Lummus (US)	Lummus proprietary ethylene process, related DGP process, computer control technology for 4 new ethylene plants	NVG	S: 1/79
Zimmer AG (W. Germany)	Polyester polycondensation plant (1.2 billion pounds/year)	$217 (DM400 million)	S: 1/79
Petroleum and natural gas development and refining			
Fluor Corp. (US)	Development of several oil-processing facilities (3 crude oil stabilizer plants, 6 vapor recovery units)	$8	S: 1/18/79

Company	Project	Value	Date
JGC, Union of California (Japan, US) (Japan, US)	2 large-scale oil refinery plants	$76.9	S: 1/18/79
	Development of underwater oilfield near Hong Kong	$1,000	N: 1/25/79
Cameron Iron Works (US)	20 blowout preventers (for land, jack-up, workover rigs)	$6	S: 1/79
Fluor Corp. (US)	Modernization of 2 petroleum processing research facilities; management and technical advisory services, equipment and materials for pilot plants at Beijing and Fushan	$11 (reimbursable cost)	S: late 1/79
Chiyoda Chemical & Engineering Construction (Japan)	Installation of units for removal of excess wax from crude oil at Shengli fields, Using Mobil dewaxing process	$15	S: 1/25/79
Chiyoda Chemical & Engineering Construction (Japan)	Residue thermal cracking processes for plant at Nanjing	$9	S: 2/7/79
Ports and related equipment			
East Asiatic Co. (Denmark)	Modernization of liner shipping services, supply of marine container equipment and services	NVG	S: 1/15/79
(Japan)	Cooperation for modernization of ports	NVG	N: 1/79
Power			
Hydro Quebec (Canada)	Large hydroelectric developments	NVG	N: 1/79
General Electric Corp., Northern Engineering Industries (UK)	4 coal burning power stations	NVG	N: 1/79
Japanese power companies	Advice on construction of four large dams and hydroelectric power stations	NVG	N: 2/79
Scientific instruments			
Varian Associates (US)	Spectrometers	$5	S: 1/16/79

2085663

35

Source: The *China Business Review*, Volume 6, Number 1, January–February 1979, reprinted with permission.

transportation, petrochemicals, iron and steel, in which international sales to China are analyzed, delegations noted, and trends assessed. Furnished too is a table of all known recent sales world wide and negotiations for sales to China, an example of which is shown in Table 2.8. A listing of all sales and negotiations for 1978 is available as a separate publication from the Council. In addition, the magazine carries reports of individual company experience in dealing with China.

There are also publications from Japan, France, Germany, and Italy that track sales and negotiations with China (if one is prepared to translate them).

Putting together a picture of the competition is not straightforward, however. Alerted by hints from Chinese economic and technology programmes, one can keep an eye on the press for mention of Chinese survey, study, or purchase missions—where they are going, which firms they are visiting, what their specialities are, what technology seems to be of particular interest. Usually the arrival of such groups suggests that China is well on its way to making a decision to purchase. For insight into the decision-making process in China leading to the purchase of foreign equipment, refer to 'Making a Decision on Purchase of Foreign Technology' by Howell Jackson in the *China Business Review*, May-June 1978.

The commercial researcher, besides finding out what the competition has sold in the past, should be keenly aware of current trends. The simplest way to acquire this knowledge is to go to China, at the invitation of a foreign trade corporation, or other organization, and chat around at the Peking Hotel. If you cannot do this, an agent specializing in trade with China, such as Jardines, WJS Inc., Biddle Sawyer, Friendship International, East Asiatic, and so on should be able to help: most maintain suites in the Peking Hotel.

Important sources of advice on what is happening in China in any given field are the China trade promotion organizations, or China branches of the various national departments of trade. In the USA, the Commerce Department's China Desk provides excellent advice on market conditions. The NCUSCT, a non-profit membership organization, has a number of industry committees, a comprehensive library with files on products traded, and export advisory services. The Sino–British Trade Council and The 48 Group in London, and similar organizations in Australia, Canada, France, and Japan, have good resources.

Market surveys
Doing Business with the People's Republic of China, noted above, is the best compendium of market surveys of Chinese industry, including, as it does, over 20 categories of technology from agricultural machinery to railway equipment. It is the only such compendium that does justice to the available information on China, although a number of individual studies or market surveys exist that gather a mass of hard-to-find data into useful assessments. A selective listing follows.

Agriculture

Many good studies exist on China's agriculture. Three excellent introductory texts are the chapters in the *Chinese Economy Post-Mao* (referred to hereafter as the JEC volume), entitled 'China's Agricultural Production', 'China Grain Trade', and 'The Evolution of Policy and Capabilities in China's Agricultural Technology'. Chapters in the earlier, 1975, JEC volume are also worth reading for a broad statistical picture, in particular 'Constraints Influencing China's Agricultural Performance', and 'The Commune System in the People's Republic of China'. The NCUSCT's *Workbook on China's Agriculture*, published in 1976, is a 200-page, strictly-market assessment for every kind of agricultural product, with details of sales made in each category, plus lists of delegations to and from China, production data for almost every kind of crop, import and export statistics, and a host of other information. The US Department of Agriculture also publishes comprehensive Chinese crop outlook reports.

Agricultural machinery

The Politics of Agricultural Mechanization by Benedict Stavis, Cornell University Press, 1978, is a good scholarly introduction to the subject, along with the 1978 JEC chapter on China's agricultural technology by Thomas Wiens. *Rural Industrialization in the People's Republic of China* by Jon Sigurdson, Harvard University Press, 1977, and a forthcoming study by the same author are especially worth reading.

Chemicals, petrochemicals

There are few adequate sources of information on this industry. The most comprehensive is Sy Yuan's 'China Chemicals', available from the NCUSCT, a reprint from the *China Business Review*, November–December 1975. *Business International* also published a study on China's chemicals in the early seventies. Reports on fertilizer production have been published by the British Sulphur Institute, the *China Quarterly* (in December 1975), in Jon Sigurdson's book on rural industrialization in China, and in the CIA's *Chemical Fertilizer Supplies* 1949–74, issued in 1975. Sigurdson's chapter in the JEC 1975 volume has a particularly illuminating section on the economics of fertilizer production, contrasting advantages and disadvantages of both big imported plants and small Chinese units.

Construction

The two major sources on this subject are the US Commerce Department's market assessment for construction equipment in China, issued in March 1976 and *China's Construction and Mining Industries*, a 430-page report, NCUSCT, March 1977. There is also a forthcoming report on the NCUSCT's construction equipment delegation(s) to China in 1978–79. Kang Chao's *The Construction Industry in Communist China*, Aldine, 1968 provides useful background information, the CIA has various monographs on the cement industry, and in the JEC's 1975 volume, Ian McFarlane contributed a chapter on 'Construction Trends in China 1949–1974' that is worth consulting.

Electric power

The best source by far on this topic is *China's Electric Power Industry* by William Clarke, head of the Commerce Department's China Desk, in the JEC 1978, Volume I. This piece updates a September–October 1977 report by Clarke in the *China Business Review* that includes a map of China's power plants and known grid lines. The JEC piece takes a comprehensive look at all technical aspects of China's electric power, and includes an excellent assessment of what China will have to do to increase its capacity and production at the rate required to meet its targets.

Electronics

Several detailed reports on China's electronics and computer capabilities have appeared, including an extensive piece by Bohdan Szuprowicz in the *China Business Review*, May–June 1976, entitled 'Electronics in China', the report by a member of a US Institute of Electrical and Electronic Engineers (IEEE) delegation to China 1978, Philip Reicher's 'The Electronics Industry in China' in the JEC's 1972 volume, Jack Craig's piece on China's telecommunications industry 1949–74 in JEC 1975, and the Commerce Department's market assessment of China's telecommunications industry.

Energy

The doyen of Chinese energy is Vaclav Smil, whose latest work appears in the JEC's 1978 volume under the title 'China's Energetics: A Systems Analysis', and whose major treatise on the subject is *China's Energy Achievements, Problems, Prospects,* Praeger, 1976. In 1975, the CIA published *China: Energy Balance Projections,* still a useful source. The CIA has also published various research papers on China's coal, most recently in early 1979. A. B. Ikonnikov's study of the Chinese coal industry is still a standard. Petroleum is mentioned below.

Forestry

New emphasis was placed by the Chinese on forestry, in the spring of 1979. S. D. Richardson's book *Forestry in Communist China,* Johns Hopkins Press, 1966, is still the best source on the subject. *People's Republic of China: Timber Production and End Uses,* CIA, 1976, should also be read.

Iron and steel

'China's Steel', by William Clarke in *China Business Review*, July–August 1975, is a basic source. Another article, by Alfred Usack and James D. Egan, published in the JEC's 1975 volume, entitled 'China's Iron and Steel Industry' is interesting but not so technically or future-oriented as Clarke's study. Considerable information has also been issued by the Japanese on China's iron and steel industry.

Machinery, machine tools
Chu-yuan Cheng's book, *The Machine Building Industry in Communist China*, Aldine Press, Chicago, 1972, is the major book on this subject, but several other reports should be consulted. These include the chapter entitled 'A Survey of China's Machine Building Industry' in the JEC 1978 volume, the Commerce Department's metalworking and finishing equipment market assessment for China, and the chapter in Szuprowicz's book on doing business with China on 'Machine-building Industries' (1978).

Minerals and non-ferrous metals
K. P. Wang is the leading expert on China in the US Bureau of Mines; his reports include *PRC a New Industrial Power with a Strong Mineral Base*, published by the US Bureau of Mines, Department of the Interior in 1975, 'China's Mineral Economy' in the JEC 1978 book, and *Mineral Resources and Basic Industries of the People's Republic of China*, Westview Press, May 1977. *The Mineral Resources of China* by A. B. Ikonnikov, Geological Society of America, 1978, carries good, though dated information. 'Aluminum Production in China' in the March–April 1978 *China Business Review* is a useful source, as is 'China's Tungsten Pricing Strategy' by Suan Tan in the March–April 1979 issue. *China's Minerals and Metals* by Peter Weintraub, available as a separate report from the NCUSCT, was published in November–December 1974. Another valuable, shorter study is the CIA's *China: The Nonferrous Metals Industry in the* 1970's issued in 1978.

Petroleum
The amount of energy expended on producing books and articles on China's petroleum industry is probably equivalent to at least several billion barrels of crude from China's leading oilfield, Daqing. Apart from the Smil works noted above, the following comprise a useful library on China's petroleum: Chu-yuan Cheng, *China's Petroleum Industry*, Praeger, 1976; Nicholas Ludlow, 'China's Oil', *China Business Review*, January–February 1974; Tatsu Kambara, 'The Petroleum Industry in China', *China Quarterly*, December 1974; Wolfgang Bartke, *Oil in the People's Republic of China*, C. Hurst & Co., 1977; Randall Hardy, *Chinese Oil*, Center for International and Strategic Studies, 1976; *China: Oil Production Prospects*, CIA, 1977; *China's Petroleum Industry*, NCUSCT, 1976; H. C. Ling, *The Petroleum Industry of the People's Republic of China*, Hoover, 1975; *China's Oil Industry Survey*, Sino-British Trade Council, 1975; and Jan-Olaf Willums, 'China's Offshore Petroleum', *China Business Review*, July–August 1977.

In a different league are a massive study by Willums and A. A. Meyerhoff, costing several thousand dollars, and an even more thorough, up-to-date, and expensive technical study by Robertson Associates of Llandudno, North

Wales. A major study of the organization, manpower, and technical dissemination channels in the Chinese petroleum industry, by Jeffrey Schultz, is due out in 1979 from the NCUSCT. The best technical reports of China's largest oilfields are articles on Taching (Daching), by Stephanie Green in the *China Business Review*, January–February 1978, and November–December 1978 on Shengli and Bohai. For anybody interested in all facets of China's off-shore oil development, Selig Harrison's book, *China, Oil and Asia*, Columbia University Press, 1977 is an outstanding, durable, and readable book which is highly recommended.

Shipping, ports
While China's shipping has been developing rapidly, useful background reading includes: 'China's Merchant Marine' by Irwin Millard Heine in the *China Business Review*, March–April 1976, three articles by Stephanie Green in the same magazine; entitled 'When will your ship come in?', 1975–76; *China's Maritime Agreements*, a Special Report of the NCUSCT, and *Chinese Merchant Ship Production*, CIA, March 1976. The NCUSCT has published a *China Shipping Manual* with known details of China's ports and shipping regulations, and the Sino-British Trade Council has put out a useful report, *Ships and Shipbuilding in China*, 1976. George Lauriat's pieces in the China Trade Report are good updates.

Transportation
There are relatively few good reports on transportation in China. The chapters by Jack Baranson and Hans Heyman on China's automotive industry and air transport industry respectively, in William Whitson's book, *Doing Business with China*, Praeger, 1974, are still good. Heyman's aviation study for the Rand Corporation is worth reading. *China's Vehicle Industry* from the NCUSCT has detailed specifications of several score of China's autos, trucks, and other vehicles. The Commerce Department and the Sino-British Trade Council have published market assessments of China's vehicle industry. The JEC 1972 study has a report, 'China: The Transportation Sector 1950–1971'. The March–April 1977, *China Business Review* has a comprehensive report on 'China's Railroads' with details, among other things, of all Peking's major railroad purchases, and of over thirty locomotive and rolling stock plants.

Business conditions in China and how to do business with the PRC
At this point, after this selective introduction to some of the resources of different sectors, the researcher, convinced there is a potential China market, should start investigating how to do business with China. The most straightforward, simplest introduction to going business with China is a booklet, *Doing Business with China*, published by the US Commerce Department; other government trade departments issue similar, helpful guides.

Beyond this, a plethora of books, including the Szuprowicz volume, have advice on starting business with the PRC. There is no perfect book as yet: most try to do too much, few are oriented to the practicalities of really doing business with China—and things change.

Addresses of China's foreign trade corporations are available in a booklet from the China Council for Promotion of International Trade (CCPIT), Peking. A more comprehensive book is published as a pocket guide to *China's Foreign Trade Organizations* by the NCUSCT. The guide, published in April 1979, has *pinyin* spelling, telex and telephone numbers of the corporations and other organizations and their branches, information on China's ministries and agencies of the State Council with cross references by product area, and also a listing by function and address of all China's known domestic corporations. It also explains the internal structure of each corporation.

The China Trade Quarterly, published in 1977 by Far East Publications in Hongkong, is a methodical compendium of China's trade organizations, addresses and contract information.

A larger volume, by several hundred pages, called *China's Foreign Trade Corporations*, compiled by Jeffrey Schultz, available from the NCUSCT April 1979, gives comprehensive details of the organization of China's trading corporations and a listing of over 1800 Chinese foreign trade officials with specialities and biographical details.

Useful chapters for importers and exporters on how to start business with China and on the Canton Fair, are found in the *Encyclopaedia of China Today*, the *China Business Review*, and in a booklet called *What China Has to Sell*, published by the NCUSCT, which lists over 900 product catalogues available from the corporations. John Kamm's *Canton Companion*, published for the Canton Fair by the Far East Trade Press in Hongkong is a thorough and useful source.

The legal aspects of doing business with China are many. The best guide on the subject is: 'Legal and Practical Problems in the China Trade' by Eugene A. Theroux, published in the JEC volume, 1975. Another piece in the JEC 1978 publication is useful: Stanley Lubman's 'Contracts, Practice and Law in Trade with China'.

Many articles have appeared on different legal aspects of the China trade. Only a few of the more salient publications are listed here. These include *Trademark Registration in the PRC*, published by the NCUSCT, 1978; *Legal Aspects of Doing Business with China*, the Practicing Law Institute, New York, 1976, with a good chapter on arbitration; Gene T. Hsiao's *The Foreign Trade of China: Policy, Law and Practice*, University of California Press, Berkeley 1977; and *Law and Politics in China's Foreign Trade*, edited by Victor Li.

The Harvard Studies Series in East Asian Law, overseen by Jerome Cohen, includes a number of excellent legal reference books on specialized aspects of business with China, such as China and international aviation regulations and China's attitude to international law.

Few good sources exist on licensing to China. Material includes that in *Les Nouvelles*, early 1977; in the *Patent and Trademark Review*, Volume 73, numbers 10 and 11, 1975, and number 1, 1976; and John Dingle's *Technical Selling in China*, Roger Williams Inc., Princeton, New Jersey, USA. A forthcoming book, written in part by Clark T. Randt of the NCUSCT, will cover the subject in depth.

Arbitration and Dispute Settlement in Trade with China and *Standard Form Contracts of the People's Republic of China* are important sources, available as special reports from the NCUSCT. An especially important article is 'Arbitration in the People's Republic of China: Case Examples Described' by Liu Yiu-chu in the *China Business Review*, May–June 1977.

Financial aspects of doing business with China are covered in a number of publications. There is a good chapter on China's banking industry by William Triplet in William Whitson's book, *Doing Business with China*. The best, most up-to-date report is 'International Finance in the People's Republic of China' by David L. Denny in the JEC 1978 Volume 1. For an idea of how China's international liabilities stand, read 'China's Foreign Financial Liabilities' by David Denny and Frederic Surls in the *China Business Review*, March–April 1977, and 'The Bank of China in the 1970's' by Howell Jackson and Dick Wilson, in the January–February 1977 issue. More practical articles in the same review, available as reprints, give the A to Z on how to finance trade with China. They are Deirdra Deamer's 'Financing Exports of Plant and Equipment to China', January–February 1979 issue, and Katherine Schwering's 'Financing Imports from China', September–October 1974 issue.

On the purely practical side, other reprints from the *China Business Review* are essential reading if you are involved in technical exports to China, including 'Giving Technical Seminars in the PRC' by Howell Jackson, 'Technical Training in Export Contracts' with the PRC by Stephanie Green and Alistair Wrightman, 'Hosting Delegations from China' by Nicholas Ludlow, and 'Industrial Standardization in the PRC' by Erik Baark.

Wages, Prices and Standard of Living of Urban Workers in the PRC by Christopher Howe, plus Howe's earlier book on the subject, *Wage Patterns and Wage Policy in Modern China*, Cambridge, 1973 are important reading for anyone contemplating an equity joint-venture in China. Susan Swannack-Nunn's *US-Business and East-West Industrial Cooperation Prospects with the PRC* from the NCUSCT is a useful starter for a firm thinking of entering a cooperation arrangement with the Chinese.

How to educate the Chinese about your products? Negotiate? How to get that invitation to China? What is the best approach? Travel information? Political background? Some of this information is covered in the sources listed above or in the appendix; more will be forthcoming in periodicals, and from the world's publishing houses, more needs to be written and made known, but armed with the information above, a company should be well on the way to framing its strategy, approach, and targets in the Chinese market.

When a firm has established its long-term goals and strategy, it is ready, as one wag reversing the Chinese proverb has put it, to take that single step that begins with 10 000 miles and start a relationship with the Chinese. Then the time has come to consult one more indispensable source: *The China Phone Book*, from Box 11581, Hongkong, which has the addresses and telephone numbers of most places you need to know in China, including state trading corporations, embassies, restaurants, and stores.

As the Chinese say: *Huan Ying*! Welcome to the Chinese trade.

3. Selling to China

IAN RAE

Before attempting to sell to China, an understanding of the market and how it is organized is essential. Certain basic facts must first be considered: it is a huge country with a population of about 1 billion, 80 per cent of whom are on the land. Despite remarkable advances over the past thirty years, China still has a very long way to go before becoming a modern industrial state. Nevertheless, industry has developed greatly and the standards of technology and technical skills are high. China makes its own aircraft, ships, machine tools, locomotives, satellites, and instruments, to name a few examples. Most aspects of living, in town or country, be it work, education, or relaxation, are organized by a government whose writ runs throughout the land. The mere fact that this vast population is fed, clothed, housed, and in work is a remarkable achievement.

China's foreign trade is only some 5 per cent of its GNP. Its chief trading partners are Japan, Western Europe, North America, and to a lesser extent eastern Europe. It exports considerably, both agricultural produce and manufactured goods. It imports technical equipment to build its economy and grain to feed its people. It imports very few consumer goods. In 1978, China's trade totalled approximately $20 billion, about $10 billion each way. Japan was by far the biggest exporter, reaching $3 billion in value, with West Germany reaching about a third of that and France, Britain, and Italy trailing far behind. The US was a substantial seller at $824 million, but much of this was made up by grain, not industrial goods. Australia and Canada were also important grain sources.

The unusual nature of the market, compared to other countries, socialist or not, makes most conventional sales methods either unsuitable or impossible. China is so organized, and so functions, that none of the normal rules apply. Chinese newspapers, journals, and other media have only just begun very tentatively to accept advertising. Buying time on TV or radio is so far rare. Direct mailing is possible, but only to a limited degree and after laborious compilation of lists, for no industrial or trade directories are published (apart from a list of major government agencies); nor, for that matter, are there any official telephone directories, though one compiled by a journalist was recently published in Hongkong (see Chapter 2 page 43). Visits to China (other than as a tourist) for business purposes are generally only possible on receipt of an invitation from the relevant organization. Detailed guidance as to whom to approach in the first instance, and how to set about things, is given by bodies sponsoring trade with China, business houses, and embassies. Selling to China is interesting, worthwhile, and profitable. It is also time-consuming and often frustrating. The Chinese like to deal with those they know, so would-be sellers must be patient as relations develop.

These opening comments should not deter the seller, provided he has the right product, from trying to get across to one of the most interesting and worthwhile markets in the world today. This is particularly so now, with the flexibility and impetus given to business by China's new policies, as exemplified in the programme of industrialization to achieve the 'Four Modernizations'. China intends to become a great industrial power by the end of this century and everything indicates that it will succeed in this aim. Effective sales promotion in China implies three things: first, an understanding of China's needs—advanced technology and equipment to suit its industrial plans; second, a general knowledge of the system of government and affairs and the ability to work within this framework and abide by it; third, some faith, as results are sometimes slow and seldom attributable.

All China's external trading relations are conducted by a series of national import/export corporations, covering the broad fields of machinery, chemicals, instruments, light industrial products, and textiles (a list is given in Appendix II). These corporations all have their head offices in Peking, with branch offices in major cities such as Shanghai, Tianjin, and Canton. They are represented abroad by the commercial sections of embassies and, in Hongkong, by the China Resources Company and other agents (see Appendix VII).

There are parallel official bodies that also deal with trade, but with its organization rather than its execution. It is not possible to deal with individuals and all buying or selling of any goods or products has hitherto been channelled via one of the China national import/export corporations (see Appendix VII).

The corporations buy according to China's requirements which in turn are determined by the State. These decisions reflect the aim, publicly stated, of modernizing the country and this must be kept constantly in mind.

The first step in making contact is to write to the corporation concerned. It is usually self-evident which is the right one from its title and the list of products it handles. If in doubt, the Chinese embassy's Commercial Section, or the body sponsoring trade with China will be able to give guidance. If in doubt as to which of the two to approach, write to both.

Introductory letters need not be in Chinese. They should be accompanied by technical data and prices, ten copies to the head office in Peking, further quantities to branches. This is important as it allows the Chinese to distribute material to interested agencies and end-users. Avoid glossy publicity brochures and reflect that the contents of an annual report, giving financial results, are of more immediate interest (although full facts about a company will be needed as negotiations develop).

These first approaches should also be copied to the Chinese embassy in the seller's country with whom contact should be maintained. Extra copies may also be sent to other bodies in Peking not directly dealing with purchases but whose role is to promote trade or advise ministries. The Centre for Introducing Literature and Samples of New Products of the CCPIT (China Council for the Promotion of International Trade) disseminates literature to end-users. The Technical Exchange Department also arranges seminars and distributes technical papers (the CCPIT and the role it plays are described later in this chapter). Professional societies, of which there are many (civil engineering, aeronautical, chemical etc.) are also interested in subject matter in their own fields. They too are in contact with the foreign trade corporations.

Depending on the product, the would-be seller can also approach some of the new specialist corporations in the fields of petroleum, chemical fibres, railways, and so on; these bodies are offshoots of the established corporations and come under the aegis of the technical ministries.

Replies will take time. This is a huge country with a large government machinery, through which just about everything must pass.

Another way of getting known is the use of regular Western publications covering industry, often sponsored by an official body, which circulate in China. These are usually fairly broad in scope, and produced on average two or three times a year. In many cases such publications do not carry advertising in the conventional sense but paid pages of technical data sheets, embellished by illustrations and diagrams. Mailing is either done direct to lists of end-users, or in semi-bulk to import corporations and similar bodies, or in bulk to the CCPIT which undertakes internal distribution. Sometimes a combination of all three methods is used. In all cases the journals are free to the Chinese reader, revenue for the publishers coming from the firms who participate.

Prominent journals include *European Industrial Report* published by Verlag und Information, *Industrie Recherche et Technologie Française*, published by the Centre Francais du Commerce Extérieur, *Dutch Trade News* published by Sembodje of Amsterdam, *British Industry* published by British Industrial Publicity Overseas Limited, sponsored by the Sino-British Trade Council, and *American Industrial Report* published by China Consultants

Limited, Hongkong. All these journals effectively transmit technical information to the Chinese. Like all forms of advertising, however oblique, results are not attributable, by there is plenty of evidence that readership is widespread and official approval is endorsed by the CCPIT's willingness, in certain cases, to organize internal dissemination.

English, or other language, literature is also of course useful but inevitably its application is more limited. All the major import/export corporations and other official bodies have translation facilities, so Chinese translation, although desirable, is not vital. Translation becomes essential for exhibition catalogues and regular journals produced in volume and widely read throughout the country.

Once the initial contact has been made, further sales promotion is feasible in the following forms: industrial and technical exhibitions held in major Chinese cities, and attended by selected mass audiences, technical seminars and symposia given for selected small audiences of high qualifications, and visiting missions (which are usually organized according to product but sometimes by organizations—chambers of commerce, for example). Representation, in the sense of a resident agent or subsidiary, is virtually impossible (though there are now a few exceptions); however, many manufacturers who are themselves unable to sustain the required effort and expense, work through trading houses based in Europe or Hongkong.

There is also the twice-yearly Canton Fair (or, to give it its correct title, the Guangzhou Export Commodities Fair). Held primarily to promote Chinese export sales, it provides a focal point for all sorts of two-way trade between China and the rest of the world; during its month-long showings, about 20 000 visitors attend. Firms attending certainly have a chance to promote sales and technical seminars regularly occur. Exhibitions may be organized on an individual, sectoral, or national basis, by Western nations (these excluded the US until the resolution of the claims/assets problem (see page 200), by the Japanese or by Eastern Bloc countries. Very recently, the first ever international exhibition was held successfully, with 12 nations participating.

Individual exhibitions, organized by a single company, are the least common. The German firm, Siemens, held its own exhibition in Shanghai in December 1978, exhibiting a complete range of sophisticated electrical equipment and expecting 60 000 visitors.

Sectoral exhibitions, offering a 'vertical coverage' of a particular industry or part of an industry have become the most popular and effective type of exhibition. Concentration on a particular aspect means that a more select audience is possible; logistically they are easier to handle than large-scale national shows; and for the same reasons there is less of a bottleneck in the ensuing sales negotiations. Over the past two years there have been a Swedish transportation exhibition, a French electronics exhibition, an Italian medical exhibition, a British scientific instruments exhibition, a French 'Petrogas' exhibition, a Swiss machine tool exhibition, and a British energy equipment show. Sectoral exhibitions vary in size but usually involve about 50 companies and receive 50–60 000 visitors.

National exhibitions were held by every one of China's major trading partners over the years 1971–75, the previous period of interest in foreign technology. They were in effect general industrial shows in which a single country put on a display of just about everything it thought could be of interest to the Chinese (and in some cases extra items purely for prestige reasons). They involved considerable protocol, were usually opened by a minister from the exhibiting country and attracted much attention. During this period a spate of such exhibitions was put on by the Swedes, Canadians, Italians, British, French, Germans, Dutch, Belgians, Swiss, Austrians, and Australians. In 1973, the British Industrial Technology Exhibition, for example, included 350 exhibiting firms, 750 British businessmen and technicians, 4000 tons of exhibits and was visited by 250 000 technicians, officials, and end-users from all over China. The German Industrial Exhibition in 1975 was even bigger. The Japanese also put on a mammoth exhibition which was held both in Peking and Shanghai.

Exhibitions, whatever their form and content are usually mounted by professional exhibition organizers who are either retained by the sponsoring government or body, or are themselves part of that government's own trade promotion network. In the latter category there is the Fairs and Promotions Department of Trade, Whitehall, London, the Netherland Council for Trade Promotion, the Hague, the Schweizerische Zentrale für Handelsforderung in Zürich, le Comité Permanent des Foires et Manifestations Economiques à l'Étranger in Paris, the Swedish Export Council in Stockholm. In the private sector, ITF, Industrial and Trade Fairs Limited of Birmingham, and IMAG, Internationaler Messe- und Ausstellungsdienst GmbH of Munich have played leading roles in major exhibitions. Similar organizations exist in most countries and when the day comes for the United States to exhibit in China the sponsor will be the National Council for US–China Trade, Washington, DC.

The actual exhibitors are usually invited to join by the sponsoring body, once agreement has been reached with the Chinese authorities over timing and scale. Usually they are subsidized by their own government as regards rent of floor space for stands, travel, and freight home for unsold exhibits. China is after all a long way away. Every exhibition employs a team of sub-contractors who are appointed by the organizers including a travel agent, stand fitters, packing and shipping agents, producers of catalogues and brochures; in addition, the organizers furnish a Head of Protocol (very necessary), a secretariat and an executive to coordinate the various technical seminars that are held concurrently. Exhibitions last on average 12 days plus a two-day preview, certain days being earmarked for smaller numbers of more senior visitors; there is an opening banquet or reception, an opening ceremony, and another party when it is all over. Exhibitions bring with them not only their exhibits but medical supplies (arguably quite unnecessary), instant coffee, marmalade (according to nation), reading matter and films; large quantities of liquor and cigarettes are allowed in duty free. The exhibitor quickly learns never to drink a whisky soda after toasts in *mao tai* at a banquet. *Mao tai* is remembered with a shudder by some and respect by all; it is the strongest liquor in existence and smells slightly of varnish.

The dramatis personae on the Chinese side fall into several categories. Direct liaison with the organizers is handled by the Foreign Exhibitions Department of the China Council for the Promotion of International Trade, a body which does exactly what its name implies. It is worth bearing in mind that the CCPIT handles all aspects of trade promotion in China short of actual business; it is headed by a very senior official, Wang Yao-ting who holds the equivalent of Cabinet rank.

Through the good offices of the CCPIT's Foreign Exhibitions Department, the organizers deal with the relevant Chinese ancillary organizations: the Foreign Trade Transportation Corporation which brings in the exhibits; the customs who clear them; the Exhibition Services Centre which hires interpreters, 'explainers', i.e., those with a technical background who demonstrate the functioning of exhibits on the stands; cleaning personnel; lavatory attendants; teamakers; the China International Travel Service which handles all travel for foreigners in the country; the Peking Arts Company, if stand fittings are made in China. There is also the hotel where exhibitors stay in a group, usually the Friendship in Peking, a large complex of 2000 rooms fairly near to the Exhibition Centre, with cars and buses to carry exhibitors to and fro. All this has to be arranged well in advance and if one includes the technical sales aspect (of which more later), it is little wonder that a major exhibition in China takes a good year to plan. Most, but not all, exhibitions are held at the Peking Exhibition Centre in the northeast of the city, built by the Russians in the fifties; other displays have been held at the Peking Agricultural Exhibition Hall, and further afield in Tianjin, Harbin, Shanghai, and Wuhan.

Just how effective are exhibitions, be they large or small? On the whole they are worthwhile, provided exhibits are chosen with care, are advanced technologically, and of course come within the scope of Chinese purchasing requirements. A few years ago, it was hard to find out what the Chinese wanted to see and thus what to exhibit, as the stock answer to any question was that they required an exhibition that reflected the advanced technology of the country in question, *voilà tout*. But times have changed and this sort of difficulty no longer remains. Other ingredients for a successful exhibition are good organization, high calibre technical seminars, ample provision of technical literature in Chinese: catalogues, brochures, pamphlets, and the like. Usually such literature is in part distributed by the CCPIT in advance; the rest is placed on the stands where it is eagerly grabbed by the visitors. This material must be in clear, modern Chinese and of technical content.

Practically every exhibition provides literature for its visitors in considerable quantity. There is always an official catalogue, often running to hundreds of pages, with an average print order of 10 000 copies. These catalogues contain lists of exhibitors and indexes of exhibits, individual data sheets for firms attending, cross-referenced indices, plan of the hall, and so on. There is often also a shortened catalogue or 'mini-catalogue' of only a few pages, giving basic information to guide a visitor round; these are usually produced in sufficient quantity to give one copy to every single visitor to the exhibition. In addition, individual exhibiting firms have their own brochures and pamphlets on their stands; there are also display panels in Chinese; instructional films are dubbed, audio-visual presentations likewise.

Normally the CCPIT distributes up to 70 per cent of all the literature produced in advance to end-users and others likely to visit the exhibition, including buying corporations; material shipped to an exhibition should accordingly be clearly marked—either for the CCPIT, or for the hall. Literature at exhibitions is popular; every visitor takes every pamphlet on offer and one can see the scramble when a new batch appears. It is not only of use at the time but is kept long after for reference. Sometimes organizers, particularly of national exhibitions, have provided complete kits, bearing the national flag as a souvenir, to be kept by visitors. Below is a summary (not exhaustive) of foreign exhibitions held in China over the last four years which indicates Chinese interests.

1976

Hungary	Telecommunications	Peking	
Yugoslavia	Machine tools	Peking	
East Germany	Electronics	Shanghai	
France	Instruments	Peking	
Sweden	Transportation	Peking	
Italy	Packaging	Shanghai	

1977

Holland	Electronics	Peking	
Japan	Industry	Peking	
Japan	Shipbuilding	Shanghai	

1978

International (12 nations)	Agricultural machinery	Peking	First of its kind Attendance 300 000
Britain	Scientific instruments	Peking	Attendance 60 000
France	Petrochemicals	Peking	
Japan	Construction/metals	Peking	
West Germany	Electrical goods	Shanghai	

1979

Switzerland	Machine tools	Peking	
Britain	Energy equipment	Peking	

Technical seminars, known in Chinese as 'technical-seat-talk', are held concurrently with exhibitions. In this case, it is the Technical Exchange Department of the CCPIT that does the organizing on the Chinese side, in conjunction with the exhibition organizers, who usually allocate one or two of their own people for this specific task. The seminars are usually held in the hotel where the exhibitors are staying, are attended by 10 to 30 highly qualified Chinese technical personnel (who often display a remarkably thorough knowledge of their field), and can last two or three days and in some cases, as a result of questions and discussion, much longer. Subject matter for seminars proposed is submitted in detail, together with full qualifications of the lecturer, well in advance. The Chinese will reject those which they consider insufficiently advanced in content; the number is seldom less than 30, and for a big exhibition, much more.

Papers given at seminars, for their very length and complexity are usually not put into Chinese beforehand but are simultaneously interpreted, material being submitted to the interpreter as far in advance as possible.

Whereas exhibitions enable thousands of end-users, officials, and technicians to view a collection of sophisticated equipment and so influence buying decisions, technical seminars provide a point of contact with a small, highly qualified team of people who also, by recommendation and interest, influence buying decisions. Implicit in the success of a seminar is the willingness to prepare and give away large amounts of technical information for nothing, for there is not always a *quid pro quo*. Nonetheless, it has been claimed that some three quarters of British firms that gave seminars in the early seventies achieved a sale within two years.

Apart from those conducted at exhibitions there are other types of seminars: there are individual company seminars held as the result of a direct invitation by a Foreign Trade Corporation, with end-users attending or not, as the case may be; similar independent seminars but hosted and organized by the CCPIT; seminars given by groups of companies. Another type of seminar, usually with little immediate commercial bearing, is that held at the invitation of one of the Chinese industrial societies.

All nations selling to China hold seminars and it is impossible to list them all, but the following lists of presentations by members of The 48 Group of British companies in late 1977 is indicative:

Smith Industries	Testing engine airframe and flight control equipment
Solartron	Computer-controlled automatic test equipment for guidance systems
Instron	Application for computer-controlled testing rigs for large-scale proving tests on prototype aircraft
Martin-Baker Aircraft	Testing of ejection seats
Smith Industries	Impact of digital technology on Smith's SEP.10 flight control systems for feeder liner and executive jet operations

Dowty Fuel Systems	Pumping systems design related to fuel system specifications
Dowty Fuel Systems	Gas turbine after-burning controls and their future prospects
Dowty Rotol	Nitrogen-supplemented liquid spring shock absorbers

If the mailing, mission, exhibition, or seminar is successful, it will lead on to actual business negotiations. These are conducted by the foreign firm on the one hand, with the China National Import Corporation appropriate to the product—machinery, chemicals, and so forth—on the other. These corporations conduct all China's buying from abroad and respond to requirements from end-users, bounded obviously by a framework of overall policy considerations and budgetary limitations.

In the case of an exhibition, as it unfolds, with crowds of visitors from all over the country (again organized by the CCPIT), so exhibitors are called forward by the corporations for discussions resulting from interest shown by end-users in particular items. These negotiations are usually for the sale of actual exhibits and there is some tension, as many deals are not concluded until the very last day. Further sales come later, though a wise man will be prepared to linger on in Peking for a week or more after closure, as by doing so he gives his Chinese opposite numbers time to contemplate, perhaps place, future business. The Chinese are thorough and slow negotiators, not the least bit impressed by the frenetic schedules of Western businessmen who want to be in Hongkong on Wednesday, in Tokyo on Thursday, and in New York for a meeting on Monday morning.

Given this, the first requirement of a would-be seller is patience and a willingness to provide his interlocutors with all the technical information they require. Discussions can be long lasting (several weeks in some cases) and no stone is left unturned. If he is not prepared for this, then he should not go. He will find the Chinese courteous and friendly, with concern for his well-being as well as his product. This will include entertainment in the form of visits to places of interest, theatres, and dinners. The latter start early, end early and should only be refused in cases of genuine extremis. It should also be added that the Chinese are shrewd and often sophisticated in Western business methods, displaying considerable background knowledge. They will, naturally, try to get the best price they can. When the talks are over and the deal signed, the seller has no worries over licences or customs as these are handled by the buyers; nor has he any worries over payment.

Resident representation in China is still not possible, though there are hopes this will alter. In fact, certain Japanese firms have had people living in Peking hotels on a more or less permanent basis for years; the Danish East Asiatic Company has maintained an executive in Peking since 1973 and the German firm of Jebsen has more recently been able to do the same. Rumour has it that certain of these foreign representatives may have their own telex.

Many manufacturers who are unable to visit China regularly work through one of the Chinese trading houses, for example, Jardine Matheson in Hongkong, Biddle Sawyer in London, Olivier in Paris, Sembodja in Amsterdam, Melchers-Ferrostaal in Bremen. Missions to China, often organized by Chambers of Commerce or similar bodies and usually by industrial category, regularly tour the country at the invitation of the corporations. While sales are not usually made on these occasions, members have a chance to make contacts and meet end-users. Equally, Chinese missions travelling abroad will often ask to meet again firms they have got to know in China.

Hongkong, while in no way the gateway to China, provides a useful jumping-off point. Many firms conduct part of their Chinese business via Hongkong subsidiaries or agents, and Hongkong provides excellent administrative back-up to those attending the Canton Fair. Any form of promotion used in Hongkong does not cross the border and media published in Hongkong does not circulate in China.

It might be useful to mention some of the peculiarities of the Chinese language. Those new to the market wonder if technical terms can be put into Chinese—and what about place names and personal names? Chinese is an ancient language that has readily adapted itself to modern usage. It is fair to say that everything that can be expressed in English can be expressed in Chinese. Written Chinese is a series of ideographs, or characters, each with its own intrinsic sound, tone, and meaning; in fact, each character is a word in its own right. Modern Chinese is usually, but not always, expressed in a combination of characters; the great variety and depth of the language has made it relatively easy to coin new phrases and technical terms. Foreign names obviously cannot be translated; they are transliterated by choosing characters which, when read aloud, sound like the name and have at best a good and at least a neutral meaning.

In recent years the written language has been reformed by simplifying many of the characters in common use, and in some cases making one character do the work of two. All China uses this simplified version and under no circumstances should the old style, still popular in places like Hongkong, be used. Likewise, translations should only be made by those abreast of current Chinese; translations by Chinese who have lived out of China for many years, or have not received a Chinese education, or both, can be disastrous. Cautionary tales in this regard are legion. There was (and this is true) the shipper who consigned his goods to Tianjian via the new port of Hsinkang but had his labels read Sinkiang, Chinese Turkestan, thousands of miles in the interior.

The chief spoken language is *Putunghua*, known in the West as Mandarin. It is the official language of the country and is spoken as the mother tongue, albeit in varying forms, by about 500 million people. The purest form is from the Peking area. There are other dialects, particularly along the south-eastern seaboard, such as Fujianese, Hakka, and Cantonese. They are very different indeed from Mandarin, but the bulk of the population in these regions uses the national language as a lingua franca. When dubbing films, care should be taken to employ a Chinese who speaks 'standard Mandarin'.

Other common pitfalls, not of language alone, could also be mentioned here, for instance the patronizing term 'Chinaman' for Chinese, as once used by a British minister in a leading speech to a Chinese audience (fortunately interpreted as *Zongguo ren,* a Chinese person, so no harm was done). One must also avoid Republic of China (Taiwan) for People's Republic of China—a mistake the Chinese genuinely find most offensive, which will at best result in a lecture.

Care too must be taken with maps; indeed, many experienced traders with China say 'no maps ever', for a slight error on the Sino-Indian frontier, or a reference, even by implication, to Hongkong as a separate country, can (or at least could) result in the banning of a leaflet or catalogue. Perhaps the most heinous crime is to make a blunder over Taiwan; it is a province of China and should be shown as such. In an excess of misguided zeal, a major firm produced, for its stand in the exhibition hall, a large wall map upon which Taiwan did not appear at all, just empty ocean. Frantic efforts to find a map with a Taiwan which could be cut out to paste over were of no avail; rescue, however, came from a large-scale map of southern Europe: Sardinia is much the same shape.

Mistakes are not all confined to the Western side. Last year, a well-known merchant had considerable difficulty over what should have been a relatively simple contract at the Canton Fair. It was only after half a day that the interpreter was changed and he found that, until then, every time he had

Table 3.1 Exports to China by leading partners

$ Million	1978	1977
USA	824	172
Japan	3 049	1 939
France	197	95
West Germany	995	502
Italy	188	86
Netherlands	132	52
UK	175	109
Canada	442	347
Australia	481	461
TOTAL	6 427	3 759
WORLD TOTAL	10 600[1]	7 100

Sources: OECD, *JETRO China Newsletter, China Business Review, China: Economic Indicators* (National Foreign Assessment Center, Washington, DC, December 1978).
Notes
1. Preliminary.

Table 3.2   Imports from China by leading partners

	1978	1977
USA	324	203
Japan	2 030	1 574
France	227	194
West Germany	367	288
Italy	200	161
Netherlands	125	94
UK	212	182
Canada	83	77
Australia	141	124
TOTAL	3 697	2 897
WORLD TOTAL	10 200	8 000

Sources: OECD, *JETRO China Newsletter, China Business Review, China: Economic Indicators* (National Foreign Assessment Center, Washington, DC, December 1978).

asked for a reduction in price this had been interpreted as an increase and vice versa.

Recent developments have made the world very conscious of China. Most national newspapers carry items almost every day, leading magazines run regular articles, and there are documentaries on TV. There are now package tours to China and the international businessman who has not yet made it to Peking may feel out of things. Inevitably, this has brought in its train people trying to cash in on the China bandwagon, either by spurious publications purporting to circulate in China but which do not, translation agencies employing unqualified Chinese writing in old-style characters, or phoney consultants who claim to have special knowledge and contacts. For the newcomer, bewildered by rival claims and without any idea of what best to do, the safe course of action is to consult the recognized body that promotes trade between his country and China: the SBTC in Britain and the National Council for US-China Trade in the USA are two examples (see Appendix III for addresses). If no official body exists he should ask his embassy in Peking for advice, or go to one of the big trading houses.

Change is afoot in China, but certain basic ingredients remain. It is still a large, backward country under a strong central government, with a fairly industrious and disciplined population, making every effort to catch up by dint of its own exertions, aided by the input of technology. It is a country where everything works according to a set of rules—you cannot 'beat' the system. Would-be sellers should plan accordingly.

Author's note: In mid-1979 The Shanghai Advertising Corporation (97 Yuanmingyuan Rd, Shanghai) was revived and now handles foreign advertising of selected products in Chinese media.

4. Receiving a Chinese delegation

PHILIP SNOW

China's startlingly ambitious plans for economic development will require the absorption of a large amount of Western technology in a short time. One of the principal ways in which the Chinese are undertaking this is through the dispatch, in rapidly growing numbers, of missions to other countries.

This has made it more and more necessary that their hosts in Western countries should acquire at least a basic idea of how to look after these missions. Trade promotion bodies in Britain, the US, and other countries are available to offer advice to companies expecting to be visited by Chinese groups, but with the numbers as great as they are now it seems desirable that there should be some general knowledge in circulation.

Looking after Chinese delegations, as potential technical and commercial partners, and simply as guests, need not be impossibly complicated, but there are certain essentials which are not always obvious, and which must be learned if a visit is to be enjoyable and successful. These include several fundamental points of courtesy and consideration which are not only relevant in the context of Chinese missions, but should be respected by anyone in personal contact with the Chinese, in his own country or in China.

Different kinds of delegation
These missions fall into various categories. There are high-level delegations headed by vice-ministers, ministers and even vice-premiers: these generally include representatives of the State Planning Commission, the State Scientific and Technological Commission, the Ministries of Machine-Building and other technical ministries, and the China National Foreign Trade Corporations. Such missions are usually empowered to conclude protocols

and agreements setting a framework for the long-term development of trade.

There are lower-level buying missions, usually composed mainly of representatives of the foreign trade corporations.

There are 'technical study groups', consisting chiefly of engineers, technicians, and researchers from factories, industrial corporations, and research institutes: the latter are in some cases directly attached to ministries, universities and the increasingly prominent 'professional societies' (such as the Chinese Mechanical Engineering Society) to which engineers from more specialist organizations may concurrently belong. The majority of missions are of this kind, and they are the most likely variety to be encountered by a company in the first instance. A spontaneous request made by such a group to visit a company indicates serious interest, and a good impression made on them may pave the way for subsequent business. However, their function is purely assessment and recommendation and they are not, as a rule, authorized to conclude any business other than the small-scale purchase of samples.

Three other categories worth mentioning are academic delegations, which may sometimes visit a company, Chinese selling missions from the foreign trade corporations, not wholly irrelevant in this context because of the mounting interest in 'compensation trading', and groups of trainee engineers, now sent more and more to spend periods with individual companies as part of a long-term contract.

The growing numbers
In 1978, the United Kingdom received at least 70 delegations of these various kinds, as against a recorded 19 in 1977 and 14 in 1976. In early 1979 missions were arriving almost weekly in the major Western countries and Japan. In the past, the UK has consistently received more delegations than any country other than Japan; the USA has been sent relatively few, but this is changing. The size of delegations varies from the 6 to 12 characteristic of most 'technical study groups' to 25 or so in the case of many high-level parties. A recent composite aviation group, with two different main interests totalled no less than 43.

High-level parties visiting the UK tend to stay for about two weeks, 'technical study groups' for the best part of a month; the latter often extend their stay by a few days to accommodate interests which have arisen, either during their tour or after the provisional finalization of the programme, but before their departure from Peking. Where the group has been invited by an individual company or organization, it may wish to use these final days to have a glimpse of the competition before returning home. Trainee engineers frequently stay for six months or longer. Groups visiting Western Europe (particularly high-level ones) may try to combine up to four or five countries in a single tour.

How visits begin

All Chinese delegations require a sponsor in the host country, and are normally invited by a government, coordinating body, (e.g., exhibition organizer or trade association), or individual company. Sometimes a Chinese organization will request an invitation, having heard of an exhibition or similar function. The commercial section of the appropriate Chinese Embassy may then approach either the prospective host, or the country's Department of Trade, or other trade promotion body.

A group may be invited during a tour: this may happen after attendance at an exhibition, a discussion at a conference, or the glimpse of a product or technique that has caught a group's eye during a visit to an entirely different company. Where a company issues an invitation at this late stage, there may be sufficient flexibility in the group's programme to accommodate it if interest is strong enough, but the company will stand a better chance if it is able to ascertain the imminence of a visit well in advance, and register its interest with the Chinese Embassy, Department of Trade, trade promotion body, or host organization. Close contact with the trade promotion bodies and study of their publications is recommended for this purpose.

Where a group makes a last-minute addition to its own programme, contact with a company may, once again, be made at second-hand, but some delegations, specialist technical groups in particular, seem to be getting more resourceful, and may at times even bypass their own overstretched embassies in making arrangements directly with a firm.

Chinese requests for visits tend to be made at abnormally short notice. Individual companies approached after arrival in the host country will often be required to accommodate a group within less than a week. Coordinating bodies may be given as little as a fortnight to draw up a programme. Organizations serious about doing business with the Chinese must be prepared to adjust to this tendency, which often reflects the urgency of a sudden requirement: whole visits may be lost to competitors through the assertion that 'we must have another month to prepare.' Two weeks should be ample time to put together a programme for a month's tour; and if an organization has expressed a particular eagerness to invite a group, it is liable to make a bad impression if it appears to retract—even by a postponement—the moment it hears that the group is ready to come.

Why receive a Chinese delegation?

From time to time, the response to a Chinese request for a visit has been one of exasperation: 'We've had them three times before and we haven't done any business. Why should we give them our technology free?'

Obviously, it is true that not every visit of a Chinese delegation results in business. Even a series of visits may be unproductive. Receiving a mission is on the whole less likely to lead to a rapid sale than, say, attendance at an exhibition or delivery of a specialist seminar to end-users in Peking, though more likely than participation in the average 'outward mission', since it gives firms full scope to display their manufacturing capabilities. It may be argued that, like any sensible businessmen, the Chinese will prefer to absorb knowledge without actually having to buy, but it should also be pointed out that a visit to a company's factory may be the only way in which the Chinese can form sufficient impression of the manufacturing processes to decide on a purchase.

Equally, the following points should be made. Chinese officials are well aware of Western criticisms on this score, and have emphasized, using a number of case histories as illustration, that the reception of a delegation is *an extremely important part* of the whole procedure that leads to trade. As China's internal policies on foreign trade have changed, even technical missions that have been sent abroad in the past year have frequently shown a readiness to talk commerce, and at the very least have invited companies to submit detailed proposals for possible future 'cooperation'. The point is often made, and bears repeating, that for various historical reasons, notably their experience with the Soviet Union in the fifties, the Chinese are extremely wary of being sold either hardware or technology, the quality of which is not the most advanced possible.

If any business is to be done, they must be convinced that what they are offered is of the highest possible technical standard. They demand an abnormal amount of technical information and seem to have demanded it from every Western firm with which they have signed contracts. To supply it may risk giving something away for nothing. To withold it, and to present a generally wary front to a mission, will certainly be unproductive. A company afraid of giving away any substantial information had best not have dealings with the Chinese at all; a company prepared to take the risk, and to offer information to perhaps two or three consecutive groups, may find that the willingness to build up a continuing relationship pays handsome dividends.

If a succession of Chinese visitors has been received and there is still no sign of progress, it is reasonable to turn the tables and suggest that you go to talk to them in Peking, but it must be stressed that a delegation's request for a visit is an indication of interest, and a subsequent request a sign that the interest is growing (or is shared by more than one Chinese body). Such requests call for a positive response.

The group

Composition of the group
Chinese delegations come in a hierarchy. There is always a 'group leader'; usually there is one 'deputy group leader', sometimes even two. These are not always officially designated as such, but their standing quickly becomes apparent. If the delegation wishes to send a small representative body to discuss the programme with senior company personnel, this is likely to

consist of the group leader and the deputy leader(s) in a kind of 'inner circle'. The technicians and researchers who constitute the rest of the party also tend to fall into a pecking order of seniority, reflected in the order of names on the official list issued by them. The interpreter will generally be last, though not if he is a senior technical man in his own right.

This hierarchical arrangement is important. It expresses the group's sense of different levels of authority and experience. The group will give warning of its hierarchy by sending the hosts a name list in advance or distributing one immediately on their arrival at a firm. Care should be taken to ensure, without in any way neglecting the junior members, that the senior members of the party are paid the full measure of attention that they anticipate.

The group leader
The leader needs the most attention of all. Unfortunately, he is often the most neglected member of the team, especially in a 'technical study group', because he is frequently not a technician himself. He may be a council member of a professional society, or even the manager of a factory, but his background is sometimes an administrative and not an engineering one. His lack of technical background tends to emerge fairly quickly, from the organizational rather than technical nature of the questions he asks, for example, 'How many people work in your factory?' 'What is your annual production?' As a result, companies are apt to bypass him in favour of his more communicative (he is usually not an English-speaker) and more apparently 'interested' colleagues. If unduly ignored, he may become somewhat restless.

This should not be allowed to happen. The leader is the decision-maker of the group. This becomes obvious in discussions with a company, when decisions are customarily referred to him. He will suggest to the group, in Chinese, what he thinks to be the next appropriate step and his line will normally prevail if the group has no firm opinion. His organizational questions will not be idle, because as the administrator he will have to consider such aspects as the logistics of setting up a production line for a particular product in China. Most important, he will have to coordinate the group's report on its return to China, and it will almost certainly devolve on him to make any commercial recommendations that may be contained in it. Such recommendations will be based on his colleagues' assessment of the technical standard of a company's goods, but he may be the only member of the group with the authority at home that will make a recommendation effective.

A particular effort should be made to talk to him, cultivate him and show recognition of his importance. He should be at the centre of any discussion which a company wishes to hold with the group, especially if its content is commercial or relates to the planning of the programme, but even if its content is primarily technical. Of the group, he is the one who should be consulted on any matter which calls for a decision.

The deputy leader(s)

The deputy leader is likely to be a senior scientist or engineer. Often, he is the oldest member of the team; often, he is also a good English-speaker with a Western education. He will probably be less self-conscious and more relaxed socially than the leader. When the group divides into two sections, for example, to cover two company visits simultaneously, he automatically becomes the 'leader' of the second section and should be accorded the full precedence due to the main leader.

Sometimes the deputy is such a dominant and engaging personality and so much at home in a Western environment that he may even appear to eclipse the leader altogether. Companies should view this development with some caution and not regard it as an excuse to forget about the leader. Where the deputy is a scientific adviser to a technical ministry, for instance, he may well carry influence tantamount to the leader's own, but his influence may equally not extend far beyond his own scientific circle.

The group members

These may derive from a number of different organizations; usually, each supplies two or three representatives. For the duration of the visit, one or two members sometimes have a specialist function, e.g., there will be an 'accountant', who comes forward to sort out the travel expenses with the host organization if the group is to pay its own way, or provides the 'shopping list' if the group wishes to purchase samples before its departure; there may also be a 'secretary' who provides lists of programme requests, technical specifications, or technical literature required.

In the main, though, the functions of the rank-and-file group members do not appear to be very distinct. This is misleading, for each member has his own speciality and each, furthermore, has specific goals he needs to accomplish to enable him to make an adequate report to his unit in China. For this reason it is exceptionally important, however difficult it may sometimes appear, for linguistic reasons and when large numbers are involved, to accord individual treatment to each member of the group. This is not only desirable from the point of view of courtesy but also essential if every aspect of a firm's technology is to be put across.

An attempt should also be made to cultivate each member of the group, since each individual memory will form part of the group's final judgement on a particular visit. On a high-level mission, an individual group member could be a vice-minister. It is sometimes apparent, when a company visit has ended, that the bulk of the group is more or less satisfied but that some quite humble engineer is unhappy. This could have more damaging effects than the discontent of one member out of ten might suggest—'Well, it seems a good company, but I couldn't find out where they got those components and I'm not sure the quality was up to that German one's...'—and great care should be taken to avoid it.

The interpreter
The interpreters on perhaps four out of five missions are perfectly competent, many first-rate. As already observed, many interpreters are technicians themselves; occasionally, the deputy leader may also be the official interpreter. Alternatively, many interpreters have been attached throughout their careers to a particular technical ministry or industry and have a thorough command of all the technology involved. The very best interpreters are apt to be sent back again and again, sometimes covering more than one speciality.

Occasionally the interpreter is inadequate; China still has rather too few linguists to go round. Where this happens he will be replaced quite fast, either by a senior technician in the group or, sometimes, by an escort provided by the Chinese Embassy.

Companies should take heart: no mission has yet been known to grind to a halt through inability to communicate. From one source or other, an interpreter always seems to emerge. Any interpreter supplied by the hosts should be tactful, and should cooperate with the interpreter rather than simply elbowing him out of the way.

Chinese Embassy representative
Visiting delegations are often accompanied by staff of the Commercial Office of the Chinese Embassy in the host country. This does not always happen nowadays, since the staff are increasingly overstretched, but where it does, they are invaluable contacts for the hosts. Their English is often admirable, and though they may disclaim an engineering background, it can extend to a remarkable grasp of technical terms and concepts. They can also provide extremely useful continuity as a channel for the group's requests for programme changes and technical information, and as 'postboxes' for follow-up literature. In spite of the growing tendency for organizations in China to make direct contact with companies, embassy contacts should be retained as parallel channels of communication, and should always be kept informed of developments.

On a protracted visit to a single company the embassy staff member may put in spasmodic appearances for important commercial sessions. This too should be encouraged, and a set of literature and samples should always be made available to him.

Trade promotion agency staff
Staff of the Sino-British Trade Council, the National Council for US-China Trade, and other such bodies try to accompany groups whenever possible. They endeavour to perform similar auxiliary functions to those of the Chinese Embassy representatives, and should be used for all those functions in their absence. Companies may also find it less inhibiting to work through someone of their own nationality, who can give them guidance on

points of protocol and hospitality, and on such needs and technical requirements of group members as may not be immediately obvious to a non-
Chinese speaker, and who can also provide some linguistic help.

Technical level of the group

It may be safely assumed that the technical level of any delegation will be
extremely advanced. This is particularly true of 'technical study groups.' For
example, the leader of one recent delegation, a 'technical' leader in this
case, read a paper to an international conference, in English, on the
'Electron Optics of Concentric Spherical Electromagnetic Focusing Systems.' Even on a high-level mission vice-ministers and others will be found
asking detailed questions on minute technical points.

Visiting Chinese technicians may be divided broadly into three genera-
tions. Many members of the senior generation (55 years old and upwards)
received education at Western universities and have remained conversant
with the development of technology in the West. They have re-emerged in
significant numbers since the 'Gang of Four' was eliminated in 1976, and
their Western experience is clearly helping to direct China's search for
foreign equipment and know-how. The middle generation (roughly the
40–55 age group) was shaped in the years of close cooperation with the
Soviet Union: the technical standards of these people are high too, though
their training may have differed in certain respects. If there is a 'problem
group', it would seem to be the 30-year-olds, whose training must in many
cases have been disrupted during the period of the Cultural Revolution. Up
till now, however, the occasional 30-year-olds that have appeared on
delegations have not compared too unfavourably with their fellows.

In general, the group will be well versed in Western technical journals and
scientific papers with a bearing on the industry which concerns it. When
touring an institute or laboratory, group members may ask to meet a
particular expert whose papers they have read. From the study of such
papers, or from companies' technical literature they have received, they will
usually have a good idea of the most prominent firms in an industry, and
their specialities. Not surprisingly, they can be erratic at times. They have
been known, probably through studying out-of-date literature, to ask to tour
a factory which has not existed for ten years; and they do sometimes ask if a
company will let them see products which it doesn't produce any longer, or
which are produced by a competitor. As contacts increase, these errors are
diminishing. In the meantime, it remains sensible to clarify a group's
inaccuracies where necessary, and to assume maximum knowledge rather
than ignorance.

Linguistic level of the group

There are few delegations in which the interpreter is the only member able
to speak a foreign language. The senior, Western-educated generation tends

to speak English or, less frequently, German or French, the middle generation Russian, while the under-40's are beginning to concentrate on Western languages again. Some representatives of all three strata speak Japanese.

Where English is spoken, it is more often technical than ordinary conversational English. Many of the old-school technicians spoke English, however, on a day-to-day basis during their studies perhaps 40 years ago at a Western university, and 'remember' it with remarkable alacrity after a few days in an English-speaking environment.

There are wide variations, but it must be stressed that *many more can understand English than can speak it.* Since most Chinese engineers apparently study a great deal of Western technical literature, English technical terms, at least, are very generally understood even by those who cannot utter in the language.

It seems to be a bad habit among businessmen, when seated at table or in a car among delegation members who they assume speak no English or very little, to talk across them to each other, often about such subjects as the planning of the programme, and the likelihood of business resulting from the visit. This is not only discourteous but may also be imprudent, since more delegates than not will probably get the gist of what is being said.

Never assume that English is not understood, even when you have no reason to suppose that it is.

Receiving the group: technical and commercial aspects

Whether as surveyors of technology, or as business negotiators, Chinese delegates often behave differently from other visitors to a Western firm. The reasons for this are old, new, and even contradictory: for instance, there is the long period of isolation, and the previous experience with the Soviet Union. Both these factors have inculcated wariness, a fear of having out-of-date or obsolescent technology 'palmed off' on them, and the consequent tendency to require abnormally large quantities of minute detail about any product or process that is thought to be of interest, and to send delegation after delegation to the same place, if need be, to convince themselves that the quality of a company and its techniques is second to none, before business can be considered. On the other hand, there is the urgency of China's new requirements, and the awareness that in order to meet them extensive purchases of Western and Japanese plant and technology must be quickly made. This means that assessments must be made fast, companies must be prepared to answer detailed questions on the spot, and to make firm and elaborate business proposals straightaway. Thoroughness, however, has in no way been abandoned: without it there can be no business.

For many firms, Chinese thoroughness alone created problems enough. Thoroughness combined with urgency is twice as perplexing. The following guidelines should help those receiving a delegation to satisfy both requirements.

Level of the hosts
The group must be accompanied throughout their visit to a company by top-quality technical staff, able to answer questions both during the factory tour and in any discussions that may follow it. A non-technical Sales Manager is not good enough: the group will sense his lack of technical knowledge very fast and the effect on their assessment of the company's quality could even be counter-productive. A real technical expert on the other hand will quickly develop a rapport with the visitors. The Sales Manager will come in useful later on if serious business discussions begin, but at that point it is desirable that the Managing Director and other senior personnel should also be present.

The programme
In the first place there has to be a programme. For a single day's visit, it may be possible for the host company to get away with a verbal rundown on arrival of what is to be shown but this is not really satisfactory. For a tour of any length, the group members will certainly require a full programme, on paper, and if not given one will signalize their need for it by continually asking, 'Where are we going?' 'What happens next?' Chinese groups tend to feel insecure if it is not made clear to them what is happening. On their arrival in a country or company they should be supplied with a detailed itinerary, clearly specifying times, places, means of transport, and what they will see at a particular firm or in a department. For a complete tour they should have at least an outline itinerary sent to them in China before their departure, listing the companies they will see and the contents of each visit.

Whether a tour or an individual company visit is to be arranged, however, the chances of preparing a programme that is totally acceptable in the first instance are slender. The group may help matters by giving the hosts an outline, when it first makes contact with them from Peking or in the course of a tour, of where it wishes to go and what it expects to do. Sometimes these initial requests may themselves be impossible to satisfy.

Even if the requests seem quite clear, it is more than likely that the delegation will wish to alter the intended programme after its arrival, especially on an extended tour. To prevent this the hosts should try to establish in advance exactly what it is that it wishes to see. But in any event, on arrival, it will certainly insist on a formal discussion of the programme for any visit of much more than a day's duration, and the hosts should not dispute the need for this. They are likely to request substantial changes in the content of a three or four week tour programme, though they generally leave the first week or so intact.

Occasional groups may make changes incessantly as the tour proceeds. New visits and other changes may be requested at as little as 24 hours' notice. This often reflects an increase in group members' knowledge as the tour has progressed, new ideas about the products or components that are really important to them, a chance encounter with a specialist from a company or institute that they wish to follow up. Host companies and organizations must be prepared for these manifestations, and be patient when they arise. It is discourteous to display exasperation in front of a group. It tends to give a bad impression of the overall competence of the hosts, and could even lead group members to suspect that something is being kept from them.

Remember: in their eyes the visitors are honoured guests and you are omnipotent, able to arrange a visit, as can sometimes be done in China, almost at the wave of a hand. The more hosts can conform to that concept the better. Sometimes a group's requests may cause some difficulty, but in the vast majority of cases the adjustments it asks for can be effected with a few telephone calls (supported, however, by written confirmation—see below).

At times a group may ask to see something that the hosts cannot or will not arrange, either because of company or government policy, or simply because the place in question no longer exists or would patently be less interesting than the group thinks. *In all cases the company should be entirely frank with the group.* The Chinese will be quite understanding if it is made clear for example that such-and-such an item is being produced for the Ministry of Defence or that a customer or subcontracting company have asked them not to release technical details. The group members will not bend the rules if the rules have been made clear to them in advance; but to restrict them when they have already started looking at something sensitive is liable to cause embarrassment.

If the company has resolved not to elaborate on a particular process except as part of a deal, it should explain politely that the supply of this technology is something it is hoping to discuss with them as part of an eventual package. However, it should in general be more forthcoming than it would normally expect to be with other potential customers, and if the group looks unhappy at this polite disclaimer and asks, 'How can we do business with you if we don't know what you've got?', the company should at least try to fit in an outline presentation or enable the group to see some products of peripheral relevance to the omitted item, in order to show the maximum possible degree of willingness. Clarity is equally necessary when the reason for not satisfying a request is one of the simpler ones mentioned above. Otherwise the group may easily suspect devious motives for withholding information where there are none.

Any kind of programme requires mutual understanding between the hosts and the group as to what is to be seen. The hosts must pay minute attention to the detail of a group's requests. If it says it wishes to see a product under manufacture, it means it wishes to see a product under manufacture, not a display area. If it says it wishes to tour a factory, it means it wishes to tour a factory, not to be shown slides. If it says it wishes to see a particular process, it means it wishes to see that process, not a 'similar' process. It may require quite painstaking questioning to establish exactly what it does want. If the host company offers 'something similar' as an alternative, this may be acceptable to the group but *the position must be put quite clearly to them in advance.*

It will be obvious that this is all the more essential where the group's hosts are coordinators for visits to their subcontractors or to a whole range of companies. An agreed and detailed written programme for distribution to both companies and the group is indispensable. This may seem overelaborate but the one time Chinese delegation members may become really angry is when, for example, they have made a long journey to a company fully expecting to be shown hardware, and found on arrival that the firm can or will do nothing except talk or show slides.

It can be equally disastrous, once the group has been given the impression that a visit or item has been laid on, to abandon it subsequently. In some cases damage has been done for years, for example, when a company has made a casual telephone arrangement to bring a group to see its subcontractor, and has then brought it to the main gate of the factory only to find that company or government regulations, unchecked by either of the persons making the arrangement, strictly prohibit their admission. Careful planning, on paper, is vital. Sometimes a company fills out a day's programme with an afternoon tour of a second factory of peripheral interest, only to find that the group is so absorbed in the morning's main factory visit and the discussions following it that the drive over to their other works has evidently ceased to be necessary; but cancelling the second visit will now be difficult: the group may well be suspicious of the perfectly innocent and sensible reasons for dropping it. *Whatever you promise you should deliver. If you think you may not deliver something, don't promise it.*

A one-day visit
The following paragraphs illustrate some typical problems that may be encountered, and points worth remembering in the course of a single day's visit to a company by a Chinese delegation.

1. The introductory talk
Following the group's arrival at a firm, when it has been ushered to the boardroom and offered refreshments, the company should give a thorough introduction to its history, organization, and products. This would be normal procedure in visits to a Chinese factory, and the group will in most cases expect it. The introductory talk should only be omitted if the group is in a hurry. It is impolite in the group's eyes, and a sign of poor preparation, for a company to embark on this opening session by demanding, 'What organization do you come from?' 'What do you want to see?' The firm should already have a clear idea of this.

Introductory talks should last for somewhere between 20 minutes and an hour. The historical part of the introduction should not be left out (the

Chinese are impressed by 'experience') but can be reasonably short. The structure of the company is well worth including at this stage. The Chinese are showing a growing interest in budgetary and accounting aspects, while basic statistics like the firm's annual turnover, and the size of the work force are essential material for high-level missions in their attempts to get a profile of the company.

Last, an outline of the firm's complete product range should be given, even if the group only appears to be interested in one or two products. Details of the other products may be passed on to potential end-users. When it comes to the products of principal interest to the group, the firm should not be afraid of giving a full account of them because they feel that the visitors 'know it all already.' The Chinese have no objection to repetition; in fact they are liable to be reassured if what a company says about a product corresponds to what they have read in the relevant technical literature, even literature received several years ago.

2. *Tour of the factory*

The main rule is *don't rush the group.* Companies with tight schedules tend to get obsessed with the notion that they must show the visitors everything and, at the first sign of lingering over a particular machine or process, will try to hustle them along. This tends to be a mistake. A carefully planned programme, with times and itinerary, is important, but it must be flexible enough to accommodate Chinese interests. If the group members are intrigued enough by what they see to start asking questions and taking notes, this is a promising sign from the firm's point of view and they should be indulged for a few minutes. Rushing them may give the impression that you are hiding something, or are not serious about doing business.

It is usually apparent when group members are interested. It is less easy to tell when they are bored, except negatively, by an absence of queries and note-taking and a tendency to ask, 'Where are we going now?' Naturally, the firm should try to attune the pace of the tour to the degree of interest shown.

The Chinese hold that 'seeing is believing' and like to see not only manufacturing processes but design work, research and development, machining, inspection and quality control, maintenance, and even the factory stores. Small firms often believe that half-an-hour is sufficient for a look round their shop floor, and amost invariably find that it is not. A minimum of an hour should be allowed for the tour of any factory: and extra time should be available for the group to come back and take a closer look at something of particular interest.

3. *Technical and commercial discussions*

The group will generally want some form of discussion at the end of a company visit. At least an hour, therefore, should be provided in the programme for discussions.

Nearly always, technical questions will have been raised in the course of the tour which the group feels have not been answered to its complete satisfaction, or which it would like to examine in far greater detail. Increasingly, however, even 'technical study groups' are anxious to talk business and may well wish to spend some time looking into the possibilities for cooperation with a firm, asking for approximate prices, and working out what the next step ought to be. The company should consequently lend authority to the occasion by producing the most senior staff it has available, but the talks should only be steered in a commercial direction after full time has been allowed for technical discussion. The group should not be pressurized into talking business if it is obviously not eager to go beyond generalities.

The company's main duty during the technical talks should be to ensure that it is making, and is seen to be making, every effort to answer the group's questions and satisfy its requirements. Its response in this respect may be vital to the success of the visit.

During the commercial discussions, the company should show that it is alert to the urgency of Chinese requirements and be prepared to take the initiative in meeting them. If it is sufficiently knowledgeable about what the group wants to be able to submit a firm written proposal on this occasion, so much the better; if not, every effort should be made to furnish it soon with a proposal, either before it leaves the country or immediately after its return to Peking.

Speed may be essential to forestall competition. It is quite wrong for a firm to take the attitude: 'When we have more background about your industry and your requirements we'll make you a proposal.' More information may be elicited nowadays than could ever be expected in the past, and the discussion period can be a good opportunity; the visitors will do their best to reply to some questions and may supply information voluntarily in the course of the talks, but the Chinese should not be expected, on returning to their parent bodies, to prepare a detailed paper on what information is required. Instead, faced with a stolid response by one company, their instinct will be to go to a competitor who is prepared to make a proposal, however hypothetical, however much based on past precedent, which at least gives specifications, approximate prices, estimated delivery times, and perhaps some suggestions, for the training of Chinese engineers. Even if it is only 50 per cent accurate, it at least provides a basis for negotiation.

Meeting Chinese requirements

1. *Technical information, literature, and samples*
One of the worst sins of companies visited by the Chinese is to promise information and then, sometimes by design but generally by accident, forget to give it. Needless to say, you should not promise information that you do not mean to give, but it is just as bad simply to forget.

A request for 'more detailed information' voiced, however mildly, by a member of the group, is likely to be of extreme importance to his part in the mission; it might mean the answer to a question he has come 6000 miles to find, crucial for his, and therefore the group's assessment of the company. He will usually be too polite, or too embarrassed, to press the company representative he has asked by repeating the enquiry. If his request has no result, he will not necessarily think that something is being concealed, but there will be an unhappy gap in his knowledge which could well tell against the firm in the group's final assessment. It is suggested, therefore, that anyone escorting a Chinese group round a factory should note any requests and check that each one is met before the group's departure at the end of the day, or at least before it leaves the country. If that is impossible, the material should be sent to them in China. A quick and thorough 'follow-up' makes a good impression on a group.

In general, the Chinese have an insatiable appetite for technical detail. Any literature given the Chinese must be as factual and technically detailed as possible. Companies should have one complete set of their latest technical literature prepared for each member of a visiting mission, as well as the embassy escort. They should see that this literature is delivered to the group as soon as it arrives in the country, either via the Chinese Embassy escort or any contact from a trade promotion agency which may be involved. Alternatively, the company can send its own representatives to welcome the visitors at the airport, and use that opportunity to hand over their literature. This will enable the group to peruse it in advance so that it will be well prepared by the day of the visit. Companies should not worry in case the group may have seen the same literature in China already. Again, repetition can be reassuring.

If literature cannot be delivered on arrival in the country, it should certainly be awaiting the group when it reaches the company. The hosts should ensure that as much supplementary information as possible is close at hand, in order to answer any questions the group may ask during or after the visit. Individuals sometimes ask questions to which you would expect them to know the answers if they had studied the company's literature. In fact, they *may* have done so and be wanting to double-check. They also like to feel that their hosts have the answer to any technical question at their fingertips. Firms should resist the temptation to fob a group off with the answer, 'You'll find it in our brochure.'

Delegations sometimes ask to buy samples to take them home with them. This may involve some risk for a company, and obviously each case must be decided on its own merits. It can, however, be an effective way of earning confidence and goodwill and it may be a good idea to present a sample to a group where the cost involved is not great.

2. *Company name lists*
The Chinese like to retain the names and positions in the company of all the persons they have met on a particular visit. A comprehensive list of all the personnel who will receive them should, accordingly, be drawn up and

distributed to each group member at the start of the visit, or at least before he leaves. The list should be in hierarchical order, since groups often ask the difference between Chairman, Managing Director, General Manager, etc. At the same time, it should include even the lowliest technician met on a tour of the works who may conceivably be the specialist on a topic of intense interest to the group.

3. Photographs
Usually, at least one member of the group will be a photographer. The Chinese like to be able to photograph the inside of factories, and will do so assiduously if they can. At the same time, the usual rule applies: the group will not object to a ban on photography if it is explained to them in advance. Some care should be taken to explain that the ban applies to all visitors to the company, and not to the group alone. If a company has stock photographs of certain processes or items of equipment, these may be appreciated by the group as a compensation.

Possible pitfalls
One of the most common stumbling-blocks to receiving a Chinese mission, as to any form of business contact with China, is and has always been Chinese sensitivity to any manifestation of a rival 'China' on Taiwan. While it looks as though this problem is diminishing fast, firms receiving Chinese visitors must observe the following fundamental rules: they must never refer to Taiwan or the Republic of China or to business with Taiwan; literature given to a group, and any wall maps they see, must not mention Taiwan or mark it as a separate country, e.g., by a blob on the map indicating an office or agency there. China must always be referred to by its correct name, the People's Republic of China, or simply China, and none other, and should never be given a name implying the existence of another 'China' as for example 'mainland China' or 'communist China'.

If the company wishes to display a Chinese flag, to welcome the group, every care should be taken to ensure that it is the correct flag, that is a red flag with a big gold star surrounded by four small gold stars in the top left-hand corner, and none other. (In London, Chinese flags may be obtained from the Guanghwa Company, Booksellers, 9 Newport Place, London WC2, telephone 01-437 3737.)

It is sad to record that every mistake implied here has been perpetrated by firms receiving Chinese delegations. In the past, this could mean the delegation walking out and their entire relationship with a company jeopardized. Nowadays, the Chinese are more aware that a reference to China as the 'Republic of China' may simply result from ignorance, and they may turn a blind eye.

Casual mention of business involving countries with which China does not have diplomatic relations, e.g., South Africa, Rhodesia, South Korea, Israel, will probably be tolerated but should be avoided.

Business with countries which China recognizes, but with which relations are hostile, e.g., the USSR, may be mentioned, in fact, reference to trade with the USSR and other eastern European countries may even be of interest as a point of comparison. But if, say, 80 per cent of a company's business is with the USSR, it is not a good idea to dwell on the relationship.

Chinese sensitivities
In general, it must be emphasized that the Chinese are not sensitive or in any way difficult visitors. Occasional spectres conjured up by businessmen, for example that they have a rooted objection to goods painted or packaged in a particular colour, are totally without foundation.

The 'hard sell' approach
It is important that businessmen should treat Chinese visitors as sophisticated professionals, on a par with themselves. This means strictly avoiding any kind of 'hard sell' approach. The tactics of occasional misguided companies that wheel out their order books in front of a group the moment they arrive can only be futile and, at worst, offensive. The Chinese are not going to do any business with a firm until they have fully and painstakingly convinced themselves of the technical quality and commercial competitiveness of their goods.

A note of modesty
There is a more subtle aspect to the same point. The Chinese have rigorous technical standards and are suspicious of being sold second-rate goods. They also, when speaking of their achievements as individuals or small organizations, though not always of their collective feats as a society, have a certain innate modesty.

Conclusion
China is changing all the time and so are Chinese delegations: they are coming thicker and faster, speaking better English, talking more business, getting more autonomous and self-assertive. Some of this is partly due to the re-emergence of the veterans: the high-powered scientists and engineers who know the West well, the 'old Europe hands' or 'old America hands'. In one recent instance, a delegation booked itself into two hotels and a university hostel directly from Peking, without going through its embassy at all. This would have been unthinkable a short while ago.

For Western companies, this profusion of visitors holds great promise but it also carries dangers. There may be a mounting tendency to look on them as 'just another Chinese party.' This must not happen. Chinese visitors set special standards for which the average Western company does not have an instinctive feel. Firms contemplating major business with China should consider acquiring Chinese language specialists to make sure that they are observed. It may be said that as delegations become more familiar with the

West, they will become more and more used to the Western way of doing things. Perhaps, but for most Chinese a Western organization is a very strange environment, and the more considerate the management, the more relaxed and responsive they will be. It may be said that they will go to the company that has the technology anyhow, but where there is a narrow choice between two competitors, it will not be surprising if the Chinese opt for one that has given them a hospitable welcome, and gone to some trouble to meet their often minute requirements, rather than another that has hustled them perfunctorily round a factory and sent them off only partially informed. More than a single contract is at issue. Often, the Chinese are looking for a company that will work with them, to mutual advantage, for a long time and in this sense their frequent talk of 'friendship' is not just jargon. Showing that you understand Chinese idiosyncrasies, displaying a friendly and cooperative spirit to a Chinese group, is not just a frill—it is the key to long-term business.

Suggested timetable for a day's visit
A standard, and generally satisfactory, timetable for a single day's Chinese visit:

10.00 Group arrives, is met by senior management and escorted to the boardroom.
10.05 Refreshments.
       Introduction to the company and its products.
10.45 Technical presentation on the main products of interest to the group.[1]
11.30 Tour of the factory.
13.00 Buffet lunch in boardroom.
14.00 Continuation of factory tour, concentrating on items of particular interest.
15.00 Technical discussions.[2]
16.00 Departure of the group.[3]
       Senior management bids farewell at main entrance.
       Group returns to hotel.
18.30 Group collected by company at hotel and taken for dinner at local restaurant.[4]
21.00 Group returns to hotel.

Notes
1. In this imaginary case the company has elected to add a full presentation on particular products. An alternative would be to confine the initial description of these products to the main introductory talk.
2. The 'technical discussions' may turn out to have a commercial content, but the company should on no account assume that commercial talks will automatically take place by specifying 'commerical discussions' in the programme.

3. The programme must make it clear to the group that their departure time is flexible or they may feel they have to hurry off at the time stated. It may be slightly preferable to allow an hour and extend it, rather than to allow two hours and find that the discussions wind up early and that the group is waiting for its transport.
4. This dinner is of course optional. The relatively early times, chosen to suit normal Chinese eating and bedtime habits, should be noted.

Suggested timetable for a half-day visit

10.00   Group arrives, is met by senior management and escorted to the boardroom.
10.05   Refreshments. Introduction to the company and its products.
10.30   Tour of factory.
12.00   Technical discussions.[1]
13.00   Buffet lunch in boardroom.[2]
14.00   Departure of group. Senior management bids farewell at main entrance. Group proceeds to next visit.

Notes
1. On such a short visit there will probably not be time for a close-focus extension of the factory tour. A clear $1\frac{1}{2}$ hours is therefore essential.
2. Again, because of the limited time, some of the technical and commercial talking may well have to continue over lunch. It is a good idea for each company visited to offer a meal, both out of hospitality and because the time can be used for discussions. In this case, the firm visited during the morning should be given the opportunity to offer lunch, and the afternoon company should consider giving dinner.

5. Law and practice in the China trade

STANLEY B. LUBMAN

This chapter surveys the practice of the principal Chinese state trading corporations which are engaged in purchasing foreign products and technology, and reviews recent developments in Chinese attitudes towards commercial law in transnational transactions. Chinese foreign trade, formerly conducted without reference to Chinese or foreign law, now seems about to become the subject of Chinese legislation which promises to be significant to foreign companies contemplating or already engaged in trade with China.

Chinese contract clauses and practice under them

A summary is set forth below of standard clauses in Chinese purchase contracts and of Chinese practice under them.[1]

Shipment

Chinese purchases from abroad usually are on f.o.b. or f.a.s. terms.[2] Although certain standard contract forms do not use the term 'f.o.b.', the clauses on these forms spell out the responsibilities of the parties in a

1. A standard Machine Purchase Contract is reproduced as an Appendix and hereafter cited as 'Machinery Contract'. For a collection of standard Chinese contract forms, see the National Council For US–China Trade, Special Report No. 13, *Standard Form Contracts of the People's Republic of China* 1975.
2. Under an f.o.b. (free on board) contract the seller is required to make available at the port of loading the goods specified in the contract, and to pay all handling and transport charges for the goods up to the time of their passing over the ship's rail. *See* Schmitthoff, *Export Trade*, 14–15, 5th edn. 1969. Under f.a.s. (free alongside ship) terms the seller is not responsible for loading, and his responsibility ends when the goods are landed alongside the vessel so that they can be loaded. *Idem.* at 12–13.

manner consistent with the common understanding of the term. For instance, one common clause states that the risk passes when the goods have 'passed over the vessel's rail and been released from the tackle.' At least three corporations—Chemicals, Minerals and Metals, and Machinery—use clauses clearly identified as f.o.b. terms. The contracts require the Chinese shipping agent, the China National Ship Chartering Corporation, to notify the seller of the arrival of the vessel a fixed number of days before the arrival date.[1] The Machinery and Minerals and Metals Corporations require the seller to notify them 30 days before the agreed time of shipment, together with details of the shipment that will allow the Chartering Corporation to book shipping space accurately.

The Chinese prefer to import on f.o.b. terms in order to ship the goods under the Chinese flag or on Chinese-chartered vessels. This, however, means that delivery by the seller, and payment, may be affected by the vagaries of Chinese shipping schedules. F.o.b. clauses may vary as to the calculation of liability for storage expenses in the event of a seller delivering cargo to the port of shipment as agreed but the Chinese vessel arriving late. The standard Chemicals Corporation form states that such losses are to be calculated 'from the 16th day after expiry of the free storage time at the port,'[2] while the standard Machinery Corporation clause simply states that if the Chinese vessel 'fails to arrive at the port of loading within 30 days after the arrival date advised by the Buyer, the Buyer shall bear the storage and insurance expenses incurred from the 31st day.'[3] Some flexibility may be shown in negotiations on this clause.

Demurrage is an item to which the seller should be particularly attentive. When the Chinese purcase on f.o.b. terms, they provide clearly that the seller is liable for demurrage if the goods are not ready when the vessel arrives at the port on time. However, the c.i.f. terms are silent on demurrage, and sellers under these terms who have not insisted on demurrage clauses suffered considerable losses when unloading of their vessels was delayed at congested Chinese ports.

Payment

1. *Standard terms*
Standard Chinese payment clauses provide that, upon receipt of the shipping advice which the seller is required to send the Chinese buyer, the buyer will

---

1. The Machinery Contract included in the appendix specifies 10 days' notice—clause 12(1)c. Contracts used by other corporations vary slightly.
2. Chemicals Purchase Contract, 'Terms of Delivery', clause 1, in *Standard Form Contracts, see* note 1, p. 77, at 25.
3. Machinery Contract, clause 12(1)c. Normally, title to the goods remains with the seller, who cannot be paid until the bill of lading has been transferred. It may be possible, however, to obtain Chinese agreement not only to pay for warehousing and insurance expenses after the 31st day, but also to pay for the goods themselves 'against a warehouse receipt.' See J. Dingle, *Technical Selling in China*, at 36, 1974.

open an irrevocable letter of credit with the Bank of China, which is payable against presentation of a draft drawn on the Bank and the shipping documents described elsewhere in the contract. The letter of credit normally is valid until 15 days after shipment, and the documents are negotiated at a Bank of China branch in the People's Republic of China. The Chinese usually insist upon confirmed letters of credit in payment for their exports, even though when they are the buyers they are well known for their reluctance to allow their letters of credit to be confirmed, such requests being taken as a reflection on the credit of the People's Republic of China.

The combined effect of the practices described above is that the seller who has shipped the goods and presented the documents loses control over both for a brief period of time.[1] Some Chinese letters of credit have reportedly contained clauses allowing inspection of the goods after they have arrived, but instances of reported inspection before payment have been rare, although deductions for alleged imperfections found on inspection have been known to occur.[2] Chinese practice apparently is not uniform, since other letters of credit clearly make the transaction a documentary one, as is customary in international trade, by providing that the Bank of China will pay by airmail transfer if the 'detailed name of the commodity, specifications, quantity, price, manufacturer, and packing shown in the documents are found, upon presentation, to be in conformity with [the contract].'

Considerable variation has occurred in the currency of payment employed, apparently in reflection of Chinese assessments of trends in international currency markets. Sometimes the Chinese have insisted on the use of their own currency as the medium of payment for their purchases. When the dollar has been weak, however, the Chinese have understandably wanted to be able to pay in US dollars.

2. Payment under turnkey contracts.

In the past, the Chinese normally discharged their obligations under turnkey contracts by cash payments. Typical contracts would provide for payment of a total of 20 to 30 per cent of the contract price at two stages prior to the first shipment of equipment, one at the signing of the contract, the other at an agreed date some months thereafter. Most of the balance of the contract price would be paid as agreed percentages of the invoice value of each shipment of equipment. The last two payments, often 5 per cent each, would be paid respectively upon acceptance and expiration of the guaranty period. Another point at which payments might be made is upon the buyer's receipt of notification from the seller that the plant is ready for start-up.

The Chinese had long expressed aversion to purchase on credit terms (except in the case of contracts for the purchase of agricultural commodities,

1. Smith, 'Standard Form Contracts in the International Commercial Transactions of the People's Republic of China' 21, *International and Comparative Law Quarterly*, 142, 1972.
2. Smith, for example, has 'been told by British businessmen that in some cases of sales to the PRC the letters of credit received only amount to 90 per cent of the purchase price, and that the balance is sometimes used as a negotiating counter.' *Idem.* at 140.

which often provide for up to 24 months' credit). In 1972, however, they began to purchase whole plants, such as Japanese petrochemical plants, on deferred-payment terms. Several deferred-payment contracts have reportedly provided for a down payment of 20 per cent, with the remainder payable at 6 per cent over a 5-year period, beginning with the completion of the plant.[1] Given the ambitiousness of China's development plans and China's limited foreign exchange reserves, it is likely that many whole plant purchases from abroad will be on a deferred-payment basis, financed by the Japanese Export-Import Bank and by European export assistance programmes such as the ECGD in the United Kingdom.[2]

The Chinese have also begun to borrow directly from abroad, a topic discussed in chapter 7. Of note here are some problems of documentation. Generally, the Chinese have expressed considerable distaste for the lengthy and complicated documentation which has become standard in Eurocurrency lending, and have insisted that foreign bankers shrink their standard 40-odd page agreements.[3] Among the specific issues on which the Bank of China's position is inconsistent with past practice are those of submission to the jurisdiction of English (or any other foreign) courts, and the choice of English (or any other foreign) law as applicable to any dispute arising out of the loan.[4]

Barter

Barter has not been employed frequently in Sino-Western trade in recent years, although the Chinese have shown a great interest recently in countertrade, which is discussed below.[5] In one barter transaction in 1973, the Chinese purchased five sets of electrical generating equipment from a British company, and reportedly paid for one with an assortment of products which included chemicals, foodstuffs, and handicrafts. Generally, however, the Chinese have not favoured barter because the products exchanged could be exported by foreigners to markets in which the bartered goods would compete with identical products sold by the PRC, usually at prices higher than the value assigned to them in a contract under which they were exchanged for goods.

1. For a discussion of the technical but important question of calculation of the interest on deferred payments, see Dingle, *see* note 3, p. 78, at 30–31. Dingle indicates that the Chinese sometimes insist on paying interest on the face value of each payment rather than on the outstanding balances.
2. In 1978, the ECGD guaranteed a $1.2 billion deposit facility signed by seven UK banks with the Bank of China. *Business China*, at 169, 1978.
3. See, e.g., 'UK Banks Negotiate China Trade Finance', *The Times*, p. 15, 17 August 1978; *Business China*, at 34–45, 7 March 1979.
4. 'China Springs a Surprise', *Far Eastern Economic Review*, pp. 50–51, 13 April 1979.
5. On barter in Sino-Italian trade, see Reghizzi, 'Legal Aspects of Trade with China: The Italian Experience', 9 *Harvard Journal of International Law* 85, at 111–12, 1968. Barter and buyback were specifically mentioned as devices which the Chinese are willing to consider in a speech by the Chinese Foreign Trade Minister, 'Foreign Trade Minister Li Chiang Comments on Growth of Trade', FBIS-78, at E1-2, 8 June 1978.

Delivery

In contrast to the studied ambiguity of delivery dates in Chinese sale contracts, Chinese purchase contracts are quite exigent. A standard machinery import clause provides a penalty for late delivery, fixed at a percentage of the contract price for each seven days up to a stated maximum, with a right given to the buyer to cancel the contract if delivery is delayed beyond 10 weeks.[1] The maximum penalty varies, but is usually no higher than 5 per cent. Contracts for whole plants also contain stiff penalty provisions. Under the standard clauses, the Chinese seem to have the right to cancel the contract for any late delivery (unless the force majeure clause applies) and to exact the penalty as well.[2]

The experience of sellers to the PRC under these clauses has not been consistent. Some, particularly steel sellers, have reported the Chinese to be unrelenting in their insistence that the penalty be paid. In other cases, the Chinese have agreed to extend the delivery time without a penalty, even though the clause did not include a grace period. The difference may depend upon the need for the particular imports and also may be affected by the parties' prior relationship and the care with which the seller has documented the reason for the delay. In one case recounted to the author, the seller was also a buyer of Chinese exports who could point to frequently delayed Chinese deliveries which had caused him economic loss.

Force majeure

Sellers frequently attempt to limit their liability for delayed delivery or non-delivery caused by acts over which they have no control, while buyers are equally resistant to the efforts. The PRC has a history of highly stubborn and successful buyer resistance; for example, the Chinese are reluctant to define in detail the circumstances that constitute force majeure, as in the standard machinery clause, which states that the seller is not liable for delay for non-delivery due to force majeure, which is not defined in the contract.[3] The clause further requires the seller to notify the buyer immediately and follow that notification with 'a certificate of the accident issued by the competent government authorities where the accident occurs.'[4] If the force majeure cause lasts for more than 10 weeks, the Chinese buyers have the right to cancel the contract.

Chinese corporations occasionally have agreed to specify some of the events which can be considered as instances of force majeure, such as 'wars, or severe natural disasters.'[5] Other force majeure clauses have been even more specific, such as one which includes 'war, earthquake, flood, fire, explosion, and other force majeure circumstances agreed upon by both

1. See, e.g., Machinery Contract, clause 17.
2. See Smith, note 1, p. 79, at 149.
3. Machinery Contract, clause 16.
4. *Idem.*
5. Reghizzi, see note 5, p. 80, (contract for the purchase of Italian goods).

parties or approved by arbitration in the case of disagreement by both parties.'[1] For ideological reasons the Chinese usually have been unwilling to specify acts of God, labour unrest, or strikes as instances of force majeure.

Regardless of the language of the force majeure clause, in practice the Chinese appear willing to recognize the principle that an intervening act beyond the seller's control may excuse him from a penalty for late delivery. Some clauses have mentioned 'any other acts beyond the control of the sellers,' and others have included a statement that the seller's liability for delay is to be limited as a result of 'other unavoidable circumstances' agreed to by the parties after the seller has invoked the clause.[2] Western European sellers who have had to invoke force majeure have stated that the Chinese generally have accepted the delay even though the actual cause was not specified in the contract.

Sellers' guarantees: inspection
Chinese buyers insist on purchasing the highest quality goods and holding sellers to the absolute letter of their agreement. Typical language requires that the seller:

> [G]uarantee that the commodity is made of the best materials, with first class workmanship, brand new, unused and complies in all respects with the quality specifications and performance as stipulated in this Contract.[3]

The guarantee period often extends to 12 or 18 months. Some negotiation is possible on the duration of the period and on when it begins to run, i.e., from unloading at the port of destination or from arrival at the site.

Standard machinery clauses require the manufacturer to present a certificate of inspection regarding quality, specifications, performance, and quantity, although the certificate is not considered final on those matters. The contract requires an additional inspection by the China National Commodity Inspection Bureau when the goods arrive. The standard clause provides that a claim may be asserted 'on the strength of the Inspection Certificate' issued by the Bureau, 'should the quality, specification, or quantity be found not in conformity with the stipulations of the [c]ontract' within 90 days after arrival of the goods at the destination.[4] A claim also may be filed if the 'damages occur in the course of operation by reason of inferior quality, bad workmanship or the use of inferior materials.'[5]

Other clauses are worded slightly differently and include 'improper design, inferior quality, bad workmanship, and the use of bad materials' as the

---

1. *Idem.* at 109.
2. For a general discussion of the vagueness of the force majeure clauses, see *ibid.* at 110. Reghizzi concludes, 'So far no problems ... seem to have arisen, and the Chinese have recognized at least two cases of *force majeure* confirmed by a declaration of the Chamber of Commerce of Milan.'
3. Machinery Contract, clause 14.
4. Machinery Contract, clause 15.
5. *Idem.*

basis for claims.[1] The sellers are responsible for 'the immediate elimination of the defects[,] complete or partial replacement of the commodity' or for a partial refund of the contract price.[2] It should be noted that liability has not been extended to cover death or personal injury caused by defects in the goods. No doctrine of product liability has yet been applied in China.

Even when contracts involve sales of whole plants or highly complex equipment, the Commodity Inspection Bureau may be given a prominent role by the contract, although special tests out of the ordinary scope of the bureau's activities may be involved. In such transactions, the standards which the plant or equipment must attain usually are derived from industrial standards common in the seller's business and which should be specified in detailed technical attachments to the contract. In contracts for the sale of whole plants, performance tests are usually carried out jointly under the instructions of the seller's personnel. Regardless of the standards used, inspections by the Chinese are rigorous. Some sellers have complained that tests used by Chinese sometimes differ from the tests normally used in the seller's country. This difficulty can be prevented by specifying in the contract the relevant tests and standards to be applied when the goods are delivered and inspected. In other cases, the equipment may be so advanced that the Chinese lack the requisite technical expertise or highly sophisticated testing equipment. Compromise has been possible in these cases, but sometimes only with difficulty.

Additional contractual protection for the seller cannot be given by providing for joint inspection by representatives of the seller and buyer. Some turnkey contracts have specified that the Chinese may send their personnel to the seller's plant during delivery of the machinery. However, the buyer will usually refuse to delegate to the Chinese inspectors authority to countersign the certificates of quality which the seller is obligated to supply. The clauses also explicitly state that the attendance of Chinese inspectors does not affect the seller's guarantee. Turnkey contracts also provide for the seller to send his own representatives to the plant site to inspect machinery and equipment at their delivery, although, again, his guarantee remains unaffected. Regardless of the inspection arrangements agreed to by the parties, it is most unlikely that the Chinese will give up their practice of subjecting imported machinery and equipment to extremely careful inspection, which may also produce annoying claims.[3]

1. Smith, see note 1, p. 79, at 147.
2. Machinery Contract, clause 15.
3. In contracts for the sale of whole plants, the parties will have agreed on the performance tests that must be run, as well as on payment of penalties by the seller according to a sale 'reflecting the importance of the failed parameter(s).' Dingle, see note 3, p. 78, at 45. The contracts usually allow the seller to repeat the test. But it has been observed that '[i]n practice, since the penalty scales representing payment as liquidated damages apply only to relatively small failures, significant discrepancies from guaranteed parameters such as output, product quality, and consumption of raw materials and utilities, will involve the Seller in making modifications theoretically without limit.' *Idem.* at 49.

Chinese finickiness about claims and their reluctance to settle them may be influenced by bureaucratic considerations. Chinese officials presumably are not eager to bear responsibility for ordering or accepting delivery of defective goods from abroad, nor do they wish to be responsible for failing to assert a claim based on defects or for wrongly settling such a claim. As a result, negotiations by Western sellers who have dealt with the Chinese over a period of years sometimes are conducted against a background of unresolved claims previously asserted by the Chinese which may serve as bargaining counters during negotiations on other contracts.

Dispute settlement

Consistent with the tenacity with which the Chinese assert and resist settlement of claims is their practice in settling foreign trade disputes. The Chinese have a record of energetically avoiding not only litigation but any third-party participation having overtones of adjudication. A standard clause provides that '[a]ll disputes in connection with this Contract or the execution thereof shall be settled [amicably] through negotiations.'[1] In the event of negotiations breaking down, the parties are limited by this clause to arbitration before the Foreign Trade Arbitration Commission (FTAC) in Peking. Some sellers have been able to obtain Chinese consent to arbitration in Sweden or in Switzerland, and a recent contract with a US seller reportedly has specified Canada as the arbitral forum. Sometimes the contract will simply provide that arbitration will be held in an unnamed third country to be agreed upon by the parties.[2] In recent years, however, the Chinese have become more willing to specify a third country as the arbitral forum, and to specify the arbitral body and the rules applicable to the arbitration proceeding,[3] although they have long been reluctant to accept choice-of-law clauses under which a foreign legal system, the seller's or that of a third country, would be looked to for the substantive rules governing the dispute. Moreover, in several transactions, a Chinese corporation not only agreed to arbitration before a named third-country body under International Chamber of Commerce rules, but also agreed that the contracts would be governed by the law of that country. However, regardless of the language of the dispute-settlement clauses, the Chinese may be expected to avoid arbitration altogether.

To date it has been impossible to obtain a detailed account of any trade arbitration involving a Chinese corporation.[4] Although many traders main-

1. Machinery Contract, clause 18.
2. Machinery Contract, clause 18, in *Standard Form Contracts*, see note 1, p. 77, at 41.
3. This opinion is based on contracts which have been shown to the author and on conversations with Western businessmen and officials of the Legal Affairs Department of CCPIT.
4. Representatives of the American Arbitration Association were told that in 1974 over 100 cases that were brought to the attention of the FTAC were settled by 'friendly negotiations', while 12 were settled on the basis of 'non-binding recommendations' made by the FTAC, and only two cases in 1974 were settled by formal FTAC arbitration. Holtzmann, H. (ed.), 'Resolving Disputes in US–China Trade', in *Legal Aspects of US–China Trade* 77, 1975. The Holtzmann account offers a fascinating recapitulation of the Chinese emphasis on avoiding arbitration and on maintaining fluid and informal devices for dispute settlement.

tain that the Chinese would regard a request for arbitration to be 'un-friendly', and that the request would endanger future business,[1] a few traders have said in private conversations that by either formally requesting or informally hinting that they were about to request arbitration, they have brought about a prompt settlement. Sometimes, however, the Chinese have been known not to respond at all. In one such case they are reported to have ignored the formal invocation of an arbitration clause while continuing to correspond with the European seller involved on all matters other than arbitration; eventually the claim was compromised. Moreover, some sellers who have negotiated a Chinese claim feel that in order to preserve the air of compromise they were forced to yield to some extent, even when they were convinced that the claim was groundless or exaggerated.[2]

Another illustration of the Chinese preference for adjudicated dispute settlement, which has recently received attention in a Sino-US dispute, is a strong emphasis on conciliation. An authoritative Chinese statement on the subject reads:

> In concrete work, the [Foreign Trade Arbitration Commission] and the [Maritime Arbitration Commission] adopt the method of combining arbit-ration with conciliation.... Experience proves that most of the cases ... can be settled by conciliation in the course of investigation or examination, prior to the arbitration proceedings or before an award is granted....[3]

A dispute between an American commodities seller and a Chinese buyer has been resolved through a form of conciliation devised by the Legal Affairs Department of the China Council for the Promotion of International Trade (CCPIT) and by the American Arbitration Association. Conciliators appointed by the two parties met in Peking in October, 1977, and arrived at a mutually satisfactory basis for resolution of the agreement in the course of a 10-day period.[4]

The cooperation between the Chinese and US sides is innovative and encouraging. However, it should be realized that if conciliation becomes institutionalized, it could become yet another obstacle in the path of an American disputant who wishes to stop negotiating and bargaining over the terms of a settlement, and wishes instead to proceed to a definitive third-party adjudication. US sellers and their advisers, while seeking to devise novel methods of bilateral dispute settlement, are also advised to continue probes and general discussions and to press for third-country arbitration.

---

1. Reghizzi indicates that '[e]ven the suggestion that a dispute be submitted to arbitration in Peking is met with disfavor.' Reghizzi, 'Law and Sino-Italian Trade', in *Law and Politics in China's Foreign Trade* 184, V, Li (ed.), 1977.
2. *Ibid.*
3. Jen Tsien-Hsin and Liu Shao-Shan, *Arbitration in China*, at 3, (mimeographed copy given to the author in Peking in March, 1978).
4. *China Business Review*, at 16, November–December 1977.

Industrial property

1. *Patents and know-how*

Contract clauses on protection of foreign patents and know-how in the PRC are particularly important since there is no Chinese statutory scheme for their protection. PRC regulations which permitted PRC citizens or foreign individuals or groups to register inventions and receive cash awards,[1] have been revised and recently published[2] but all inventions, apparently including those unregistered, become the property of the PRC. Accordingly, at the moment, a foreign seller can protect his rights in his industrial property only by bargaining for a contract clause that will afford him protection.

The China National Technical Import Corporation, which negotiates for the purchase of whole plants, is likely to be involved in negotiating the clause. In a few rare occurrences, the Technical Import Corporation has purchased technology without also buying equipment but generally, purchases of technology occur in the context of a whole-plant purchase. Practice apparently varies on whether the licence has a specified portion of the contract price assigned to it, or whether it is included in that price,[3] but apparently payments of royalties are rare. The provisions covering patents and know-how make the agreement a lump-sum sale. The actual payments may be completed at the time the plant begins operations or may be included in the instalments paid under deferred-payment terms.

The foreign seller of technology has thus far been required to rely on the contract to protect him against use of his industrial property in ways extending beyond the scope of the contract, either by Chinese duplication of it or by Chinese disclosure or subsequent unlicensed transfer. Officials of the CCPIT Legal Affairs Department, with whom this question has been discussed, have acknowledged that the Chinese side must be willing to provide the protection, and officials of the Technical Import Corporation, which has negotiated licences with foreign licensers, has concurred. In some contracts, the Technical Import Corporation has agreed never to disclose the licensed technology; in others, non-disclosure has been limited to a period of years. The original licence usually assumes a fixed periodic output at a disclosed number of plants, but the Chinese sometimes wish to use the licensed process in other plants.

In varying language, the Technical Import Corporation has agreed not to duplicate a plant utilizing the process covered by a licence, subject to a

1. Regulations of 3 November 1963, 'Concerning Awards for Inventions', 1964, 13 *Chung-Hua Jen-Min Kung-Ho-Kuo Fa-Kuei Hui-Pien* (FKHP) (compilation of Laws and Regulations of the People's Republic of China), 241. For English translation, see US Consulate, Hongkong, 'Survey of the China Mainland Press', No. 3117, 11 December 1963, at 6.
2. *China Issues Revised Regulations on Awards for Inventions*, NCNA (English), at 25, 17 January 1979.
3. This variation has been described to the author in private conversation with representatives of European and American companies who have discussed licensing with the Technical Import Corporation. It has also been reported in 'How China Buys Foreign Technology', *Business International* at 396, 5 December 1972.

Chinese right to improve the plant or plants covered by the licence and to increase production at those plants without any obligation to the seller. The Technical Import Corporation has at times sought to obtain the licenser's approval of unlimited use of the licensed technology. One licenser retained the technology for production of a vital catalyst, and can measure Chinese production by their purchases of the catalyst from the licenser.

Consistent with its preference for lump-sum purchases, the Technical Import Corporation has often been willing to forego the right to make use of future improvements of a process by the licenser if further payments would be required. Certain licensing agreements, however, require the licenser to continue to inform the Chinese licensee of improvements for a stated period of time, often as a minimum until the plant begins operations. On the other hand, the Technical Import Corporation has been unwilling to disclose subsequent Chinese improvements.

It should be noted that the situation reviewed immediately above is likely to change. Chinese officials have expressed to foreign visitors their view that China needs a patent law; Chinese have been sent to Japan to study the patent system, and this author was told during visits to Peking in February and March 1979 that a patent law was being drafted.

Even if a patent law is adopted, foreign sellers will have to rely on their contracts to impose a prohibition on the PRC against exporting products manufactured by factories supplied by the sellers. It is difficult to determine how readily the Technical Import Corporation will agree to this restriction. The author has been informed that in at least one agreement with a Japanese licenser, the Corporation has agreed that the products would not be exported.

2. Trademarks

Although no known contract has involved the use of a foreign trademark in the PRC, Chinese policy toward trademarks reflects their general attitudes toward industrial property.[1] A Chinese statute specifically permits a foreign enterprise to register marks to which it has rights in its own country,[2] if that country has reached an agreement with the PRC on the reciprocal recognition of trademarks.[3] The nationality of the applicant appears to be the criterion governing ownership by a foreign country.[4] The language of the statute seems to make it possible for protection to be given to an applicant

---

1. For a discussion of China's application of trademark laws and regulations, see Randt, Trademark Law in the PRC: Case Fables with Morals for Western Traders', US–China Business Review, at 3, May–June 1974.
2. Regulations of 10 April 1963, Concerning the Control of Trademarks, 13 FKHP 162, 1964 hereinafter cited as 'Regulations on Control of Trademarks'); Rules of 25 April 1963, Concerning the Implementation of the Regulations Governing the Control of Trademarks, 13 FKHP 164, 1964 (hereinafter cited as 'Implementing Regulations').
3. Regulations on Control of Trademarks, § 12(1).
4. See 'Implementing Regulations', §§ 16, 20. These regulations make specific reference to the certificate of nationality which foreign enterprises must file. Idem.

from a country that has not formally concluded an agreement, but that protects Chinese trademarks by virtue of its own laws, as is the case with the United States.[1]

Indeed, early in 1978 the Chinese government announced that registration of foreign trademarks in Peking would be permitted according to the principle of reciprocity. As a result, US trademarks may now be registered in Peking although the United States and China have not concluded an agreement on the subject. CCPIT has also announced that reciprocity will determine other aspects of registration. Formerly, for instance, registrants in Peking had to file copies of their original certificates of registration, but now that requirement will be dispensed with whenever it would not be imposed on foreign applicants by the registrant's country. The author was informed in early 1979 that 'several hundred' US trademarks had been or were in the process of being registered in Peking.

Recent developments in Chinese trade law

That the term 'trade law' should come to be used in China is itself a novelty. Hitherto, contract negotiations were conducted with foreigners in a legal semi-vacuum. No legal system was referred to in the contracts. However, the vacuum was not complete because negotiations were always conducted against a background of Chinese commercial practice with which foreigners were usually not acquainted in depth.

Processing and compensation trade contracts

Since mid-1978, Chinese trade officials have indicated that they are now extremely interested in forms of business activity which are new to the China trade. These include contracts under which the foreign side provides all raw materials or components, and the Chinese side processes or assembles the product in return for a processing fee. They also include countertrade arrangements or, as the Chinese prefer to call it, 'compensation trade' which deserves particular mention here because the Chinese seem to have embraced the concept with great enthusiasm.

Under compensation trade contracts the foreign side provides equipment, machinery, technology, know-how, and training, while the Chinese side provides the land, building, and workers. Variations are possible because in some circumstances the foreign side may even supply steel to be used in constructing a new factory, and in large projects may also send managerial

---

1. According to one report, a Chinese trademark was registered several years ago in the United States by an American distributor of the trademarked product. See Sobin, 'Good Health: The First Chinese Mark Registered in the US', US–China Business Review, at 3, November–December 1975.

It should be noted that the registration process is simple and inexpensive, consisting of filing a single application with the Legal Affairs Department of CCPIT, which must be given a power of attorney by a notarized document. The fee for regulation is a nominal RMB 20 (RMB = Renminbi, the currency of China), approximately $32.00 at the rate of exchange prevailing in late May 1978.

quality control, and inspection personnel to live or remain for a time in place at the factory.

Under these arrangements, the capital goods supplied by the foreign contract partner become Chinese property upon delivery and the Chinese pay for them, together with any other items, such as know-how, for which a value is mutually agreed solely in terms of goods produced at the factory. Obviously variations are possible here since, before the factory has begun full production and even afterwards, the foreign partner could be repaid by other 'non-resultant' goods produced elsewhere.

To date, the Chinese have exhibited their customary reluctance to negotiate complicated contracts. Many of the transactions have involved relatively small quantities of equipment and machinery, and have also been concluded between Hongkong garment and other light industrial manufacturers. Because of the limited scope of the capital goods and because Chinese were on either side of the table, contract documentation has been very sparse. The would-be partner in a compensation trade agreement would be well advised to negotiate carefully about such matters as responsibility to maintain and insure equipment after it is delivered to China, quality control standards and procedures, including inspection by the foreign buyer's personnel, pricing, interest on any financing which the foreign side has to supply, exclusive rights to purchase and market the product, areas where the product may or may not be marketed, and dispute settlement, to name some obvious issues.

Negotiations and conversations about compensation trade in China during the first half of 1979 suggested that, although Chinese interest was great, inexperience and understandable caution, particularly in large transactions, were causing progress to be slow in spreading the use of this type of transaction. One of the largest reported contracts involved Harper's, the Ford dealer in Hongkong, which contracted to supply a plant at which tourist buses would be assembled in Guangdong for purchase by Harper's to sell in Hongkong.

At the time of writing, legislation was being drafted to state uniform principles applicable to compensation trade according to conversations with Chinese trade officials in Peking. Discussions also suggested that it was recognized that the Bank of China might have to provide bank guarantees in some of the major transactions, which might pose a difficulty. Compensation trade is attractive to the Chinese because it requires no foreign exchange outlays by China; however, if a Bank of China guaranty is needed, the Bank's obligations increase, thereby requiring the Bank to balance competing demands for its support.

Joint ventures

A not-surprising development in trade with China has been Chinese willingness, first experienced in mid-1978, to consider foreign equity joint ventures. By May 1979, no joint venture agreement had been negotiated in detail (as opposed to in principle), and many questions remained unsettled. Negotiations and conversations demonstrated, however, that the Chinese were willing to consider permitting the foreign partner to own up to 49 per cent of the venture (and, in some cases, perhaps, more), and that they were willing to promise to protect the right to repatriate profits after payment of taxes. Details were to be regulated in an Investment Law, which was being drafted, promulgation of which was regarded as a prerequisite to the final negotiations of any agreements.

Many joint ventures were under discussion in 1978–79, with both sides working hard to clarify their assumptions and requirements. Completion of the Investment Law, foreigners were told, was a task to which high priority was being given. The prediction may be ventured that the new legislation is likely to be fairly general, and to raise many questions of interpretation and application as Chinese negotiators and Western businessmen alike try to cope with the creation of forms of business activity new to the China trade. If the emphasis on joint ventures continues, however, the legal rules will be a significantly novel feature of the China trade. It may be noted that the author was told that plans were being made to draft a statute or other rules intended to apply to contracts as well as to joint ventures, but such legislation was not likely to appear in the very near future. Still, the acknowledgement that it is being contemplated is itself an expression of a noteworthy change in the attitude of Chinese trade officials towards the relationship between law and international commerce.

SPECIMEN CONTRACT

No. _____

Peking. Date: _____

The Buyers:

CHINA NATIONAL MACHINERY IMPORT AND EXPORT CORPORATION, Erh-Li-Kou, Hsi Chiao, Peking, China. (Cable Address: 'MACHIMPEX' PEKING)

The Sellers:

This Contract is made by and between the Buyers and the Sellers; whereby the Buyers agree to buy and the Sellers agree to sell the undermentioned commodity according to the terms and conditions stipulated below:

1. *COMMODITY, SPECIFICATIONS, QUANTITY AND UNIT PRICE:*

2. *TOTAL VALUE:*

3. *COUNTRY OF ORIGIN AND MANUFACTURERS:*

4. *PACKING*: To be packed in strong wooden case(s) or in carton(s), suitable for long distance ocean parcel post, air freight transportation and to change of climate, well protected against moisture and shocks. The Sellers shall be liable for any damage of the commodity and expenses incurred on account of improper packing and for any rust attributable to inadequate or improper protective measures taken by the Sellers in regard to the packing. One full set of service instructions for each instrument shall be enclosed in the case(s).

5. *SHIPPING MARK*: The Sellers shall mark on each package with fadeless paint the package number, gross weight, net weight measurement and the wordings: 'KEEP AWAY FROM MOISTURE', 'HANDLE WITH CARE', 'THIS SIDE UP' etc., and the shipping mark:

6. *TIME OF SHIPMENT:*

7. *PORT OF SHIPMENT:*

8. *PORT OF DESTINATION:*

9. *INSURANCE:* To be covered by the Buyers after shipment.

10. *PAYMENT: for/by*
    (1) In case by L/C: The Buyers, upon receipt from the Sellers of the delivery advice specified in Clause 12(1)(a) hereof, shall 15–20 days prior to the date of delivery, open an irrevocable Letter of Credit with the Bank of China, Peking, in favor of the Sellers, for an amount equivalent to the total value of the shipment. The Credit shall be payable against the presentation of the draft drawn on the opening bank and the shipping documents specified in Clause 11 hereof. The Letter of Credit shall be valid until the 15th day after the shipment is effected.
    (2) In case by Collection: After delivery is made, the Sellers shall send the shipping documents specified in Clause 11 hereof, from the Sellers' Bank through Bank of China, to the Buyers for collection.
    (3) In case by M/T or T/T: Payment to be effected by the Buyers within seven days after receipt of the shipping documents specified in Clause 11 of this contract.

11. *DOCUMENTS:* The Sellers shall present to the paying bank the following documents for negotiation:
    (1) In case by freight:
        3 Negotiable copies of clean on broad ocean Bill of Lading marked 'FREIGHT TO COLLECT'/'FREIGHT PREPAID', made out to order, blank endorsed, and notifying the China National Foreign Trade Transportation Corporation at the port of destination.
        In case by air freight:
        One copy of Airway Bill marked 'FREIGHT PREPAID' and consigned to the Buyers.
        In case by post:
        One copy of Parcel Post Receipt addressed to the Buyers.
    (2) 5 copies of Invoice with the insertion of Contract No. and the Shipping Mark. (In case of more than one shipping mark, the invoice shall be issued separately).
    (3) 2 copies of Packing List issued by the Manufacturers.
    (4) 1 copy of Certificate of Quantity and Quality issued by the Manufacturers.
    (5) Certified copy of cable/letter to the Buyers, advising shipment immediately after shipment is made.
    (6) The Sellers shall, within 10 days after the shipment is effected, send by air-mail two sets of the abovementioned documents (except Item 5) one set to the Buyers and the other

set to the China National Foreign Trade Transportation Corporation at the port of destination.

12. *SHIPMENT:*
   (1) In case of f.o.b. Terms:
   (a) The Sellers shall, 30 days before the date of shipment stipulated in the Contract, advise the Buyers by cable/letter of the Contract No., commodity, quantity, value, number of package, gross weight and date of readiness at the port of shipment for the buyers to book shipping space.
   (b) Booking of shipping space shall be attended to by the Buyers' Shipping Agents Messrs. China National Chartering Corporation, Peking, China. (Cable address: Zhongzu Peking)
   (c) China National Chartering Corporation, Peking, China, or its Port Agents, (or Liners' Agents) shall send to the Sellers 10 days before the estimated date of arrival of the vessel at the port of shipment, a preliminary notice indicating the name of vessel, estimated date of loading, Contract No. for the Sellers to arrange shipment. The Sellers are requested to get in close contact with the shipping agents. When it becomes necessary to change the carrying vessel or in the event of her arrival having to be advanced or delayed the Buyers or the Shipping Agent shall advise the Sellers in time. Should the vessel fail to arrive at the port of loading within 30 days after the arrival date advised by the Buyers, the Buyers shall bear the storage and insurance expenses incurred from the 31st day.
   (d) The Sellers shall be liable for any dead freight or demurrage, should it happen that they have failed to have the commodity ready for loading after the carrying vessel has arrived at the port of shipment on time.
   (e) The Sellers shall bear all expenses, risks of the commodity before it passes over the vessel's rail and is released from the tackle. After it has passed over the vessel's rail and been released from the tackle, all expenses of the commodity shall be for the Buyers' account.
   (2) In case of c. & f. Terms:
   (a) The Sellers shall ship the goods within the shipment time from the port of shipment to the port of destination. Transhipment is not allowed. The contracted goods shall not be carried by a vessel flying the flag of the country which the Buyers cannot accept. The carrying vessel shall not call or stop over at the port/ports of Taiwan and/or the port/ports in the vicinities of Taiwan prior to her arrival at the port of destination as stipulated in Clause 8 of this Contract.
   (b) In case the goods are to be dispatched by parcel post/air-freight, the Sellers shall, 30 days before the time of delivery as stipulated in Clause 6, inform the Buyers by cable/letter of the estimated date of delivery, Contract No., commodity, invoiced value, etc. The Sellers shall, immediately after dispatch of the goods, advise the Buyers by cable/letter of the Contract No., commodity, invoiced value and date of dispatch for the Buyers to arrange insurance in time.

13. *SHIPPING ADVICE:*
   The Sellers shall, immediately upon the completion of the loading of the goods, advise by cable/letter the Buyers of the Contract No., commodity, quantity, invoiced value, gross weight, name of vessel and date of sailing etc. In case the Buyers fail to arrange insurance in time due to the Sellers not having cabled in time, all losses shall be borne by the Sellers.

14. *GUARANTEE OF QUALITY:*
   The Sellers guarantee that the commodity hereof is made of the best materials with first class workmanship, brand new and unused, and complies in all respects with the quality and specification stipulated in this Contract. The guarantee period shall be 12 months counting from the date on which the commodity arrives at the port of destination.

15. *CLAIMS:*
    Within 90 days after the arrival of the goods at destination, should the quality, specifica-
    tion, or quantity be found not in conformity with the stipulations of the Contract except
    those claims for which the insurance company or the owners of the vessel are liable, the
    buyers shall, on the strength of the Inspection Certificate issued by the China Commodity
    Inspection Bureau, have the right to claim for replacement with new goods, or for
    compensation, and all the expenses (such as inspection charges, freight for returning the
    goods and for sending the replacement, insurance premium, storage and loading and
    unloading charges, etc.) shall be borne by the Sellers. As regards quality, the Sellers shall
    guarantee that if, within 12 months from the date of arrival of the goods at destination,
    damages occur in the course of operation by reason of inferior quality, bad workmanship or
    the use of inferior materials, the Buyers shall immediately notify the Sellers in writing and
    out forward a claim supported by Inspection Certificate issued by the China Commodity
    Inspection Bureau. The Certificate so issued shall be accepted as the base of a claim. The
    Sellers, in accordance with the Buyers' claim shall be responsible for the immediate
    elimination of the defect(s), complete or partial replacement of the commodity or shall
    devaluate the commodity according to the state of defect(s). Where necessary, the Buyers
    shall be at liberty to eliminate the defect(s) themselves at the Sellers' expenses. If the
    Sellers fail to answer the Buyers within one month after receipt of the aforesaid claim the
    claim shall be reckoned as having been accepted by the Sellers.

16. *FORCE MAJEURE:*
    The Sellers shall not be held responsible for the delay in shipment or non-delivery of the
    goods due to the Force Majeure, which might occur during the process of manufacturing or
    in the course of loading or transit. The Sellers shall advise the Buyers immediately of the
    occurrence mentioned above and within fourteen days thereafter, the Sellers shall send by
    airmail to the Buyers for their acceptance a certificate of the accident issued by the
    Competent Government Authorities where the accident occurs as evidence thereof.
    Under such circumstances the Sellers, however, are still under the obligation to take all
    necessary measures to hasten the delivery of the goods. In case the accident lasts for more
    than 10 weeks, the Buyers shall have the right to cancel the Contract.

17. *LATE DELIVERY AND PENALTY:*
    Should the Sellers fail to make delivery on time as stipulated in the Contract, with
    exception of Force Majeure causes specified in Clause 16 of this Contract, the Buyers shall
    agree to postpone the delivery on condition that the Sellers agree to pay a penalty which
    shall be deducted by the paying bank from the payment under negotiation. The penalty,
    however, shall not exceed 5 per cent of the total value of the goods involved in the late
    delivery. The rate of penalty is charged at 0.5 per cent for every seven days, odd days less
    than seven days should be counted as seven days. In case the Sellers fail to make delivery
    ten weeks later than the time of shipment stipulated in the Contract, the Buyers shall have
    the right to cancel the contract and the Sellers, in spite of the cancellation, shall still pay the
    aforesaid penalty to the Buyers without delay.

18. *ARBITRATION:*
    All disputes in connection with this Contract or the execution thereof shall be settled
    through friendly negotiations. In case no settlement can be reached, the case may then be
    submitted for arbitration to the Arbitration Committee of the China Council for the
    Promotion of International Trade in accordance with the Provisional Rules of Procedures
    promulgated by the said Arbitration Committee. The Arbitration shall take place in Peking
    and the decision of the Arbitration Committee shall be final and binding upon both parties;
    neither party shall seek recourse to a law court or other authorities to appeal for revision of
    the decision. Arbitration fee shall be borne by the losing party. Or the Arbitration may be
    settled in the third country mutually agreed upon by both parties.

19. *SPECIAL PROVISIONS:*

IN WITNESS THEREOF, this Contract is signed by both parties in two original copies; each party holds one copy.

THE BUYERS:

CHINA NATIONAL MACHINERY IMPORT AND EXPORT CORPORATION

By _____
Title _____
Date _____

THE SELLERS:

By _____
Title _____
Date _____

6. Financing the China trade

NICOLAS WOLFERS

Historical and institutional background

The Bank of China was originally established in 1912 and has always been primarily responsible for international business. It acts as the overseas arm of the People's Bank of China, which functions both as China's central bank and as its predominant domestic commercial bank. While the People's Bank handles its foreign transactions through the Bank of China, it lays down international policies and rates of exchange itself. However, Exchange Control is administered by the Bank of China though no foreign exchange regulations applicable to commercial transactions are published in view of the system which operates.

With the establishment of the People's Republic of China in 1949, the Bank of China on the mainland was reconstituted and its Head Office moved from Shanghai to Peking. Its current articles of association state that it is a corporation of joint public-private ownership, with limited liability. Private shareholders, though possibly nominees of the People's Bank or the Chinese government, still hold a minority shareholding in the Bank of China, thought in the early seventies to be as high as one third, although this may well have fallen in 1975 when, doubtless as a reflection of the Bank's increasing activity, paid-up capital was increased to RMB 400 million from the figure of RMB 19.8 million set in 1962. The Bank of China has the status of a Special Agency of the State Council, to which it is constitutionally responsible.

The Bank of China has branches in London, Hongkong, and Singapore, and in June 19 opened a branch in Luxembourg. It will probably not be long before the expanded development of international trade and finance leads to the opening of branches, or at least representative offices, in New York and Tokyo. In China itself the Bank of China operates at least 32 branches in major cities.

Table 6.1 Bank of China Balance Sheet as at 31 December 1976 and 1977 (in RMB million)

Assets	1977	1976	Liabilities	1977	1976
Cash	49.01	43.00	Due to banks	6 652.24	7 076.11
Due from banks	11 606.20	10 544.76	Deposits	12 735.00	10 562.17
Bills discounted and remittances bought	2 210.29	1 956.28	Remittances and drafts outstanding	120.35	107.23
Loans and overdrafts	5 498.14	5 761.44	Sundry accounts payable and accounts payable under forward contracts	673.48	596.67
Securities and investments	77.44	63.48	Other liabilities	156.93	144.65
Land, buildings, furniture and equipment	176.88	123.69	Collection for customers	427.68	419.57
Sundry accounts receivable and accounts receivable under forward contracts	879.22	764.55	Letters of credit and guarantee	8 496.49	7 654.00
Other assets	816.76	96.41	Trust liabilities	285.11	396.26
Collections receivable for customers	427.68	419.57	Total liabilities	29 547.29	26 956.65
Customers' liabilities under letters of credit and guarantee	8 496.49	7 654.00	NET WORTH		
Trust assets	285.11	396.26	Capital	400.00	400.00
Total assets	30 523.22	27 832.45	Surplus	191.83	146.45
			Reserves	258.72	216.99
			Net profit current year	125.38	103.37
			Total net worth	975.93	866.80
			Total liabilities and net worth	30 523.22	27 823.45

Table 6.2 Profit and loss statement for the years ended December 31, 1976 and 1977

EXPENSES	1977	1976
General expenses	151.87	118.54
Depreciation and amortization	92.17	73.74
Net profit	125.38	103.37
Total	369.43	295.64
INCOME		
Interest, commissions and other income	369.43	295.64
Total	369.43	295.64

Source: From the report of the Board of Directors, Bank of China, Peking.

In addition, this account of China's overseas banking structure, as it may affect foreign companies planning to do business with China, would be incomplete without mention of the 12 other banks controlled by the People's Republic of China, listed in Table 6.3.

The Bank of China's main Hongkong branch supervises the activities of the Chinese-controlled banks mentioned above. The Kwangtung Provincial Bank also has a branch in Singapore.

Table 6.3 Other Chinese-controlled banks in Hongkong

Name of bank	Number of branches	Location of head office
Bank of Communications	13	Peking
China and South Sea Bank	10	Shanghai
China State Bank	8	Shanghai
Chiyu Banking Corporation	5	Hongkong
Hua Chiao Commercial Bank	6	Hongkong
Kincheng Banking Corporation	9	Shanghai
Kwangtung Provincial Bank	11	Canton
Nanyang Commercial Bank	12	Hongkong
National Commercial Bank	6	Shanghai
Po Sang Bank	2	Hongkong
Sin Hua Trust, Savings and Commercial Bank	15	Shanghai
Yien Yieh Commercial Bank	9	Shanghai

Source: US Government Research Aid No. CR77-13-37, July 1977.

The two British banks currently represented in the People's Republic are the Chartered Bank (headquarters in London), part of the Standard Chartered Banking Group, and the Hongkong & Shanghai Banking Corporation (headquarters in Hongkong). Both these banks have branches in Shanghai.

By 1979 the Bank of China had a wide variety of international correspondent banking relationships, and the mutual trust and experience built up over the years through such relationships was crucial to the confidence with which the Bank of China could now respond to the financial requirements of the 'Four Modernizations'. The eagerness with which international bankers were offering their services to the Bank of China to help supply the foreign exchange needs of modernization was greatly due to the excellent reputation which the Bank of China had built up over a long period as a thoroughly reliable counter-party and paying agent, and as a most well-managed organization.

The caution with which China approached the possibilities for tapping the international financial markets was due in part to the old interpretations of the concept of self-reliance, but the underlying reasons could be found in China's history. 'He who is bitten by a snake will be afraid of a straw rope.' This old Chinese proverb was frequently quoted to explain the hesitant attitude towards accepting foreign loans. The snake was the heavy debt incurred by the former Imperial Government, and the straw rope the present opportunity for foreign currency borrowing. This was why the Bank of China was at first only prepared to accept deposits from foreign banks, rather than borrow outright, and why its deposit-taking stance was balanced by placing deposits with its close friends among the foreign banks. This was also why the Bank of China would always see to the maintenance of a conservative attitude to borrowing obligations which the People's Republic undertakes abroad, so that debts could be serviced without difficulty or delay regardless of any temporary economic problems which might put pressure on China's international cash flow. The soundness of this attitude also helped China to obtain fine terms and prime conditions in the international financial markets.

In fact, China's attitude to foreign loans has long been more flexible than its former ideological stance might at first sight imply. When the Soviet Union was assisting China's development programme in the fifties, Russian sales of plant and equipment to China were financed in part by loans of over $1 500 million, which the Chinese repaid in full by 1965. In the sixties and seventies plant imports from Japan and the West were often financed on a deferred-payments basis, usually five years from plant completion, though these loans were always supplier credits. From the early sixties, there have also been a number of 12 to 18-month loans to China to finance its imports of grain from Canada and Australia.

China has not objected to the principle of other countries taking on foreign loans. China has made loans to a variety of Third World countries, such as Tanzania, Pakistan, Sri Lanka, and Malta, though this was often in the context of China's overall foreign aid programme.

Nor, of course, has the principle of borrowing been questioned in a domestic context, where the People's Bank, grouping together most of China's pre-1949 commercial banks, with over 12 000 branches and many more sub-offices, receives deposits from a broad range of organizations and individuals and lends to agriculture and industry, in close coordination with the planning authorities. However, deficit spending is strongly discouraged and if possible, accounts are balanced throughout the economy and transactions settled on a non-cash basis. The main aim of strict control of the money supply has been to achieve stable prices, in contrast to the appalling hyper-inflation of 1937 to 1949, which preceded the creation of the People's Republic and when currency in circulation rose by 140 billion times and prices eight-and-a half times faster than in the nightmare Weimar inflation of 1923 in Germany.

Yet, ideological misgivings did persist so far as foreign capital was concerned, and it was only in August 1978 that an article in the influential *Guangming Daily* confirmed statements in July that the new interpretation of self-reliance was fundamentally in harmony with communist ideology. The article, called 'What is Lenin's view of introducing advanced technology and foreign capital?' found parallels in Stalin's statement of Russia's economic needs and priorities in the period of early industralization:

> In 1921 Lenin knew industry was not developed in our country and yet the peasants were in need of commodities, and he also knew that industry could not be developed immediately. He recognized therefore at that time that the best among all the feasible measures which could be taken was to attract foreign capital, to use it for the development of industry. Unquestionably that was the correct way.

The Renminbi, and China's currency preferences
The currency of China is called *renminbi* (abbreviated to RMB),[1] meaning 'people's currency', and the basic unit is the *yuan* (abbreviated to Y). The yuan is divided into 100 *fen*, or cents, 10 cents being known as a *jiao*, or colloquially *mao*. Notes are issued by the People's Bank of China, in denominations of Y10, Y5, Y2, and Y1, and of 5, 2, and 1 jiao, and coins in denominations of 5, 2, and 1 fen.

It is necessary for visitors to declare all foreign currency, travellers' cheques, etc., at the port of entry. These will be listed on a Bank of China form and any subsequent conversion of foreign currency or travellers' cheques into local currency must be made through a branch of the Bank of China and the currency declaration form stamped accordingly. On leaving China, travellers will only be allowed to convert into foreign currency the Chinese currency balance shown on their declaration form.

According to the Chinese, at least 60 countries trading with China have used the renminbi as the unit of settlement for some or all transactions. While this Chinese preference allows them to avoid international exchange

1. As at 9 April 1979, £1 = RMB 3.26, US $1 = RMB 1.57.

risks, it has at times been an obstacle for China's trading partners. Proceeds of exports to China can be converted into foreign currency, but the Chinese government is against any form of free dealings in RMB overseas. Some limited forward facilities are available, but the Chinese Ministry of Finance, which has done its best to establish the international acceptability of the RMB, is not thought over-keen to encourage their use. Forward cover facilities are mainly available to importers of Chinese products, who can obtain forward quotations from selected banks in London, the Continent, and Hongkong and from the overseas branches of the Bank of China.

By way of illustration, in February 1977 a spread of forward premium was announced by the Bank of China for purchases of RMB against the US dollar (see Table 6.4). These rates were only obtainable by foreign trading companies and businessmen holding firm contracts with the Chinese State Trading Corporations.

However, in 1979 it seemed most unlikely for forward cover to be provided by the Bank of China for periods of over six months. Earlier, forward yen–RMB contracts had also been made available, followed shortly afterwards by a period of considerable fluctuation in the yen which could have only served to underline the uncertainties faced by those concerned with international trade. In practice, many traders hedge in sterling, dollars, and other convertible currencies, and the Chinese in many cases accepted contracts denominated in dollars and some other currencies.

The RMB's external parity is decided unilaterally by the Chinese authorities, and the daily rate is obtainable from the People's Bank of China, the Bank of China and the New China News Agency. The international value of the RMB used to be linked informally to sterling but is now thought to be based on a basket of some 15 of the world's main currencies, the formula for which is not known. It may well be that this basket is made up on some trade-weighted basis, and the RMB has seemed to be quite closely linked to the world's strongest currencies. For extended periods, the value of

Table 6.4 Spread of forward premium offered by Bank of China: February 1977

Period	%
One month	0.9
Two months	1.7
Three months	2.5
Four months	3.0
Five months	3.5
Six months	4.0

Source: *International Currency Review*, Volume 10, Number 2, 1978.

the RMB remained in line with the Deutschmark, the Dutch guilder, or the Hongkong dollar.

The Chinese change the value of the RMB very frequently to reflect world monetary conditions. Until 1974 there was a single rate for purchases or sales of the RMB currency, but thereafter the Bank of China announced buying and selling rates, with a usual spread of around 0.5 per cent. Tables 6.5 and 6.6 illustrate the movement of the RMB over a 14-month period against four leading currencies, the US dollar, the £ sterling, the Hongkong dollar, and the yen.

When China was generally importing on cash or near-cash terms, its main concern was to minimize risk by matching payments and receipts, currency by currency, where business was not denominated in RMB. However, when China began to borrow in the international markets, it expressed a strong preference for obtaining loans denominated in US dollars. This was partly to avoid a proliferation of obligations in different international currencies, partly for the convenience of dealing in the world's main trading and reserve currency, which should always be readily marketable in large amounts and for long maturities, and partly because of the dollar's recurrent periods of weakness since the sixties. Provided the dollar continued on a weakening trend, the Chinese would have done well to finance imports and general purpose requirements for the modernization programme in dollars, rather than in harder currencies; the debt service charge in higher interest rates would have been more than offset by the lower relative burden of capital repayments.

In mid-1979, the six-month Eurocurrency interest rates were around $10\frac{1}{2}$ per cent per annum for US dollars, $7\frac{1}{2}$ per cent for Dutch guilders, $1\frac{3}{4}$ per cent for Swiss francs, $5\frac{1}{2}$ per cent for Deutschmarks, $8\frac{1}{2}$ per cent for French francs, 12 per cent for Italian lira, $10\frac{3}{4}$ per cent for Asian dollars, 6 per cent for Japanese yen, and $11\frac{1}{4}$ per cent for sterling. This was the interest rate background against which the Chinese were judging between different methods of finance and between different currencies, so far as commercial loans were concerned. The range of choice between currencies was a wide one, and there were many imponderables. The longer the term of borrowing, the wider the possible disparities between relative interest and exchange rates then and at the time of repayment. Since the Chinese seemed to be opting for commercial Eurocurrency loans with a 'bullet' form of repayment, (i.e., all at the end rather than in equal semi-annual instalments over much of the life of the loan, following a grace period), this exchange rate risk: reward factor was further increased. The relative interest rates between currencies have often been a good guide to future, as well as present, strength or weakness, but not invariably, since underlying conditions may of course change.

All in all, however, in recent years China has shown a marked preference for commitments in US dollars. This must have been enhanced by normalization of Sino-US relations and the probable solution of the frozen assets

Table 6.5 Bank of China spot buying rates

Date	US $100	£100	HK $100	¥100 000
31 December 1976	189.26	318.08	39.00	643.80
3 February 1977	192.11	329.91	40.22	663.01
11 March	190.97	326.65	40.22	694.95
5 April	190.20	326.65	40.22	690.93
10 May	188.12	324.47	40.22	678.23
9 June	188.12	324.47	40.22	678.23
7 July	186.99	321.67	40.22	700.20
2 August	184.57	317.76	40.22	630.94
6 September	185.31	320.62	40.22	690.94
6 October	184.57	321.90	39.86	699.23
4 November	182.17	327.99	39.18	722.89
9 December	177.29	326.34	38.79	737.41
4 January 1978	172.87	329.15	37.94	710.59
31 January	169.94	329.15	37.49	703.05
4 March	164.40	321.34	35.02	693.64

Table 6.6 Bank of China spot selling rates

Date	US $100	£100	HK $100	¥100 000
31 December 1976	188.32	316.50	39.03	640.58
3 February 1977	191.15	328.27	40.02	659.71
11 March	190.01	325.21	40.02	671.59
5 April	189.26	325.03	40.02	687.49
10 May	187.18	322.85	40.02	674.85
9 June	187.18	322.85	40.02	674.85
7 July	186.05	320.07	40.20	696.70
2 August	183.65	316.18	40.02	687.50
6 September	184.39	319.02	40.02	687.50
6 October	183.65	320.30	39.66	695.75
4 November	181.27	326.35	38.98	712.29
9 December	176.11	324.72	38.59	733.73
4 January 1978	172.01	327.51	37.76	717.53
31 January	169.10	327.51	37.31	699.55
4 March	163.58	319.74	35.34	690.18

Source: *International Currency Review*, Volume 10, Number 2, 1978.

problem between the two countries. The disinclination of China to incur yen or Deutschmark obligations for some time held up signature of business which would be financed in these two major hard currencies. The difficulty was that most finance arranged with the support of national credit insurers is denominated in the respective national currency. Yet, it is such finance, rather than commercial Eurocurrency bank loans, which would usually carry preferential rates of interest and a greater degree of certainty for China's planners, since interest rates would be fixed, while on Eurocurrency loans they are usually floating, on a six-monthly rollover basis. Official export finance is also often available for longer overall maturities than commercial bank loans.

In order to obtain access to attractive finance of this kind, largely tied to national exports of capital goods and related services, China must deal with national agencies such as Hermes in West Germany, Coface in France, Ducroir in Belgium, ECGD (the Export Credit Guarantee Department of the Department of Trade) in the United Kingdom, or the Japanese or US Export–Import Banks. But most of these agencies have no legal powers to guarantee, fund, or insure credits in currencies other than their own. This is a particular barrier for Hermes, which is limited to the Deutschmark, and also for the Export–Import Bank of Japan, the largest part of whose financial resources are in yen and only a relatively small, special allowance in US dollars. That leaves only ECGD, the major proportion of whose support for large-scale capital exports has, since 1976, been in US dollars rather than sterling. Given the fact that the US Eximbank could probably only hope to obtain legal sanction from Congress for export finance to China towards the end of 1979 at the earliest, Britain had a certain advantage in terms of China's currency preference.

Moreover, it will be remembered that national credit insurers agreed to be bound by the International Consensus Guidelines (or 'Gentleman's Agreement') as to minimum payments by delivery and interest rates and maximum credit periods for officially supported export credits on terms of two years or more. For China, the minimum interest rate for two to five-year credits was $7\frac{1}{4}$ per cent and for over five years $7\frac{1}{2}$ per cent. These rates would apply equally to yen or Deutschmark credits from or with the support of the national agencies, as for credits in weaker currencies. Therefore, China would not even gain an interest rate advantage were it to incur yen or Deutschmark obligations in this way. Even when Japan was believed to have offered China yen funds at rates below the consensus (for purposes which fall outside its terms of reference), the same unwillingness to take on eventual commitments to repay yen was apparent. For instance, after almost six months of intermittent discussions, China had at the time of writing, in April 1979, still not accepted a major long-term Eximbank loan at $6\frac{1}{4}$ per cent for 'mineral resource development untied to Japanese exports' or even 3 per cent 20-year finance from Japan's Overseas Economic Cooperation Fund (OECF).

Economic and financial parameters

Because of the homogeneity of China's culture and people, there is a tendency to think of China as a single massive unit. However, study reveals a considerable diversity of local tradition, language, diet, resources, geography, and way of life, as well as a strong sense of pride in the local or regional unit, and not only in the Chinese nation as a whole.

Even though official statistics for 1977–78 became available during 1979, it would still be a difficult task to assess a country as vast and varied as the People's Republic of China, where not only geographical distance but difficulties of terrain and inadequacies of infrastructure hinder the prompt collection of up-to-date and comprehensive data. Attempts at quantification are therefore partly a matter of guesswork, deduction or extrapolation, and should be viewed as such.

Yet, the more heavily China borrows, the more lenders may require reliable, regular, and up-to-date information in order to monitor their commitment. The keenness of bankers to be among the first to lend to China, coupled with the fact that China at present has low indebtedness and bankers little exposure to the country, has allowed lenders to go ahead without the complete country assessment information which would be usual otherwise. China's reputation and the size and strength of the country have seemed to provide enough assurance. But in years to come, as China's estimated debt service ratio rises and some of the above initial factors no longer apply, China's relative credit rating and the terms it can command may well be enhanced by the provision of official statistics on a regular basis, especially as this would be a good way for China to keep the world in touch with the progress of its programme of modernization and industrialization.

China's greatest asset is its people, estimated at over 1000 million in number, generally well motivated, literate, energetic, and quick to acquire new skills and training. The high density of the population in certain areas, the relatively low wage levels and standard of living compared with most of China's Far Eastern neighbours, its strong cultural foundation, and the fact that 80 per cent of the population is still in agriculture (though only around 60 per cent of the Gross National Product comes from that sector), could all be preconditions for successful industrialization. However, the very size of the country and its population also brings problems, and a massive effort is needed in training after the years of disruption in China's education system. Moreover, it is no easy matter to institute an effective system of material incentives, when for so many years individual bonus payments have been out of fashion.

In addition China is rich in minerals, being the world's main producer of wolfram (tungsten ore) and third largest producer of coal, which provides about 80 per cent of total domestic energy requirements. There are also large deposits of iron ore, bauxite, copper, lead, zinc, antimony, and of non-metallic minerals such as salt, magnesite, and the raw materials for cement. Most important, there are hydrocarbons, both in the form of crude oil and of gas, and exploration onshore and offshore may yet reveal still larger reserves, since the discovery and exploitation of hydrocarbons as a major resource in China is only a relatively recent development of the last decade or so. China is currently self-sufficient in oil, although many of its oil fields produce oil with a high wax content, which is more difficult and expensive to refine. However, adjustments can be made for this in new refineries being built in China, and in Japan which, under the terms of its $20 billion trade agreement to 1985, will become a major recipient of Chinese oil in future years. Some of these mineral resources will naturally be absorbed by China's own industrialization. Exactly how much is impossible to quantify at this stage; for instance, China is particularly short of some minerals, such as cobalt for steel production, and is already a net importer of copper, lead, and zinc.

China also has great agricultural wealth, with crops such as cotton, jute, flax, rice, sugar, tea, wheat, barley, maize, and millet, some of which is surplus to domestic needs and can be exported regularly. Animal products such as frozen rabbits, feathers and down, and pigs' bristles are also substantial exports, though overall agricultural export potential is simply not large and regular enough to cover more than a small part of China's planned imports to 1985.

While many of the projects of the original modernization plan were in heavy industry, such projects often have a long lead time, and by mid-1979 increasing emphasis was being placed on light industrial products, which have a quicker pay-back period. It seems likely that China was intending to earn part of the foreign exchange needed for imported plant through expanded exports of such goods as textiles and consumer electronics, both fairly labour-intensive industries for which workers can be trained quickly. For instance, China was negotiating with the EEC to increase textile exports. However, this is already an area in which domestic European producers feel threatened by Asian competitors, and in these and other light industrial products the problems of protectionism in potential importing countries must not be underestimated. Nevertheless, in terms of total world trade, China's overall export targets seemed not unreasonable, provided it did not rely too heavily on the high penetration of any one national market with any one manufactured product, as Japan has sometimes done.

The original 1976–85 programme called for the investment of around $600 billion. Some reports looked to imports over the period 1978–85 of over $200 billion (assuming 30 per cent average annual growth), others put the figure as low as $100 billion (assuming 15 per cent average annual growth). At all events, the figure is substantial and unlikely to be covered by China's increased exports, which on the lowest forecasts might only reach $90 billion over the period (an average rate of just under 10 per cent), though more optimistic forecasts envisage over double that figure.

Visible exports earned China around $10 billion in 1978, after $7.85 billion in 1977, (an 8 per cent increase on 1976), while imports reached just over $10 billion against $6.45 billion in 1978, (a 7 per cent increase on 1976). In the first half of 1978 alone, imports were up 60 per cent on the first half figures for 1977, while exports were up 29 per cent, but the rate of imports seems to have accelerated in the second half of 1978, which also saw the start of the upsurge in the world price of key commodities regularly imported by China, such as copper. In 1976, a trade surplus of $1.2 billion was achieved, and in 1977 of $1.4 billion, but in 1978 the trade account is likely to have achieved break-even, at best, and will probably start to move increasingly into deficit until 1980, when the trade deficit may reach $3.7 billion according to a JETRO estimate, recovering to a small surplus of $10 million in 1981.

Assuming China's present GNP to be in the range of $400 billion, with exports accounting for 2–2½ per cent, a 7 per cent GNP growth rate in real terms would raise the GNP at today's prices to $1000 billion by 1990 and, if exports can be achieved at double the GNP growth rate, they will account for 4–5 per cent of the GNP by 1990. This would give China annual exports in 1990 of $40–50 billion, and perhaps around $20–30 billion in 1985. However, export growth rate of just under 10 per cent (the growth rate assumed in the lowest forecast mentioned above for the 1978–85 period) would give exports of only around $15 billion in 1985. China's long-term GNP growth trend over the past 30 years has been around 6 per cent, so an acceleration of real GNP growth to 7 per cent in a stable and encouraging domestic and international political climate seems reasonably conservative. Although their economies are very different from that of China, with few raw materials but without such vast organizational and infrastructural problems, it may be remembered by way of comparison that both Japan and South Korea averaged over 10 per cent annually during the decades of most rapid industrialization or reconstruction.

In certain areas the Chinese economy may well again prove vulnerable to disruption and damage by earthquakes, floods, droughts, or other natural disasters, as in the past, and climatic conditions can wreak havoc on growth rates when so much of the GNP is agricultural.

The major part of the investment under China's modernization programme will have to come from domestic savings, currently not at a high level after the years of austerity, but in 1979 a campaign to encourage higher savings and their mobilization through the banking system was already under way, with increased annual interest rates for accounts with the People's Bank not unattractive on a tax-free basis, in a country with minimal inflation and a limited choice of consumer goods. In spite of their relatively low per capita incomes, the Chinese already seem to have a high propensity to save, as have the peoples of other Far Eastern countries with a similar cultural background, and the marginal propensity should rise with the growing incomes which modernization should bring about. In addition, the Construction Bank was restored, as an entity independent from the People's Bank, to oversee the efficient allocation of at least $45 billion a year on investment in industry, agriculture, and technology up to 1985. The Agricultural Bank was also reconstituted.

Yet, if modern plant and machinery are to be imported at the rates still under discussion, the trade deficit will need to be covered somehow. In 1978 alone, the West reportedly received plant export contracts for about $4.5 billion, and imports of at least $20 billion more were currently being considered. US Secretary of Commerce, Juanita Kreps, had predicted imports of $70–85 billion of capital equipment between 1979 and 1985, including $50 billion of complete plants, but this was before the general reappraisal of plan targets in early 1979.

An invisible surplus estimated by US Department of Commerce sources at $1 billion in 1978, rising to $2.7 billion in 1985, helps make up the likely foreign exchange short-fall, but only marginally. The modernization of China's existing hotel capacity and some new building should allow China to earn foreign exchange from a growing number of tourists. To conserve foreign exchange, China prefers f.o.b. quotations for import and c.i.f. or c. & f. quotations for export contracts, in order to use Chinese-owned or chartered carriers. The continued growth of the Chinese merchant fleet, over 10 million dwt, which at present transports around 50 per cent of China's trade, will be another significant currency earner; so will income from the shipping agencies, insurance companies, retail outlets, property holdings, banks, and the new finance companies which the People's Republic controls in Hongkong. Remittances from an estimated 20 million overseas Chinese to relations on the mainland may presently amount to $1 billion and have recently been positively encouraged by the Chinese government, though this flow may decrease as links between families weaken over time.

In July 1978, China's gold and foreign exchange reserves were revealed by Vice-Premier Li Xiannian as over $2 billion and at the end of 1978 were generally thought to be between $4 and $5 billion. This was the view of Midland Bank International in their *Spotlight on China*, in which they estimate China's reserves to be divided about equally between gold and currencies. The end-78 increase in the price of gold would therefore have boosted the value of the reserves, though cash payments in late 1978 and early 1979 may have offset this benefit, so that by mid-March a *Far Eastern Economic Review* commentator felt that the reserves might have fallen back to $2 billion again. Since then, they will have been boosted by China's commercial Eurocurrency borrowings, which on a commitment basis would have raised them to over $3 billion. The greater the extent of China's borrowing, the more important it will become to consider the reserves figure on a net as well as a gross basis. However, this sort of reserve level compared favourably with a current import level of about $10 billion, so that reserves seemed to cover three to four months' imports and perhaps more. In considering the composition of the reserves, it is important to remember the break-down of China's trade country by country, the bilateral trade balances, and the currencies in which trade may have been transacted, as well as the fact that 82 per cent of trade is with non-communist economies.

It may have been a sharp drop in the reserves in the spring of 1979 which led the Chinese government first to freeze around $3 billion worth of plant import contracts with Japan, and then to accept a succession of Eurocurrency loans from commercial banks. After a week, seven separate loans for a total of $1,175 million had been mandated or signed, though not actually utilized by being drawn down (see section on Commercial Eurocurrency Finance below). To this figure should be added an estimated $2 billion of China's existing international liabilities.

The announcements led to renewed discussion of the extent to which China could safely borrow to finance the foreign exchange short-fall relating to the achievement of the modernization programme. Estimates ranged from a figure for a total accumulated external debt of $6 billion in 1982, rising to $35 billion in 1985 from one US source, to a figure of $15–20 billion in 1985 from another. A Japanese source estimated $1.07 billion in 1979, peaking at $6.9 billion in 1983, and falling to $3.13 billion in 1985 when the debt-service ratio would be 12.4 per cent.

These figures give an idea of the range of possibilities, even the largest of which might conceivably be sustainable if exports developed very favourably, the economy grew in a political climate of peace and stability, and the total borrowings included a sizeable element of officially supported preferential rate national and international agency finance, possibly also from overseas aid organizations. The estimated debt figures can be compared with end-78 estimates of accumulated indebtedness for Comecon of $60 billion, for Mexico of $33 billion, for Indonesia of $12 billion, for the Philippines of $8 billion, and for Iran of $5 billion. China's economic parameters seemed to justify a debt-service ratio of 10–13 per cent, with 17–20 per cent somewhat on the high side.

However, having whetted the world's appetite with billion-dollar project possibilities in China and canvassed the world's salesmen for details of the latest plant and technology in a wide variety of fields, the Chinese were, in spring 1979, narrowing down the choice to more modest though still momentous proportions. The foreign exchange shortfall in this more manageable business schedule could almost certainly be fully covered through the efforts and resources of the international banking community.

Options for payment, finance, and the generation of foreign exchange
Short-term business

The most usual form of payment is by irrevocable Letter of Credit, opened by the buyer through the Bank of China and payable against presentation of sight draft and shipping documents. Confirmed Letters of Credit are not usually requested or allowed since payment difficulties have not been encountered. The frequent stipulation that the Letter of Credit is to be available for payment at a particular branch in China of the Bank of China means that payment is only made when the documents have been checked and accepted at that branch. China is not a party to the International Chamber of Commerce's Uniform Customs and Practice for Documentary Credits, but follows them unofficially. In the case of amendments to credits, beneficiaries in China normally advise non-acceptance but do not advise acceptance. All charges in connection with documentary credits, (e.g., advising, amendment, confirmation, negotiation, post and cable expenses), must be borne abroad. In addition, it should be mentioned that some short-term business is transacted with the Chinese on open account. All ECGD's normal short-term facilities are, of course, available for business with China, as would also be the case for Europe's other credit insurers.

Invoices, shipping documents (bills of lading), insurance policies (certificates), and other commercial documents issued in China are not usually signed by hand but may bear a facsimile signature. There are no Chambers of Commerce, and authentication of documents by foreign consulates is not acceptable. The China Council for Promotion of International Trade issues certificates of origin and certifies documents if required. Invoices usually incorporate combined certificates of origin, packing, weight and measurements lists, unless the credit specifies separate documents. Sanitary specifications and quality certification are usually issued together. Standard trade contracts are issued by the trading corporations and are printed in Chinese and English with each language equally valid. Contracts are brief and straightforward to avoid linguistic and other misunderstandings. Strict adherence to the provision of any contract is expected and it is in the businessman's interest to ensure that all the particulars of any agreement entered into are included. It is important that China's official designation, the People's Republic of China, be used on invoices, the labels for goods, and all correspondence.

Should any disagreement arise, the State Trading Corporations prefer to settle disputes through bilateral negotiation, but in particularly difficult cases they may submit the matter to the Foreign Trade Arbitration Commission of the CCPIT, or for arbitration in Switzerland or Sweden. This also applies for medium and long-term business.

Finally, an example is given of a short-term commodity credit, for which the term is usually 12–18 months: Lloyds Bank Limited quotes as a typical case a $150 million grain contract with Canada in February 1976. 25 per cent of the value was to be paid on loading the vessel, and the remainder 18 months later, with interest being paid at current market rates.

Medium and long-term business
Purchases of industrial plant by China have often been made on the basis of deferred payments, a down-payment of 10 to 35 per cent being followed by repayment of the remainder over a period of up to five years after

completion of the plant. An alternative method might be by way of progress payments made while the plant is actually being installed, so that payment has been effected by the time of completion. ECGD's normal supplier credit facilities would be available in the usual way, as would those of Europe's other credit insurers.

However, a major new development took place in the City of London on 6 December 1978 when ten British banks signed with the Bank of China seven separate ECGD 'deposit facilities' set up to provide preferential rate finance for UK exports of 'off-the-shelf' capital goods and related services (as opposed to project contracts). These facilities totalled $1.2 billion and were provided by Midland Bank Limited with $400 million, National Westminster Bank Group with $300 million, Barclays Bank International with $150 million, Standard Chartered Bank Limited with $100 million, S. G. Warburg & Co. Ltd in conjunction with Lloyds Bank International Limited with $100 million, Kleinwort Benson Limited in conjunction with the Bank of Scotland with $100 million, and Williams & Glyn's Bank Limited in conjunction with the Royal Bank of Scotland Limited with $50 million. These facilities were the first inter-bank facilities of their kind to be concluded with the Bank of China, supported by an official credit insurance organization.

To qualify under the terms of the deposit facilities, contracts had to have a minimum value of $5 million and be approved for financing by 6 December 1979, though an extension to this date could be negotiated if adequate utilization of the facilities seemed assured. Up to 85 per cent of the contract would be financed through the deposit facility, with the remainder, or 'front-end', payable from the buyer's own resources. The credit period was five years from mean delivery date, final delivery date, or installation date, as ECGD considered appropriate, and the rate of interest was fixed at $7\frac{1}{4}$ per cent throughout the period. Remuneration to the British banks was in the form of a flat-deposit placing fee.

The 'deposit facility' was to work in broadly the same way as an ECGD General Purpose Line of Credit and documentation was reduced to a minimum. At the time the deposit facilities were negotiated, the Chinese were not yet ready to accept direct loans; so the transfer from the British bank to the Bank of China in London of the appropriate deposit, against the usual shipping and other documents from the exporter, avoided the ideological problem and only added one stage to the normal operation of a General Purpose Line of Credit. Payment to the UK exporter was to be made by the UK bank on receipt of the appropriate notification from the Bank of China in London. If the exporter were able to negotiate progress payments into his supply contract (with a State Trading Corporation), the 'deposit facility' could be used to make these available to him as agreed.

The 'deposit facility' was followed in March 1979 by another major step forward. During his visit to China, the then Secretary of State for Industry, Mr Eric Varley, signed with the Chinese Minister of Foreign Trade a $5 billion Credit Agreement valid until 31 March 1985, guaranteeing that ECGD would provide official support for British exports to China up to that value. The $5 billion figure, set as an attempt to quantify China's future credit requirements, included the $1.2 billion deposit facilities, and should be seen in conjunction with the Sino-British trade agreement signed at the same time, which set a target for two-way trade to 1985 of £7 billion, (then equivalent to $14 billion).

By that time the Bank of China had agreed to most of the principles for buyer credit, and for the sake of simplicity ECGD's draft Loan Agreement had been shortened at the request of the Chinese from 44 to 7 pages. Guideline rates and conditions were also agreed, with credit of up to five years at $7\frac{1}{4}$ per cent fixed and of over five years at $7\frac{1}{2}$ per cent. Large project business might obtain up to eight years and very large project business up to ten years. However, these rates and terms could only continue if there were no change in the 'International Consensus'.

The agreed cover for such buyer credits, to be used in support of project contracts with mainly UK capital goods and related services, was up to 85 per cent of eligible UK value. A small degree of flexibility might be shown in the case of an unavoidable foreign element, especially if from other EEC countries. 85 per cent is definitely a maximum percentage of cover, and the actual percentage will have to be agreed case by case. Defence equipment usually obtains lower rates of cover, and the OECD guidelines for the export of ships require a maximum of 70 per cent. As for all buyer credits, the minimum allowable size of the credit is £1 million, but both the Bank of China and ECGD preferred that all the buyer credits should be in US dollars. Repayments would be by way of equal semi-annual instalments, starting six months after the appropriate date chosen for the start of the ECGD credit term.

By mid-1979, Japan had not agreed a financial package in support of the Sino-Japanese trade agreement signed in February 1978, which set a yen target of $20 billion equivalent for two-way trade to 1985. A much higher target had subsequently been set for 1990. The package currently being negotiated by the Japanese was thought to consist of: $1 billion in consensus terms supplier credits, half in yen from Japan's Eximbank and half in dollars from Japanese commercial banks; $2 billion equivalent in 15-year yen finance from Eximbank to finance oil and other resource projects in China (at $6\frac{1}{4}$ per cent, below the consensus but not tied to purchases of Japanese equipment); a $2 billion syndicated four-and-a-half-year bank loan from a consortium of 22 Japanese banks led by the Bank of Tokyo at $\frac{5}{8}$ per cent over the London Interbank Offered Rate for dollars (LIBOR); and a $6 billion six-month revolving dollar loan from Japanese commercial banks at $\frac{3}{8}$ per cent over LIBOR. The Chinese had asked for rates of $\frac{3}{8}$ per cent and $\frac{1}{8}$ per cent over LIBOR respectively for these last two facilities and were maintaining objections to yen finance, although the yen had begun to weaken due to the world oil crisis of early 1979, which could reassure the Chinese about borrowing yen. A final compromise on the margin for the commercial bank facilities seemed likely to be $\frac{1}{2}$ per cent and $\frac{1}{4}$ per cent respectively.

West Germany had still not arranged finance, due to the inability of Hermes under its statute to provide credit insurance other than in Deutschmarks. France had signed a 60 billion French franc trade agreement in early December 1978 with a then dollar equivalent target for two-way trade to 1985 of $14 billion, (the same as Britain's allotted figure). At the time the official French credit insurer, Coface, was thought to have signed a FF 30 billion ten-year credit agreement.

Italy was thought to be close to signing an eight-year credit agreement for $1 billion, and Denmark and Sweden similar agreements. The US Eximbank was not yet empowered by Congress to lend to China, but legislation was in preparation to remedy this position. However, if and when Eximbank can lend, its exposure to China may well be given a surprisingly low limit, for the 1979–85 period, of $1.5 billion in direct loans, (usually 45 per cent of total export contract value). By way of comparison, its largest commitment in direct loans to any single country at the end of 1978 was $1.3 billion to Mexico. On the other hand, US exporters could also count on the support of PEFCO or other large private institutional lenders, and of a resilient surety market. Meanwhile, news had just come in of a C$2 billion agreement between the Export Development Corporation of Canada and the Bank of China.

Commercial Eurocurrency finance

The first commercial bank loan for China to be arranged by a Western bank was signed on 30 March 1979 by the Bank of China and Midland & International Banks (MAIBL). The only terms disclosed were that it provided $175 million for 5 years. The loan was placed among the shareholders of MAIBL, and the proceeds were not tied to any specific project or exports from the West.

Shortly afterwards, it was announced that a group of Arab banks led by the Union de Banques Arabes et Françaises (UBAF) had received the mandate for a $500 million $3\frac{1}{2}$-year loan to the Bank of China at a margin of $\frac{1}{2}$ per cent over LIBOR, with 'bullet' repayment. Midland Bank and Standard Chartered Bank then separately announced the establishment of commercial credit lines to the Bank of China of $100 million each, followed by announcements of lines of $100 million each by Lloyds Bank International, National Westminster Bank Group and Barclays Bank. The Lloyds Bank 5-year facility was expected to have a margin of $\frac{1}{2}$ per cent over LIBOR— with drawing at the discretion of the Bank of China and the finance to be used partly in payment for British exports. The National Westminster Bank Group loan was to be drawn within six months and to be used for the import of capital goods. Midland Bank's five-year loan was untied to any project or to Western imports; it had a 'bullet' repayment. Standard Chartered's five-year 'bullet' loan had a $\frac{1}{2}$ per cent margin. The documentation for all these loans was believed to have been reduced to a minimum.

These developments bore out the willingness of the banking community to support China's modernization programme on the finest terms. Some of the loans were general purpose and could be used by the Bank of China in any way to further China's development, including as front-end finance for ECGD loans, others had to be used specifically as front-end finance for imported capital goods. As a result, the Chinese could now buy from Britain on a 100 per cent financed basis, with the down-payment to the supplier funded on a five-year basis. As with the ECGD agreements, they represented a commitment, but until actual draw-down by the Bank of China, not a utilization of funds.

The criteria of Eurobond market investors are usually very different from those of lending bankers, but the enthusiasm with which the bankers greeted opportunities to fund China's development could be mirrored in the attitudes of at least the institutional capital market investors. Although a bond or floating rate note issue would be unlikely to raise more than a maximum of $100–200 million, as compared with the 'jumbo' $1 billion or $2 billion loans possible in Eurocurrency syndications, if well managed other issues could follow, and China would gain the benefit of the very long maturities available to capital market instruments. This could be especially useful were China keen to avoid bunching in debt-service payments or debt maturities.

Additional project cover

Tendering for large projects, of course, involves problems other than the raising of finance. ECGD has introduced a number of special schemes, some temporary and some long-term, to reduce the risks for British suppliers and contractors. All these forms of cover would be available in the case of business in China: Tender to Contract Cover, Project Participants Insolvency Cover, Joint & Several Cover, and Cost Escalation Cover (very relevant in China where fixed price contracts are the norm and only rarely can contracts be signed on a cost-plus basis). It has not been usual for the Chinese to require any form of bonding, but should this ever occur, ECGD provides cover for a variety of the risks of performance bonds, tender bonds, advance payment and progress payment bonds, and against the unfair calling of bonds.

Other Western countries have adopted a variety of different approaches to the problems of large project contracts, and the increasing cross-frontier integration of European industry strengthens the case for establishing a European Export Bank. China is a market where the joint European approach could prove welcome on political as well as economic grounds, and where a European Export Bank would therefore be able to play a useful role.

Compensation trading and joint ventures

In addition to the methods of payment or finance mentioned above, China is considering a number of alternative ways of marketing its exports and gaining access to imported plant and technology, of avoiding the disbursement of foreign exchange or of finding new methods to generate it. By mid-1979 even joint ventures were possible, and some basic legislation was passed by the June 1979 National People's Congress. The variety of combinations and permutations was so great that this section will merely give some explanations of the main Chinese terms, as listed in JETRO's March 1979 China Newsletter:

Simple processing method: under this formula, foreign manufacturers bring raw materials into China for processing. The goods manufactured belong to the foreign manufacturers and China receives a commission for its work. This is also called 'work on consignment'.

Raw material working formula: under this formula, foreign manufacturers bring in equipment and use Chinese factories. The goods manufactured will be owned by the foreign manufacturers, but 20–30 per cent of the commission charge for China's work will be deducted every time, so that the equipment becomes Chinese property in three years or so.

Compensation trade formula: foreign manufacturers supply the entire plant and China carries out production within the framework of its national economic development plans. The plants will be compensated for by deductions from China's commission charges for its work. This formula is best applied to large factories, and when this method is used China may share in the management. Both this and the raw material formula are forms of product sharing, or 'product-buyback' as it is called in East–West trading.

Package buying of parts and assembly materials: the foreign contracting firm supplies all parts and packaging materials, and a Chinese factory is paid by the foreign firm for its processing and assembly work. This form of industrial cooperation may also be called 'product-buyback', or, in Japan, 'joint venture knock-down production'.

Partial purchasing of parts and raw materials: the foreign firm supplies some parts or a portion of raw materials and a Chinese factory the remainder. This can also be a form of 'product-buyback'.

Improvement trade formula: China accepts orders to turn out manufactured goods from supplies of raw materials.

Component order formula: China is made responsible for producing parts for machinery and equipment.

Trademark attached formula: China exports products under the brands of ordering firms.

Accessory utilization formula: China accepts orders to manufacture clothing and craft articles on being supplied with the accessories for such production.

Design consignment formula: China will produce to order in accordance with the design designated by foreign firms.

Package designated formula: China will produce finished articles after being supplied with packaging materials.

Assembly trade formula: China manufactures the finished articles after receiving supplies of equipment and semi-finished goods.

The above are all forms of work on consignment, except that the last resembles a joint venture under Japanese definition.

Total job formula: foreigners take charge of 'commercializing' articles from design to production and also take responsibility for employee training.

Barter formula: China pays for its machinery and equipment purchases with its mineral resources or other goods.

Joint venture formula: the two sides, China and the foreign interests, make capital subscriptions in kind to set up a firm to produce goods, or even services. Foreign ownership on a large scale may be allowed. It was reported that the Chinese have even proposed allowing $100 billion of direct investment in joint ventures by foreign companies by 1985.

Joint production along the lines of certain of the above formulae has already begun in China just over the border from Shenzhen, with the foreign partners usually Hongkong Chinese or the Hongkong subsidiaries of Japanese companies.

Other sources of finance

At the end of September 1979 China announced a keen interest in obtaining to international development agency finance from sources such as the World Bank and the Asian Development Bank, though certain diplomatic hurdles would first have to be crossed. The advantages of such finance are its long maturities and low interest rates, coupled with the improved terms usually available from the commercial banking sector under co-financing arrangements. At the same time it accepted a $15 million loan from the UN.

If China needed to obtain further finance on even longer terms and lower rates of interest, this might be forthcoming from international and national aid organizations such as the European Development Fund, or in Britain the Overseas Development Ministry. This Ministry now reserves 5 per cent of its annual budget for 'trade-aid' funding where trade criteria are predominant but combine with aid objectives. Such sources could be very helpful to the beneficial funding of China's modernization programme, and could significantly lower the debt service burden.

Finally, China has now decided that it is interested in joining the International Monetary Fund, which counts Rumania and Yugoslavia as members, as well as 103 other countries. This could certainly be of advantage and a further source of funding, though diplomatic obstacles would again have to be cleared. China may yet feel that IMF membership would entail too much of an infringement of sovereignty and too much statistical groundwork.

Conclusion

Historic changes took place in 1978–79, which should lay the foundations for a stronger and more prosperous China in the future, and a major world economic power by the end of the century in spite of the many problems which must first be overcome. The Chinese were approaching this historic challenge with due realism and considerable ingenuity. It therefore came as little surprise when, in mid-1979, the Bank of China made its debut as a lender in the Eurocurrency markets, joining six Western banks in a seven-year $42 million loan for Sun Hung Kai Securities, a Hongkong company with close Peking ties, to finance an office tower in central Hongkong. The margin on the loan was thought to have been $1\frac{1}{8}$ per cent. This and other new developments were welcomed by the international banking community, for the further opportunities they gave for establishing a full and equal partnership with the Bank of China.

Many other options also now seem to be open. Within a few years of ECGD's deposit agreements of December 1978 and the Secretary of State for Industry's Credit Agreement of March 1979, it could well be that the Chinese will themselves set up a national credit insurance agency or an Eximbank. It is possible that joint ventures will not only be discussed within China's borders but in terms of project collaboration in third countries, which could prove a further important way for China to augment its foreign exchange reserves, as other countries have already begun to do.

At all events, it is certain that in the future there will be many possibilities for Britain and its European partners to work with China for the advancement of national economic development, and, as the world's largest international financial centre, the City of London is sure to continue to play a key role.

Note

The cable address for all branches of the Bank of China in China and abroad is CHUNGKUO followed by the name of the city, except for that of the Bank's headquarters, which is HOCHUNGKUO PEKING. For contact by telex, the number for the Head Office is 716307 and answerback Chungkuo PK 307, though to make contact from the UK it is necessary first to dial 201 and to make the call through the operator. The digits 716 indicate Peking.

The address of the Head Office is San Li Ho, Peking, People's Republic of China; of the London Branch: 8–10 Mansion House Place, London EC4, Telephone 01-626 8301; of the Hongkong branch: Bank of China Building, 2a Des Voeux Road, Hongkong; and of the Singapore branch: Battery Road, Singapore 1.

Recently the Bank of China has also opened up in 107 Shaftesbury Avenue, London W1, Telephone 01-734 7785, to cater for the needs of the adjacent Chinese community.

7. Shipping with China

C. M. O'CONNOR

There is a long history of overseas shipping links with China and the tea clipper races of the 1870s are well known. China itself has a long maritime tradition befitting a country with thousands of miles of coastline and its sailors have contributed in large measure to maritime developments world wide. The Chinese, therefore, continue to have a thorough understanding of shipping today and are naturally keen to play a full part in the seaborne carriage of their overseas trade. Shipping services, of course, should rely on the cargo interests which are their customers and reflect their requirements and terms of trade. Thus, contracts of sale specifying ports of loading and discharge, influenced by points of origin and consumption or other trade requirements, will produce, either individually for full loads or collectively for smaller parcels, the pattern of vessels' loading and discharging itineraries.

It is, therefore, relevant at this point to examine the structure of China's transportation set-up. This follows the national corporation style outlined elsewhere in this book for manufacturing and trading activities (see Chapters 3 and 9 and Appendix VII). China's own ship-owning operations are under the China Ocean Shipping Corporation (COSCO) which also controls non-Chinese flag operations. This corporation works under the Ministry of Communications which also covers related activities, such as the work of the harbour authorities, and the China Ocean Shipping Agencies Corporation which undertakes all ship agency functions in Chinese ports. However, there is an important distinction in regard to charter operations which fall under the control of the China National Chartering Corporation (generally known as: ZHONGZU, its cable address), which works together with its associated organization, the China Foreign Trade Transportation Corporation, both under the Ministry of Foreign Trade. These corporations, as their names imply, cater for the overall land and sea transport requirements of the trading corporations for both imports and exports. They may use COSCO vessels (or their associated fleets), ZHONGZU chartered vessels, or foreign flag vessels. There can clearly, therefore, be a difference of emphasis in the approach to shipping questions by the two ministries and in turn their subordinate corporations.

There are five basic types of deep-sea shipping involved in the China trade: dry bulk, tankers, reefers (which provide controlled temperature conditions), liners, and passengers.

Dry bulk

This is the tramp sector which operates on a daily hire basis (time charter) or a full-load tonnage basis (voyage/charter). Ships are selected for the specific requirement—bulk carriers for grain, ore etc, and 'tween-deck ships[1] for general cargo carriage on time-charter basis. The scale of the activity of the Chinese in this world charter market makes them a prominent force, and the fact that their operations are under one central control heightens this dominance in the grain, ore, and time-charter markets (these markets are otherwise composed of a multiplicity of the private sector competitive interests). Such business is invariably on Charter Party terms.[2]

Tankers

This sector principally covers the bulk shipment of petroleum products, though in addition it includes the carriage of edible oils and fats, and chemicals on a 'parcel' tanker basis, i.e., vessels capable of giving segregated carriage for part loads of these types of liquid. The petroleum business is, of course, a special entity on its own and currently in a state of change with the recent rapid development of China's own oil resources.

Reefers

This covers China's exports of refrigerated cargoes, i.e., those requiring carriage in controlled temperature conditions. A proportion of this traffic moves in full loads in chartered, fully refrigerated vessels, i.e., fixed on tramp terms as for dry bulk. The balance moves in COSCO's own vessels or foreign flag liners which have part reefer capacity as mentioned below.

Liners

This sector caters basically for less than full loads and so is likely to be of interest to the widest range of those interested in the import and export trades with China. It should cover the required frequency and range of ports for all such items of trade: general cargo, refrigerated, bulk liquids in parcel

---

1. 'Tween-decks have intermediate decks in cargo-carrying spaces to provide separate stowage.
2. The Charter Party is the document which prescribes the terms under which a vessel is fixed for period or voyage.

sizes. More discussion of how this presently stands under current Chinese shipping policies will follow.

Passenger
Non-Chinese interest is in the cruise sector such as John Swire & Sons' successful operations with their *Coral Princess* from Japan and Cunard's calls with the *Queen Elizabeth II*. The Chinese have purchased a number of passenger-carrying vessels, mostly of the combined freight and passenger type, for example the former Peninsular and Orient ship *Cathay*, carrying 250 passengers and about 5000 tons of cargo. There are also numerous specialized vessels for the traditional river services, including modern vessels built in China. The Chinese passenger fleet seems to be concerned solely with its own business and does not appear to be traded on the international passenger market. However, with the opening up of the tourist trade, this situation could alter, especially if the very large overseas Chinese market were tapped.

For a proper understanding of the Chinese shipping scene it is necessary to consider Chinese trading policy as a whole. The present state trading organizations almost invariably sell c.i.f. or c. & f. and purchase f.o.b. Thus, in the shipping context they control the routing arrangements for both their imports and exports. This underlies and indeed explains their shipping arrangements, whereby for full loads they nominate their own vessels, or fix time-chartered vessels, or voyage(s), or chartered vessels for their own account. For less than full loads they nominate the carrying vessel which may be their own COSCO vessel, their time-chartered vessel, or a foreign-flag liner.

The controlling corporation in this respect is the China National Chartering Corporation (ZHONGZU), and the policy is to increase the proportion of foreign trade carriage in Chinese flag vessels and to minimize freight costs over the whole of foreign trade shipping operations. This is achieved in two ways. The first is the aggregation of part cargoes to produce full loads from the least number of load/discharge ports, thereby minimizing the operating costs of both their own COSCO vessels and their time charters. The second is stipulating for foreign-flag liner operators rates according to their own ZHONGZU tariff which relate to this present method of operating and the tramp market rates (which have of recent times been exceptionally low).

The result of this policy has been sucessfully to produce low freight rates (probably only 60 per cent of the equivalent HK/Europe rates), but with the not inconsiderable disadvantage of poor delivery performance in both directions, which clearly affects export and import prices. As an example, in the past, manufacturers of heavy equipment for China geared to a specific loading port have had to wait a matter of months after the goods were ready for dispatch from their factory for a shipping opportunity from that port. This is doubtless a matter of calculated policy, but China's trading partners need to take account of the time-lag between the execution of orders, time of payment (normally when shipped Bills of Lading are available), and the completion of delivery. The cost of extra financing involved must come into the account of the f.o.b. export or c.i.f. import prices, as indeed must the uncertainty of time of the delivery of Chinese exports at the port nominated in the c.i.f. contract.

Another consequence of this shipping arrangement is to limit the participation of foreign liner companies as they mostly work on a part-loading basis, within a competitive liner schedule covering other areas, and hence are inhibited from waiting whilst cargoes are aggregated. Furthermore, on such a liner-type operation, they have difficulty in operating viably at rates which are based on the tramp market.

In the past, these terms of trade have covered the vast majority of cargoes carried on liner terms between Europe and China. However, there have been notable exceptions: refrigerated cargoes from China (exceeding lots of say 200 B/L tons[1]) and bulk liquids in liner deep tanks (say up to 2000 tons). The first have been covered by special Contracts of Affreightment (contracts which lay down conditions of carriage) where the buyer may have purchased f.o.b. and thereby been responsible for securing shipping space. The second are invariably covered by Contract of Affreightment and purchases can be f.o.b. or c.i.f.

In the case of large bulk shipments dealt with on a 'tramp' basis, the evidence points to few cases of the non-Chinese trader being able to buy f.o.b. or sell c.i.f. There is, however, the exception of tanker business where the Chinese may not always control the shipping (for example, where barter arrangements—say oil for ore—may be in question), or where they do not have the specialized tonnage required—such as 'parcel' tankers with coated or stainless-steel tanks.

Looking to the future, continuance of the present Chinese policy of liberalization of trade may necessitate a review of present shipping policy. Better delivery performance may be needed, requiring faster and more frequent shipping opportunities which are commonplace in other sectors of world seaborne trade. This consideration applies with even greater force to the need to give comprehensive carrying capacity for all cargo requirements, such as hazardous cargo, reefer cargo, and bulk liquids. This is illustrated by the fact that British imports of Chinese vegetable oils have in the past been inhibited by a lack of deep-tank capacity for liner-size parcels, in for example the 100/2000 tons range. To be competitive, China may need to trade on more equal terms in this way. This would lead to more efficient liner operations but would, of course, be more expensive.

However, self-sufficiency underlies all China's trade policy and it is worth at this point reviewing how this stands in the shipping context. Since 1949, the Chinese have by any reckoning achieved the most remarkable progress in the economic development of their country, given their very difficult

1. Tonnage on which freight is paid.

initial circumstances. In terms of priorities, communications for foreign trade were relatively low, against the most urgent need for domestic viability and, in particular, the feeding of the large population. However, in more recent times, they have been able to advance this sector by improving road and rail links to the ports, reconstructing harbours on a large scale, and acquiring a large ocean-going merchant marine.

With not inconsiderable acumen, the Chinese made substantial purchases of second-hand tonnage during the 1977–78 depression in the sale and purchase market: in one recorded 18-month period alone they acquired 150 vessels at a probable cost of around £500 million. Of these, about two-thirds were 'tween-deckers with a general cargo capability, and the balance were bulk carriers suitable for grain, ore, or the like. Tanker purchases were small. Reputedly, COSCO's deep sea fleet now breaks down as follows:

General cargo 60 per cent
Bulk ore/grain 20 per cent
Tankers 15 per cent
Passenger and special purpose 5 per cent.

As regards harbour work, a plan for 50 new berths in the major ports over the last four years is probably 60 per cent completed. The serious earthquake in 1976 at Tangshan in north China undoubtedly set back these developments. More recently, the Danish East Asiatic Company has announced contracts for major communications improvements, including harbour works involving container facilities, though these have been 'postponed', like other contracts during China's 'readjustment' period. However, the Chinese are currently still stretched to keep pace with the expansion of seaborne trade, particularly heavy grain imports, and are still hampered by port facilities restricting the size of vessels that can be accommodated. But it is probably the inadequacy of road and rail links which is now the major inhibiting factor in smoothing the flow of imports and exports and, in particular, in clearing port congestion. This still remains a problem.

It remains to be seen, therefore, what course China will steer in shipping policy, balancing the goal of self-sufficiency against the practical requirements of competitive foreign trade, involving greater use of foreign (trading partners') shipping services. Lastly, there remains the question of China's cross-trading[1] aspirations where their current activity is fairly minimal

It is clear how Chinese government involvement in shipping takes place through the Ministries of Foreign Trade and Communications. There is, however, the additional defence interest which impinges on foreign shipping through the somewhat stringent regulations governing the conditions for vessels transiting Chinese ports, and making coastal inter-Chinese port passages.

1. Cross trade: seaborne carriage between countries not of the flag of the carrying vessel, for example, in this context, Chinese vessels carrying rubber from Singapore to West Germany.

The main concern of foreign shipowners relates to the restrictions on the use of navigational aids in Chinese estuarial waters: prohibition on the use of echo depth recorders, limitations on use of radar, are examples. As ships become larger and more complicated, and hence more expensive, this risk increases as does the value of cargo per vessel.

As far as Britain is concerned, various representations have been made through the Chinese trade and communications ministries for some amelioration, to bring Chinese practice in line with the West so that British ships could enjoy the same use of facilities as is open to Chinese vessels navigating in and out of British ports. These have not yet been successful but it is hoped that current discussions on a United Kingdom–People's Republic of China Maritime Agreement may cover this aspect in terms of legislating for equal and fair treatment of each party's vessels and personnel.

This agreement has been under discussion for some time and such agreements have been concluded by the Chinese with various western countries from as far back as 1974, for example with West Germany, Belgium, Holland, and the Scandinavian countries. In the case of EEC countries, such agreements have relevance to the Trade Agreement signed in May 1978 between the European Economic Community and the People's Republic of China.

The purpose of such maritime agreements is mutually to develop maritime transport by the strengthening of friendly relations and cooperation based on most-favoured-nation treatment for both contracting parties in each other's territory. Thus, there should be no discrimination against each others' vessels in terms of entry conditions, charges, and the like; equally, facilities for crew should reflect recognition of each party's legislation, for example documentation of personnel.

Last, the maritime activity of the parties within the scope of the agreement should be in accordance with the principle of equal treatment and mutual benefit. This last facet, of access to traffic, will be seen to present some difficulties in the face of the present Chinese policy for terms of sale/purchase and control of routing/freighting arrangements.

Current conditions have, therefore, tended to limit the foreign liner companies participating in the carriage of China's foreign trade. Such foreign lines have clearly to be acceptable to ZHONGZU and must use the rates of freight prescribed in the ZHONGZU tariff for cargo controlled by ZHONGZU. These rates are in general on the same conditions as international liner conference tariffs. However, China does not recognize adjacent area international conferences such as the Far Eastern Freight Conference (FEFC) and hence foreign owners do not have the same participation in rate-fixing arrangements.

Serious port delays have in the past also influenced liner participation as they have effectively prohibited the integration of Chinese services within liner schedules covering a spread of countries, leaving such services to cover Chinese ports only. The result of this has been a lower frequency and speed of services, as it has prevented the normal liner concept of frequent part load/discharge over sufficient spread of load/discharge areas reasonably to fill the ships. This may be illustrated by reference to the European trade. There, Rickmers, East Asiatic, and Toho are the only foreign liner operators participating in the trade, providing about three sailings per month, whereas the FEFC comprises some 30 lines providing daily sailings from, say, Hongkong or Japan.

Thus, even if a non-Chinese trader is able to retain control of routing, the choice and frequency of service is very limited. In addition, with the relatively small volumes involved, such infrequency, even allowing for COSCO's own or time-chartered sailings, means the necessity of considerable transhipment at the European end of the trade: this factor may also be influenced by discharging costs, such as in certain UK ports whence transhipment has taken place via Rotterdam. This may be illustrated by the fact that whilst China's exports of liner cargoes may emanate from the three major ports of Tianjin/Xingang, Shanghai, and Qingdao, tariff destinations in northern Europe total some 30 ports. UK trade in 1977 by weight was 184 000 tons imports from China and 59 000 tons exports to China—not much more than the equivalent of one ship load per month in each direction.

One important exception should be noted in the liner business and that relates to Hongkong, whence South China exports are carried on through Bills of Lading from such ports as Canton, Shantou, and Xiamen. These cargoes are coasted to Hongkong and transhipped to regular liner services loading at Hongkong, though the ZHONGZU direct-China-base-port rates are used. These Hongkong services include fully cellular[1] services such as Trio and Scan/Dutch to Europe. So far these cargoes arrive in break bulk in Hongkong where they are packed into the liner operating companies' containers. This would clearly be one suitable area for extension of box facilities into China. However, the Chinese have not so far shown signs of great interest, particularly in feeding arrangements, though there have been improvements in the rail connections between Hongkong and Canton. To date the Chinese have not wished any imports from Europe to China to be transhipped in this manner.

Such then is the background to the current situation in the various freight sectors. It may be helpful to amplify it by reviewing the practical shipping requirements which will face importers and exporters in the China trade.

Dry bulk

Substantially, this is a matter of imports into China in the grain, ore, pig iron, and fertilizer markets, with shipment controlled by ZHONGZU on behalf of the importing corporation. Thus, f.o.b. sellers are required to present their cargoes 'free on board' at the port of loading in accordance

1. Operated by vessels with container-guide facilities in all cargo spaces.

with the custom of the port and trade. Currently, for example, in some grain trades to China such as US Gulf, this involves the f.o.b. exporter in some loading costs and, in certain ore trades, the exporter uses (and pays for) his own, or contracted, ore-handling installation for loading purposes.

The precise obligations involved in f.o.b. delivery must clearly be established in each case. Proper completion of f.o.b. delivery will enable the issue of Mates Receipts against which B/L's may be taken up, thus facilitating negotiation of payment for the goods. In the rare event of a c.i.f. sale, the exporter would be obliged to provide for sea carriage and unless regularly involved in 'Baltic' operations,[1] would be advised to make use of the services of a chartering broker.

Bulk exports from China, in this category, are mostly confined to government-to-government barter arrangements, such as rice to Sri Lanka against rubber from Sri Lanka. There is, however, still a significant movement of Chinese coal, mostly to Japan. Last, there could be business with an overlap to the tanker sector with barter deals which might trade Chinese oil against ore.

The ports in China principally used are:—

Qinhuangdao ⎫
Shanghai   ⎬ for grain
Dalian   ⎪
Xingang   ⎭

Shanghai   ⎫ for ores and pig iron.
Zhanjiang ⎭

Tankers

China is now a net exporter of oil (waxy crude): 1978 exports were 13 million tons of which 7 million tons went to Japan and 1.5 million to Hongkong. Trade to Japan is said to be due to increase to 9 million by 1981 and 15 million by 1982. Trade deals with US, Philippine, and Italian interests have also been reported.

Shipments (mostly from Dalian and Qinhuangdao) are in Chinese-owned or controlled tankers, but in view of the limitations of their tanker fleet this could involve arrangements with their trading partners such as the Japanese. However, the Chinese customarily like to retain control of the shipping, though they recognize cases where this is impossible in terms of lack of suitable ships. This has been the case, for example, with imports into China of refined products such as benzine, requiring specialized or part (product) tanker capability. A major inhibiting factor in the development of Chinese oil exports is the limitation of the size of the oil loading ports: these have at best capacity for 50 000 ton tankers and the generality of berths probably

---

1. Chartering operations as commonly traded on the Baltic Mercantile and Shipping Exchange.

much less. This falls very far short of the capacity needed for VLCCs (very large crude carriers) or ULCCs (ultra large crude carriers)—sizes much preferred by many oil buyers.

In the development field, a pilot project for LNG (liquified natural gas) has been planned in conjunction with the Japanese (Kawasaki and C. Itoh) for operation by 1984. LPG (liquified petroleum gas), as a refinery product, is probably a more distant prospect. However, logistically, LNG traffic with Japan has economic attractions. The shipping possibilities in this field are currently rather too remote for sensible comment. Nearer in time scale are the prospects for the offshore supply shipping sector.

It is appropriate in this context to include a reference to the important role played by classification societies, which provide internationally accepted standards and monitor them. They are active, not only in ship survey/ classification work, but also in industrial work in the field of inspection, standards control and the like, for projects particularly in the offshore oil business. Lloyds Register of Shipping has been particularly prominent in establishing reciprocal arrangements for marine work with its equivalent classification body in China and also in promoting its capacity in the industrial field, especially for harbour projects and oil rigs.

There remains the non-mineral oil sector, which may assume greater significance if China expands its exports of agricultural produce. Bigger exports of rape seed, cotton seed, wood and tung oils, for example, would exceed the capacity available in the deep tanks of liner-type vessels. This would then be of interest to specialized parcel tanker operators such as Panocean–Anco Ltd., who can provide such part-load facilities with tanks in the range of 250/2000 tons at regular frequency, with a capability per vessel of 10 000 tons or more. In the reverse direction, such parcel-tanker business is already operating into China, for example with tallow from the US and Australia. Thus, possibilities exist for parcel tankers which operate in a liner way with regard to frequency, by integrating China into their services on a global pattern.

Carriage conditions for liquids follow the pattern dictated by f.o.b. or c.i.f. sales. Normally, installations are responsible for pumping in and the ship for pumping out, but precision is needed in establishing relative obligations for the availability of ship and cargo, pumping, etc., case by case. Specialist shipping advice, available from lines or their agents or brokers should be sought where necessary. In the liner and parcel tanker field, carriage is customarily on a Bill of Lading basis, complementary to a Contract of Affreightment and/or Charter Party which spells out the obligations of the parties involved, relative to the particular commodity carried and the arrangements for payment of freight.

Reefer
Imports into China requiring controlled temperature carriage—such as medicines requiring 'chill' carriage at say 40°/45° F—are currently small.

Expansion of trade may increase the demand, but it seems likely to remain within the capacity of 'reefer' chambers in conventional liner vessels.

Exports are, however, much greater in volume, varying from bulk shipments of frozen fish, pork, and egg yolk in lots of several thousand tons to smaller liner-size parcels of these and other agricultural produce, such as rabbits, game, and whole egg.

Full loads are dealt with on a tramp basis as earlier described. Part loads may be carried on Bills of Lading or, for larger f.o.b. purchases, on Contracts of Affreightment linked to Bills of Lading. Broadly, the Bills of Lading cover the general conditions of carriage, whereas the Contract of Affreightment deals with the more specific requirements of carriage of the cargo in question, for example, in the case of frozen cargo, the maximum acceptable delivery temperatures and the range of the carrying temperature. It would also include the provisions for payment of freight.

Liners

This sector is likely to concern the greatest number of actual or potential traders with China and, on the assumptions described earlier, the pattern of events relating to shipping is likely to be as follows:

Exports to China

1. The f.o.b. sale contract will provide for a shipping period, with the seller usually required to apply to the ZHONGZU agent in the country of shipment (Lambert Bros Ship Agencies Ltd, in the UK) for shipping instructions, when the goods are ready for dispatch to the port of shipment.
2. Such instructions will be forthcoming from ZHONGZU on behalf of the importing corporation nominating the ship, date of loading, and port of loading, with provision for the exporter to give full cargo details to the local ZHONGZU agent in the country of shipment—the UK ZHONGZU agents operate a cargo consolidation centre at Ilford so that, in consultation with ZHONGZU Peking, they can organize vessel nominations.
3. This enables detailed calling forward instructions to be issued by ZHONGZU local port agents.
4. Upon shipment, shipped Bills of Lading should be issued by the loading port agent of the vessel—the ZHONGZU agent in the case of Chinese-controlled vessels.
5. If, as is often the case, payment for goods depends on production of Bills of Lading under the terms of the Letter of Credit, then payment will not be made until shipment has taken place and shipped Bills of Lading issued.
6. Delivery/forwarding arrangements up to f.o.b. will normally be the responsibility of the exporter who will need to instruct his supplier accordingly, if appropriate.

As explained earlier, delay may be encountered in a ship being nominated though many contracts allow for an automatic extension period in these circumstances. However, the pursuit of enquiry with the importing corporation, with perhaps the intermediary of the Chinese Commercial Attaché's Office (see Appendix II), may hasten shipment. Availability of a shipping opportunity may be speeded up by acceptance of another loading port where an earlier vessel may be available. This can be examined in consultation with ZHONGZU's and the vessel's agents in the country concerned. Of course, failure to meet the nomination can involve material further delay and possibly some liability for dead freight[1] or demurrage (ship costs for delay or vacancy due to non-arrival of cargo).

Against this background, it may be advisable to sell 'f.o.b. any UK port', rather than f.o.b. one specified port. The possible extra inland delivery costs to the port of loading may be more than offset by the time saved, particularly where payment for the goods depends on shipped Bills of Lading, and a request for alteration of a loading port named in the contract may involve considerable extra delay.

Imports from China

1. The buyer's c.i.f. contract should provide for the shipping period and ZHONGZU will route the cargo under advice to the overseas buyer.
2. The goods should be released to receivers at the port of discharge by the ship's agents, against surrender of the Bills of Lading. In the case of Chinese-controlled vessels, the agents will be ZHONGZU's agents in the country concerned.
3. C.i.f. delivery will be regarded as complete at ship's tackle, so receivers must allow for those receiving charges customary at the port of discharge, for example wharfage and handling charges from ship's tackle to road wagon.

Again, there may be delay in shipment which may be ameliorated by the pursuit of enquiries, as for exports. However, unlike exports, Chinese Bills of Lading for imports are claused 'direct or with transhipment': transhipment may add to the delivery time though transhipment expenses in these circumstances would be the responsibility of Chinese sellers.

These are the special features facing importers and exporters in the China trade and it is assumed that the normal export/import procedures are well known to such potential traders, including forwarding, customs requirements, and the like.

Last, there is the shipping service likely to be available in the China/Europe trade:

---

1. The freight that would have been paid had the cargo arrived in time.

1. The Chinese-owned or associated fleets comprise:

COSCO
COSCO Associates such as: China Merchants Steam Navigation Co. Ltd
Hongkong, Nan Yang Shipping Co. Macao
COSCO Joint Ventures: Chinese Tanzanian Joint Shipping Co., Chipolbrok (Joint Chinese Polish Shipping Co.)
2. Chinese chartered vessels operated by ZHONGZU.
3. Foreign flag liners: Rickmers, East Asiatic, Toho.

In the north-European trade, the frequency provided by these services
currently averages:

COSCO Associates and Joint Ventures ⎫ 3 sailings per
Chinese Charters   ⎭ month

Rickmers 1 sailing per month   ⎫
East Asiatic 1 sailing per month   ⎬   3 sailings per
Toho 1 sailing per month   ⎭   month

The average voyage time from last port China to first port Europe is 25
to 30 days and the Chinese ports used are normally: Shanghai,
Tianjin/Xingang, Qingdao, Huangpu, and the European ports: 1–2 per
month out of Antwerp/Hamburg, Immingham/Liverpool, UK, and an occasional Scandinavian port.

In this attempt to give some practical illustrations of the shipping requirements involved in the present China trade, I have not tried to cover the legal
or claims aspects. These are separate subjects and are touched upon in the
chapters on Chinese law and insurance.

There remains the question of the future. In the short term, as illustrated
earlier, expansion of China's trade, particularly into a more competitive
world environment, could necessitate improved liner services. Already,
some containerization development is discernible—to Japan, the USA and
Australia, dictated largely by customer requirements. Increasing dock labour
resistance, and hence higher costs in the USA and Australia, to handling
break-bulk cargoes is spreading elsewhere. More manufacturers and end-
users have adapted their goods-handling techniques to deal with containers,
and it is increasingly inconvenient and expensive to revert to the labour-
intensive methods of handling on a break-bulk basis. However, containerization cannot by any stretch of the imagination be considered a natural for
the Chinese in their present conditions, as the system requires a suitable
infrastructure if real value is to be achieved for the heavy investment
required. Road, rail, and inland waterway links to the ports are still far from
capable of container distribution and the Chinese are only now getting their
ports modernized to the conventional cargo handling level.

In addition, China has a very large workforce and so has no need to seek
capital intensive alternatives for existing labour-intensive activities. It has

also recently acquired a large fleet of vessels, primarily suited to break-bulk cargo operations. In any case, material items traded with China, such as ores, crude minerals, iron and steel, are not particularly suited to containerization.

The pace of development in shipping services, therefore, may depend upon how the Chinese wish to meet these competitive pressures for mechanized handling. They might either provide for them or discount their prices further to take account of inadequacies of delivery. This would seem to indicate a possible compromise solution: more use of foreign liners with part 'combi'[1] capacity for containers; greater use of existing container services from adjacent areas, e.g., Hongkong and Japan, and introduction of ro-ro (roll-on/roll-off) services with their own or chartered ro-ro vessels or those of foreign operators: it may in certain trades be possible to use such vessels for containers and 'wheeled'[2] operations, where landside facilities in China are still inadequate for lift-on/lift-off combi or fully cellular container vessels.

Further ahead, the pace seems likely to depend upon the progress of development of inland road and rail communications, the development of ports, and the willingness of the Chinese to enter into cooperative arrangements with other container operators to develop economic global network arrangements.

In view of China's avowed intention to lift its economy to the level of the most advanced of the industrialized nations, undoubtedly in the long term its transportation will reflect the most efficient modern transport technology adapted to its particular requirements.

1. i.e., with combined capacity for unitized, containerized, or break-bulk cargoes.
2. Cargo which can be moved on its own or temporarily provided wheels.

8. Insurance and China

A. LAGOPUS

Almost by definition, a communist country does not need insurance but of course the requirements of overseas trade dictate that there should be at least one insurance company which can provide the appropriate facilities.

Prior to 1 October 1949, there were several indigenous Chinese companies, such as the China Insurance Company and the Taiping Insurance Company, but after this date the People's Insurance Company of China (PICC) was formed and operates alongside the Bank of China under the wing of the Finance Ministry. The 'China', the 'Taiping' and a company called the Ming An Insurance Company now operate as subsidiaries/joint ventures in Hongkong. It is worthwhile noting that reference to an insurance company list will show that the 'China' and the 'Taiping' still operate in Taiwan, even apparently using the same telegraphic titles as the Hongkong-based companies, despite the obviously very different management.

The comparison of a communist state with insurance is a valid one since the definition of an insurance fund may be briefly 'a fund created by the premiums of the many out of which the claims of the few may be paid.' In a communist state such as China, therefore, the national exchequer becomes the insurance fund and as a result, China, as a general rule, does not feel it is necessary to insure any domestic assets, no matter how valuable they may be and despite the fact that they may have had to expend a great deal of valuable foreign currency to purchase them.

In addition, the Chinese have been known to insure certain buildings such as embassies and monuments to friendship between China and the country concerned, often known as friendship halls. Importantly it is believed that the PICC have recently begun to offer insurance coverage for certain construction projects where foreign countries are involved. Details of these insurances are known for the reason that the nature of the insurance cover

133

must inevitably vary from instance to instance and reflect the private circumstances of the organizations concerned. These insurances will depend on factors such as the nature of the project, the manner of financing, and the requirements of those providing the finance, as well as the area or areas from which material and equipment are obtained.

This change of heart regarding the insurance or erection risks has almost certainly been dictated by the switch, on the part of the Chinese, from a policy of buying out of capital and income to a policy, in many instances, of long-term financing in its various forms. In other words, an asset for which they have already paid would be regarded very differently, from an insurance point of view, from an asset which, if it suffered complete destruction, would have to be re-financed, whilst they continued to pay for an asset which no longer existed. Of course, a loss need not mean total loss of the asset itself. A casualty causing sufficient damage to preclude use of the asset for an appreciable length of time, need not of itself be severe but could cause loss of an item of equipment which might take months to replace. This alone from China's point of view deserves serious consideration.

The insurance of China's ships with the PICC is necessary because of the very considerable third-party liability which can arise out of the operation of a cargo ship, be it a dry cargo or a tanker. Even the responsibility for the removal of the wreck of a ship from a harbour or restricted waterway can create the need for a substantial premium fund and if this is to be set up, it should have the 'bread and butter' base of premium generated by the insurance of the ships' hulls.

The same principle applies to aircraft, of course, particularly on international routes where it is likely that from a liability point of view some very expensive passengers might be carried. It might be expected that, as the volume of visitors using China's domestic air services is already quite large and will surely increase, then their domestic aircraft and liabilities would also be insured, but at present this is not the case and only China's aircraft and associated liabilities which fly international routes are insured by the PICC. Those individuals or companies who might expect to obtain compensation arising out of the loss of a relative or an employee as a result of the crash of an aircraft flying a domestic route may well be able to recover from the airline but it would not be backed by a policy of liability insurance. In the circumstances, it is advisable to take out alternative insurance protection for an appropriate amount.

The insurance of cargo and transit risks is an essential part of international trade, bearing in mind the fact that payment for shipment of cargo is often not made until the arrival of the goods at their destination, or until the formal documents are in the hands of the bank financing the transaction. It is normal practice for any cargo to be insured and since the circumstances surrounding the insurance of every commodity or product are different to some extent, depending upon the voyage, the carrier, and the required breadth of insurance cover and other factors, it is obviously impractical within the scope of this chapter to go into detail which is best left to one's insurance broker or adviser to supply.

At one time, it was the practice of the Chinese trading corporations to buy on an f.o.b. basis and sell on a c.i.f. basis, but this has now been relaxed and in certain instances it is possible to arrange one's own cargo insurances, whether buying from or selling to China. The reasons for this are mainly due to difficulties experienced by the shippers, traders, and manufacturers. One of the difficulties arose out of the fact that, in the event of dispute over a claim or other matter, arbitration and any other legal process had to take place in China. Another was that goods reported as damaged after arrival in China had to be surveyed by Chinese surveyors. Not that there is anything wrong with Chinese surveyors or their methods, it is just that often it is expedient and helpful to be able to appoint independent outside surveyors and this was not practical so far as the Chinese were concerned. Perhaps the strongest reason was that banks or other financial institutions are notoriously careful when it comes to the wording of a shipper's policy or insurance certificate, and due to the unfamiliar wording of the Chinese clauses they were frequently reluctant to accept the Chinese insurance. Inevitably, the Chinese corporations found that it was easier to let the shippers and others arrange their own insurances, which, although it did not solve the problem of damage surveys, meant that disputes over claims could be conducted on home ground and moreover the banks were happy.

Since April 1972, the PICC has used its own clauses both for the insurance of ships' hulls as well as cargo against marine and war risks. Copies of these clauses are appended and insurance technicians will see the differences between the PICC clauses and those clauses which are in general use throughout the rest of the world. The interpretation of the PICC clauses and determination of any likely practical differences is a matter which, in the ultimate, would be determined by a court of law and obviously this is a step which most parties to a transaction try very hard to avoid. However, as each shipper's requirements for insurance vary, his insurance broker should be in a position to give an informed opinion based upon his knowledge of those requirements.

Clauses which have been in general use for very many years in the UK and in the West generally have had their construction tested and interpreted constantly and as a result, when a claim occurs, an adjuster is normally able to state firmly what has or has not been covered. The Chinese clauses, having been in existence only since April 1972, have not been so exhaustively tested although the officials of the PICC say that in practical effect there is no difference between their clauses and those in general use elsewhere. Western insurance technicians would disagree and would point to the fact that a Chinese ship would continue to be fully insured against war risks in time of war involving China and another of the so-called great powers, at a peacetime rate of premium, while the ship of any other country under similar circumstances would have had the war element of the coverage cancelled and reinstated at a premium which properly reflected the circumstances. This of course is a matter which would only affect the insurance company (or their reinsurers). The shipowners, in this instance the Chinese, would be quite pleased with the situation. So far as the cargo clauses are concerned, it will be seen that the PICC uses only one set of clauses for all and any type of cargo, whereas elsewhere highly specialized clauses have been drafted to specific major commodities such as bulk oil, frozen meat, and so on.

It can be said, however, and despite the PICC's statement that its clauses offer the same protection as others, where goods have been insured by PICC by policy, subject to their own clauses, shippers have sometimes elected to take out an insurance policy in their own country on a 'difference in conditions' basis. This policy would pay in the event that a claim was not paid under the PICC policy but which would have been paid under a policy issued by an insurance company in the shipper's own country, on the usual clauses. This is not to say that there is any question of the PICC seeking to evade a valid claim under its own policy, but simply that a claims adjuster may interpret the clauses on a certain basis and without a court judgement, and his opinion would be generally accepted as a matter of course by the parties concerned. Naturally, his opinion could be in favour of the shippers as easily as it could be in favour of the PICC, depending on the circumstances.

Fortunately, there are signs that the general relaxation of the political attitudes of the People's Republic of China will extend to normal commercial and financial transactions, including insurance, and problems such as those mentioned above, which many shippers and traders felt that they had had in the course of doing business with China, may be amended if not eliminated.

Over the last two years, particularly, the scope of the PICC's activities has grown. It has set up claims payment agencies and policy service agencies in many countries, and shippers and traders in the United States and Japan, as well as the United Kingdom and Europe, should find that they have no difficulty in the translation and handling of insurance arranged with the PICC. Although at this stage it is too early to say, it is possible that the clauses and policy wordings used for insurances which they underwrite could be brought into line with those used internationally. So far as the Chinese are concerned, of course, this would represent a considerable change and it is impossible to say when any such change might take place. It is also possible that legal difficulties which have existed in the past, arising from the general requirement for arbitration and the settlement of disputes to take place in China, could be relaxed. Again, this is not something which can be forecast with any accuracy.

In line with this general relaxation, by the spring 1979, it seems likely that the PICC will have to discuss with the various Chinese trading and operating corporations the nature of an insurance programme or programmes which would meet the needs of the corporations, or their contractors or partners in any particular project, bearing in mind the increasing number of projects subject to long-term credit and finance.

In addition to these domestically generated overseas trade insurances, the PICC are writing an increasingly wide portfolio of international reinsurance business of all classes, both from their own many direct insurance company contracts, as well as from international insurance brokers. They are particularly interested in accepting business relating to erection and contractors' projects overseas, aviation and marine business of all kinds, and by these means and by the exchange of reinsurance business, they are consolidating their position as an important member of the world insurance market.

It should be mentioned that like every other insurance company the PICC reinsures a proportion of its incoming portfolio of business. Although it is capable of absorbing a very great deal of the business it accepts, it is nonetheless sensible of the PICC to cede a proportion of the business it accepts, in order to reduce and spread the load of possible liability and in order to encourage a volume of reinsurance business in exchange. By this means they are widening the geographical base of premium upon which the company operates. Naturally, the classes of reinsurances are restricted to those accepted by the PICC—marine hull and cargo, and international aviation hull and liabilities.

It will be appreciated that political events in China over the last 18 months have created a climate in which China's economy and the need to modernize have accelerated at a rate hardly thought possible just two or three years ago, and there seems no doubt that insurance, along with other related activities, will be brought much more into line with international practices. By this is meant that the Chinese consumer, corporate rather than private, will be likely to purchase insurance, thus providing the PICC with a much wider base of business from which to operate. This factor, if combined with a change by the PICC to the use of those policy wordings and clauses which are in general use internationally, will create a much wider acceptance of their position as the only insurers of the business of one third of the world's population.

Those expecting or hoping to have business dealings with the trading or operation corporations of the People's Republic of China, or wishing to do business with The People's Insurance Company of China, may contact the company direct at:

22, Fan Di Xi Lu,
Peking,
The People's Republic of China.

Telex: 22102 PICC CN
Cables: 42001

or through their own insurance broker or adviser. It may also be helpful to know that the PICC has several representatives operating within the Insurance Division of the Bank of China, in London. The address is:

The Bank of China,
Insurance Division,
8–10 Mansion House Place,
London EC4.
Telephone: 01-626 8301

THE PEOPLE'S INSURANCE COMPANY OF CHINA

HULL CLAUSES

With a view to meeting the requirements for the development of the shipping enterprise and according to the principle of equality and mutual benefit, this Company writes Hull Insurance, the Clauses being as follows:

1. Scope of Cover

This insurance is classified into Total Loss Cover (Time and Voyage) and Comprehensive Cover (Time and Voyage). This Company shall undertake to indemnify the Insured for loss of or damage to the ship insured according to the risks insured and the provisions of these Clauses.
  (1) Total Loss Cover
    This Company shall be liable for total loss of the insured ship caused by:
    (a) Natural calamities and/or accidents;
    (b) Latent defects in Hull and Machinery;
    (c) Negligence of the Master, Crew, Pilots or ship repairers.
  (2) Comprehensive Cover
    This Company shall be liable for total or partial loss of the insured ship caused by:
    (a) Natural calamities and/or accidents;
    (b) Latent defects in Hull and Machinery;
    (c) Negligence of the Master, Crew, Pilots or ship repairers.
  This company shall further be liable for the following liabilities and expenses arising from the foregoing events:
    (i)   Contribution to General Average;
    (ii) In case of collision, the indemnity assumed by the insured ship towards the loss to the other ship in collision and the goods aboard such other ship, dock, wharf or other fixed structures, and delay to or loss of use of such other ship or fixed structures and salvage expenses incurred in connection therewith, but in no case shall the amount so indemnified exceed the insured amount of the insured ship;
    (iii) Salvage expenses;
    (iv) Expenses for pursuing recovery from third parties, reasonable expenses for ascertaining the loss or damage within the scope of Cover and the expenses for examining the ship's bottom after grounding.
  Partial losses caused by the events in sub-sections (a) to (c) under section (2) hereinabove shall be subject to the deductible franchise stipulated in the Policy for each and every voyage (a voyage is meant a sailing from port of sailing to port of destination).
  Ships may be insured for Total Loss Cover or Comprehensive Cover on application and may also be insured against additional risks upon consultation.

2. Exclusions

This company shall not be liable for
  (1) Loss or damage caused by unseaworthiness of the insured ship;

(2) Loss or damage caused by the negligence of the Shipowner and his representative and by the intentional act of the Shipowner and his representative and Master;

(3) Maintenance repairs to the hull and machinery of the insured ship, expenses for painting, wear and tear and corrosion;

(4) Risks covered and excluded in the Hull War Risk Clauses of this Company;

(5) Demurrage of the insured ship and other indirect expenses;

(6) Expenses for removal or disposal of obstructions.

3. Trading Limit

The prior agreement of this Company shall be obtained in case the insured ship sails out of the trading limit stipulated in the Policy, and an additional premium may be charged by this Company when so required.

4. Period of Insurance

(1) Time Insurance

Longest duration one year, the time of commencement and termination being subject to the stipulation in the Policy.

In the event that the insured ship is sold or transferred during the currency of insurance, the insurance shall become terminated forthwith unless such sale or transfer is agreed to by this Company in writing. Where the insured ship is sold or transferred in the course of a voyage, the insurance may be extended until the completion of such voyage.

(2) Voyage Insurance

To be subject to the voyages stipulated in the Policy. The time of commencement and termination to be dealt with according to the following provisions:

(a) With no cargo on board: To commence from the time of unmooring or weighing anchor at the port of sailing until the completion of casting anchor or mooring at the port of destination.

(b) With cargo on board: To commence from the time of loading at the port of sailing until the completion of discharge at the port of destination, but in no case shall a period of thirty days be exceeded, counting from midnight of the day of arrival of the ship at the port of destination.

5. Cancellation of Insurance and Return of Premium

(1) Time Insurance

(a) Where the insured ship is sold or transferred or the insurance thereon is cancelled during the currency of insurance, a premium to be calculated pro rata daily shall be returned to the Insured.

(b) Where the insured ship undergoes repairs in dock or shipyard or is laid up in port for a period exceeding thirty consecutive days, 50% (fifty percent) of the premium, to be calculated pro rata daily, for the period during which the insured ship is under repairs or laid up shall be returned to the Insured.

(2) Voyage Insurance

In no case shall the insurance be cancellable once it commences.

6. Treatment of Loss

(1) In the event of accidents to the insured ship which fall under the scope of Cover, the Insured shall notify this Company immediately and take all possible measures to minimise the loss to the insured ship. The prior consent of this Company shall be obtained before repairs are carried out. This Company shall be entitled to make deductions of unreasonable repairing costs and other expenses.

The Insured shall cause the insured ship to undergo periodic overhaul and repairs and be well kept, so as to make her in good technical condition.

(2) Where the insured ship is in collision with other ships, the Insured shall obtain the prior agreement of this Company on the liability resting with both parties and the amount of recovery which he ascertains with the party concerned.

7. Claim and Subrogation of Rights

(1) In the case of a total loss of the insured ship, the full insured amount of the insured ship shall be indemnified.

(2) Where no news is received of the whereabouts of the insured ship over a period of six months after the date on which she is expected to arrive at the port of destination, it shall constitute an event of missing of ship.

Where the insured ship is missing or it is estimated that the aggregate of the amount of loss to the ship, salvage expenses, cost of repairs and other necessary disbursements will exceed the insured value of the insured ship, it may be deemed a total loss, and the full insured amount of the insured ship shall be indemnified.

(3) In the case of a partial loss to the ship, this Company shall be liable for the reasonable costs of replacement and repairs.

(4) In the case of loss of or damage to the insured ship, should the insured amount be lower than the sound value of the ship, the contributions to the general average and the salvage expenses to be paid by this Company shall be calculated in the proportion that the insured amount bears to the sound value.

(5) In submitting his claims for loss, the Insured shall, in case third party liability is involved, subrogate the right of recovery from the third party and transfer the necessary documents to this Company.

8. Treatment of Disputes

All disputes arising between the Insured and this Company shall be settled by friendly negotiations on the principle of seeking truth from facts and of fairness and reasonableness. Where a settlement fails after negotiation and it is necessary to submit to arbitration or take legal actions, such arbitration or legal actions shall be carried out at the place where the defendant is domiciled.

HULL WAR RISK CLAUSES

1. Scope of Cover

This Company shall be liable for loss of or damage to the insured ship, expenses and liabilities caused by:

(1) War, hostile acts or armed conflicts;

(2) Seizure, detainment, confiscation or blockade arising from the events in (1) hereinabove, but such claim shall be dealt with only on expiry of six months from the day when such events arise;

(3) Conventional weapons of war, including mines, torpedoes or bombs.

2. Exclusions

This Company shall not be liable for loss of or damage to the insured ship caused by:

(1) Requisition, pre-emption, detainment or confiscation by the government of the country of which the Insured is a national;

(2) Atomic or hydrogen bombs or nuclear weapons of war.

3. Termination of Cover

(1) Should the insured ship be used for serving a war of aggression launched by imperialism, this insurance shall terminate automatically from the time of the outbreak of such war.

(2) In respect of time insurance this Company shall be entitled to issue to the Insured, at any time. notice of cancellation to terminate such war risk insurance upon expiry of fourteen days from the day on which such notice is issued.

Note: These Clauses are the additional clauses to the Hull Clauses of this Company. In case of conflict between any clauses in these Clauses and the Hull Clauses, these Clauses shall prevail.

THE PEOPLE'S INSURANCE COMPANY OF CHINA
OCEAN MARINE CARGO CLAUSES

With a view to developing friendly trade dealings between China and the peoples of various countries in the world and according to the principle of equality and mutual benefit, this Company writes Ocean Marine Cargo Insurance, the clauses being as follows:

1. Scope of Cover

This insurance is classified into three forms—Total Loss Only (T.L.O.), With Average (W.A.) and All Risks. Where the insured goods sustain loss or damage, this Company shall undertake to indemnify therefore according to the risks insured and the Provisions of these Clauses.

(1) Total Loss Only (T.L.O.)

This Company shall be liable for

(a) total loss of the insured goods caused in the course of transit by natural calamities—heavy weather, lightning, floating ice, seaquake, earthquake, flood, etc. or by accidents—grounding, stranding, sinking, collision or derailment of the carrying conveyance, fire, explosion and falling of entire package or packages of the insured goods into sea during loading or discharge, etc.;

(b) Sacrifice in and contribution to General Average and Salvage Expenses arising from the foregoing events.

(2) With Average (W.A.)

This Company shall be liable for

(a) total or partial loss of the insured goods caused in the course of transit by natural calamities—heavy weather, lightning, floating ice, seaquake, earthquake, flood, etc. or by accidents—grounding, stranding, sinking, collision or derailment of the carrying conveyance, fire, explosion and falling of entire package or packages of the insured goods into sea during loading or discharge, etc.;

(b) Sacrifice in and contribution to General Average and Salvage Expenses arising from the foregoing events.

(3) All Risks

In addition to the liability covered under the aforesaid Total Loss Only and With Average Insurance, this Company shall also be liable for total or partial loss of the insured goods caused by shortage, shortage in weight, leakage, contact with other substance, breakage, hook, rainwater, rust, wetting, heating, mould, tainting by odour, contamination, etc. arising from external causes in the course of transit.

Goods may be insured on Total Loss Only or With Average or All Risks conditions and may also be insured against additional risks upon consultation.

2. Exclusions

This Company shall not be liable for

(1) Loss or damage caused by the intentional act or fault of the Insured;

(2) Loss or damage falling under the liability of the Consignor or arising from normal losses of the insured goods;

(3) Loss or damage caused by strikes of workers or delay in transit;

(4) Risks covered and excluded in the Ocean Marine Cargo War Risk Clauses of this Company.

3. Commencement and Termination of Cover

This insurance shall take effect from the time the insured goods leave the Consignor's warehouse at the place of shipment named in the Policy and shall continue in force in the ordinary course of transit including sea and land transit until the insured goods are delivered to the Consignee's warehouse at the destination named in the Policy. The Cover shall, however, be limited to sixty days upon discharge of the insured goods from the sea-going vessel at the final port of discharge.

4. Survey of Damage to Goods and Presentation of Claim

(1) The Insured shall take delivery of the insured goods in good time upon arrival thereof at the destination or port of destination named in the Policy and shall undertake to:

apply immediately for survey to the surveying agent of the claims settling agent stipulated in the Policy should the insured goods be found to have sustained loss or damage. In case this Company has no surveying agent or claims settling agent locally, a local competent surveyer may be applied to for survey;

obtain forthwith from the Carrier or relevant Authorities (Customs and Port Authorities, etc.) Certificate of Loss or Damage and/or Short-landed Memo and lodge a claim with the Carrier or the party concerned in writing should the insured goods be found short in entire package or packages or to show apparent traces of damage.

(2) The Insured shall submit the following documents when presenting a claim to this Company:

Original Policy or Certificate of Insurance, original or copy of Bill of Lading, Invoice, Packing List and Tally Sheet;

Certificate of Loss or Damage and/or Short-landed Memo, Survey Report and Statement of Claims.

When third party liability is involved, the letters and cables relative to pursuing of recovery to and from the third party and the other essential certificates or documents shall be submitted in addition.

(3) The time of validity of a claim under this insurance shall not exceed a period of nine months counting from the time of completion of discharge of the insured goods from the seagoing vessel at the final port of discharge.

This Company shall undertake to indemnify the Insured for the reasonable expenses incurred by him for having immediately taken effective measures in salving and preventing further loss of the insured goods after damage was sustained but the amount of such indemnity together with the amount of the claim shall not exceed the insured amount of the damaged goods.

5. Treatment of Disputes

All disputes arising between the Insured and this Company shall be settled by friendly negotiation on the principles of seeking truth from facts and of fairness and reasonableness. Where a settlement fails after negotiation and it is necessary to submit to arbitration or take legal actions, such arbitration or legal actions shall be carried out at the place where the defendant is domiciled.

THE PEOPLE'S INSURANCE COMPANY OF CHINA
OCEAN MARINE CARGO WAR RISK CLAUSES

1. Scope of Cover

This Company shall undertake to indemnify for the loss of or damage to the insured goods consequent upon the undermentioned causes:

(1) Loss or damage caused by war, hostile acts or armed conflicts;

(2) Loss or damage caused by seizure, detainment, confiscation or blockade arising from the events in (1) hereinabove, but such loss or damage shall be dealt with only on expiry of six months from the day when the loss or damage arises;

(3) Loss or damage caused by conventional weapons of war, including mines, torpedoes and bombs.

This Company shall further be liable for

Sacrifice in and contribution to General Average and Salvage Expenses arising from the events enumerated in (1) and (3) hereinabove.

2. Exclusion

This Company shall not be liable for loss or damage caused by atomic or hydrogen bombs or nuclear weapons of war.

3. Commencement and Termination of Cover

This insurance shall attach from the time the insured goods are loaded on the sea-going vessel or lighter at the port of shipment named in the Policy until the insured goods are discharged from the sea-going vessel or lighter at the port of destination named in the Policy, but in case the insured goods are not discharged from the sea-going vessel or lighter the longest duration of this insurance allowable on the insured goods upon arrival at the port of destination shall be limited to 15 days counting from midnight of the day of their arrival at such port.

This insurance shall cease to attach when the insured goods are discharged from the sea-going vessel or lighter at the port of transhipment, but in case the insured goods are not discharged from the sea-going vessel, the longest duration of the insurance allowable on the insured goods upon arrival at such port shall be limited to 15 days counting from midnight of the day of their arrival at such port. The insurance shall reattach when the insured goods are loaded on the on-carrying sea-vessel at the port of transhipment.

4. Automatic Termination of Cover

Should the insured goods be used for serving a war of aggression launched by imperialism, this insurance shall terminate automatically from the time of the outbreak of such war.

Note: These Clauses are the clauses of an additional insurance to the Ocean Marine Cargo Insurance. In case of conflict between any clauses of these Clauses and the Ocean Marine Cargo Clauses, these Clauses shall prevail.

9. Importing from China

A. H. CAVE, MBE

Since Western traders made the first tentative approaches in the early fifties to resuming imports into the West from China, there has been a steady increase in the volume of trade which in recent years has reached significant figures. The year 1978 will long be remembered both by importers and exporters as the year in which China announced dramatic changes in its foreign trade programme. These changes are likely to affect significantly the level of trade between China and the West for the next decade.

In 1978, Chinese exports totalled $10.6 billion, $1.7 billion up on the 1977 figure of $7.9 billion. Apart from Hongkong, which at about $2.2 billion was the biggest importer, the leaders were Japan, West Germany, the USA, France and the UK. Hongkong's Chinese population and dependence on its natural hinterland in the Chinese province of Guangdong make it an enormous market for foodstuffs and simple consumer goods, while Japan benefits from its proximity to China and the complementarity of the two economies.

Even after 'readjustment' to the economy announced by Chinese leaders in the spring of 1979, China's economic plan still provided for the development of agriculture and industry at a fast rate. This involved imports by China from Japan and the West on an unprecedented scale. To give some idea of the expected demand, arrangements have been made between the Bank of China and a British consortium of banks whereby amounts up to a total of $1.2 billion will be deposited with the Bank of China for repayment over five years, at an annual interest rate of $7\frac{1}{4}$ per cent. The deposits will be guaranteed by the Export Credit Guarantee Department of the Department of Trade and will be used by the Bank of China to pay cash to UK exporters. In addition, by April 1979 China had borrowed a total of over $500 million from Western banks in non-project-related finance, and the British, French, and Italian governments had guaranteed substantial credits required (see Chapter 6).

Until 1978 China imported capital goods and materials from the West only against cash payment or medium-term suppliers' credit (see Chapter 6) which it did not regard as borrowing, calling it simply 'deferred payments' to accord with its policy of self-reliance. The importance of this change of policy to importers from Europe and the USA is that, in the long term, China will have to step up its exports substantially over a much wider range of natural and manufactured products. There are new opportunities both for the experienced trader and for the newcomer. In 1978, China ran a deficit of $400 million on its visible trade which will increase pressures to sell more goods abroad. It is only by a further increase in exports that China can support the massive development of its imports which is envisaged in the coming years.

In a major speech during 1978, Li Qiang, Chinese Minister for Foreign Trade, outlined the new economic plan and stated: 'Our imports should be based on our ability to pay. Only if we have the ability to pay can we increase our imports. That is to say, only if we increase our exports simultaneously can we import more goods.'

Thus, although making provision for financial medium-term facilities to increase imports, China recognized that a substantial improvement in exports over the next few years will be necessary to meet repayment arrangements.

The future expansion of trade
The development of exports from China was seriously curtailed in recent years when the economy suffered badly from political intervention by the so called 'Gang of Four', Chairman Mao Zedong's wife and her three Shanghai colleagues. Development of trade was further disrupted by the earthquake in 1976 at Tangshan in north China. It was not until August 1977 at the Eleventh Congress of the Communist Party of China that trade was given a new emphasis. The more liberal and outward-looking attitude to the growth of Chinese industry, and the expansion of foreign trade which followed, stemmed largely from the appointment of Deng Xiaoping as Vice-Chairman of the Party. It was at this stage that the economic modernization programme began to have an important effect on trading policy.

Broadly speaking, China's exports consist of textile items, food, other light industry products, crude oil, chemicals, metals, and minerals. In 1977, the latest year for which a breakdown is available, nearly a quarter of China's exports were yarn, fabric, clothing, and footwear (important items in trade with Europe and the USA), and another 12 per cent was taken up by light manufactures. This category covers consumer goods like the extremely popular handicraft and art goods, as well as sports goods, musical instruments and similar.

A further 20 per cent of exports was composed of meat, fruit, vegetables, and rice, and while much of this went to Hongkong and South-east Asia, in general it forms an important element in trade with Europe and, increasingly, the USA.

With the growth of China's oil industry, crude oil has come to play a growing part in the export trade. In 1977 it took up 10 per cent of the total, and petroleum products another 3 per cent. However, none of this has been sold to Europe and only a small quantity to the USA. The main market for crude is Japan and, for petroleum products, Hongkong.

A high proportion of goods offered by the Chinese in the past has been of an acceptable standard to buyers in the West, and in some cases the quality of the products offered has far surpassed that of imports of similar materials from other countries. This applies particularly to items such as certain foodstuffs—frozen prawns and (specially bred) white rabbit meat are examples of impeccable quality. Other items such as silks, carpets, and certain perfumery oils cannot be matched from any other source of supply.

The range of edible oils and oilseeds offered for export varies each year according to seasonal situations and is also determined to some extent by home requirements. Qualities are well known internationally and Chinese exports are normally made through established merchant houses specializing in this market.

Among foodstuffs, besides the more usual mandarin orange segments and pineapple, there is an interesting range of other fruits largely obtainable only from China such as lychees, loquats, and longans which have rare and exotic flavours.

Recently, China has started to export wine to Western countries. The range of white wines produced in the Peking area is quite good, but other regions also produce some very drinkable whites and reds. The latter, however, need to be carefully selected for Western markets as they differ widely in flavour and strength.

China exports teas world wide, from the strong black tarry flavoured large-leaf teas such as Lapsang Souchong to the delicately scented green teas such as jasmine tea.

China also sells culinary spices which are used extensively in Chinese cooking, and the essential and aromatic oils used by most of the world's leading perfumery houses, such as cedarwood, geranium, and vetivert.

Animal by-products include bristles, casings, hides, leather, furs, lambswool, camelhair, cashmere, a wide range of feathers, and the famous Tianjian and Peking carpets.

China exports a wide range of textile fibres, both natural and synthetic—Chinese silk yarn and fabrics are famous. There is a wide range from which to choose. In the field of cotton piece goods, the demand in Europe is only limited by quota restrictions. Linen from Irish mills is exported to China for the making up and re-export of embroidered table sets.

A wide range of art goods including ivory, jade, and wood carvings, jewellery, paintings, porcelain, and lacquerware is also on offer.

Household goods made from bamboo, rattan, wicker, and straw are another feature.

Chemicals available range from industrial and agricultural chemicals to pharmaceutical products, colour pigments, paints, and printing inks.

China has tremendous resources in metal ores and minerals. Products offered for export, apart from basic metals such as antimony, zinc, tin, and mercury, include many semi-manufactured articles made from steel and non-ferrous metals.

A wide range of building materials such as terrazzo tiles, marble slabs, and mineral colours are included in the range.

The light industry of China is constantly increasing the range of manufactured articles offered for export. It includes a variety of musical instruments, sports goods, toys, and leather goods. China also exports paper, paperboard, and stationery. Some very good cameras are made in China, together with a full range of photographic equipment.

However, increasing requirements for home consumption have often led to shortages of products for export, even in some cases where continuity of supply was essential for the establishment of regular trade.

Packing has often been a problem and in some cases has involved re-packing in the buying country to buyers' requirements. Chinese export packing is generally robust and adequate for sea transport but, particularly in consumer goods, lacks the sophistication and appearance that Western buyers require.

Most goods developed for export from China, particularly manufactured and consumer goods, are shipped in the packing normally provided for internal distribution and, while the strength of the packing (usually wooden cases) has been adequate, the cost of heavy packing for movement of goods internally has been high and presentation does not match the imports of similar items from other countries. In the middle seventies, experienced importers made clear their needs to Chinese Export Corporations, feeling at times that their proposals for the improvement of quality packing and presentation of export products fell on deaf ears.

The Chinese Export Corporations have long been aware of this limitation and, under the new and more flexible policy, they are now prepared to pack regular lines in accordance with buyers' requirements and to use labels bearing the buyers' trademark. This is a big advance but will take time to bring into effect. A special foreign trade corporation—the China National Export Commodities Packaging Corporation—has been established to carry out research for the development of quality packing for export commodities, to meet international market requirements. It is therefore the responsibility of the importer to specify his packing requirements and to send samples of packing materials to China, where necessary by arrangement with the exporting corporation.

When, in early 1978, the Chinese adopted detailed plans for the expansion of exports, Western traders found to their astonishment that the new proposals took into account all past grievances. Furthermore, the Chinese appeared alive to the need to establish new export lines and were seriously considering joint ventures and buyback arrangements. In short, the new plan envisaged, besides a willingness to discuss and conform to the buyer's requirements:

1. The setting up of production specifically for export of certain lines including, where necessary, the import by China of some of the components or ingredients not readily available from home resources. Thus, an importer interested, say, in the import of footwear could supply machinery, lasts, designs, and samples to China, together with detailed technical specifications and, in return, could secure regular footwear manufactured with Chinese raw materials.

   It is important in setting up an operation of this nature that the terms are very clearly set out and it would be difficult to do this without a visit to China and detailed technical discussions with suppliers (see Chapter 10).

2. Improved quality control, delivery, and packaging.

3. Counter-purchase contracts with Western manufacturing and trading companies who were prepared to supply plant, equipment, and technology on a medium-term financial arrangement to be covered by a counter-purchase of the agreed products. This is a similar operation to that mentioned under 1. but intended to cover a bigger type of operation in which all or part of the raw materials can be exported to China.

Thus, the door is open for the future expansion of trade.

A general approach to importing from China

It is important for the newcomer to appreciate that when it comes to trade there is a fundamental difference between China and most other countries. If he is to be successful, he must take the time necessary to understand the organization and the trading methods appropriate to the development of good relationships and understanding.

The Chinese officials with whom Western importers will negotiate are mostly experienced international traders. They are well-balanced individuals with a good sense of humour, though they dislike facetious remarks which are not always well interpreted and can therefore be misunderstood. They dislike the verbose negotiator who tries to tell all his story in the first five minutes (often forgetting to pause for translation). If you negotiate calmly and courteously, you will be met by equal courtesy from the other side.

The Chinese export trading organizations

The Ministry of Foreign Trade in Peking is the arm of the government concerned with major policy decisions and the overall administration of the various trading corporations.

The China Council for the Promotion of International Trade (CCPIT) has its head office in Peking and sub-councils in all principal cities of China. The main objectives of the CCPIT are to undertake activities for the promotion of good economic and trade relations between China and other countries, as well as increasing understanding and friendship.

To implement these objectives, the Council arranges visits abroad of Chinese officials concerned with the import and export trade. It also receives officials and delegations from foreign economic and trading circles. Other activities include attendance at international conferences on trade and economics, arranging of exhibitions of Chinese goods abroad and exhibitions of foreign goods in China. There are some other important sections of the Council such as those concerned with transport (including sea transport) and trademark registration. It also incorporates a foreign arbitration commission and maritime arbitration commission (see Chapter 3).

Chinese trading corporations (see Appendix III) are organized on a commodity or product-group basis and each corporation is responsible both for the export and import of the range of goods handled. The head office of each corporation is situated in Peking and has branches in all main cities of China. Unlike trading organizations in other planned-economy countries who have centralized their trading organizations within their capital, the branches of the Chinese trading corporations are free to negotiate and conclude contracts directly with buyers and suppliers overseas. In Peking, apart from the head offices, there are some branches handling local products for export. This arrangement has very distinct advantages for the trader, since the negotiators in each branch have specialized knowledge of the product of their own region and must also have close contacts with the production and supply organizations.

There are other corporations within the Ministry of Foreign Trade Structure providing services to export and import, such as the China Ocean Shipping Corporation and the China Ocean Shipping Agency which deal with cargo and passenger services, chartering, booking of cargoes, and shipment, and act as agents for ocean-going vessels calling at Chinese ports. Since, however, the Chinese trading corporations now normally offer goods for export on c.i.f. and c. & f. terms, it is unlikely that many importers will be involved with these corporations.

Marine insurance on goods exported from China is normally handled by the People's Insurance Company of China (PICC) (see Chapter 8).

The Chinese export organizations and commodities handled

The organizations for handling exports from China consist of a number of national export/import corporations, which act as negotiators and intermediaries between the supplying corporations and buyers overseas. Each corporation has a list of the commodities offered for export. The list varies from branch to branch, since each deals with the products grown or produced in the region in which its particular branch is situated. The main branches concerned with foreign trade on a substantial basis are situated in the following cities:

Peking
Dalian
Tianjin
Hangzhou
Shanghai
Qingdao
Canton
Nanning

In the early fifties, one corporation known as the China National Import and Export Corporation was formed to handle foreign trade, but this soon became a series of specialist corporations covering particular ranges of import and export products.

Methods of establishing import business

The importer who wishes to buy goods from China on a regular basis has a choice of several methods by which he can secure offers and negotiate business. The one he chooses will depend to some extent on the volume and frequency of his requirements, and the need to make funds available to finance purchases throughout the two/three-month sea journey from China.

Companies new to China trade should:

1. Study the list of items which China can offer for export and identify the corporation handling the goods in which they are interested.
2. Make an application to the appropriate office of the Chinese Commercial Counsellor for an invitation to visit the Chinese Export Commodity Fair which is held twice annually in Canton (entry via Hongkong) as follows:

Spring Fair—15 April to 15 May
Autumn Fair—15 October to 15 November.

   Letters of application should give full particulars of the company's trade interest and should specify the commodities in which it has an interest. Once an invitation has been received, application may be made to the Consular Office of the Chinese Embassy for a visa. On arrival in Hongkong, the invitation card should be presented to the China Travel Service (Hongkong) Limited who will make the necessary arrangements for the journey into China. It is advisable, however, on receipt of the invitation, to cable the Travel Service advising them of the date of arrival in Hongkong, the date on which the importer wishes to enter China, and the approximate duration of his stay.
3. A visit to the Chinese Export Commodity Fair will enable importers to contact the branches of the corporation handling the goods they wish to import, to see samples and, one hopes, sign their first purchase contract.

About 25 000 buyers from over 100 different countries visit the Fair on each occasion. It provides a unique opportunity to assess the type, availability, and price of various Chinese products.

4. Join one or more of the trading organizations which arrange regular visits for parties of importers to China, and apply for a place. Advice on this subject may be obtained from the Sino-British Trade Council in the UK or Chambers of Commerce and similar organizations in other countries.

Another method by which a newcomer may purchase goods from China is by arrangement with one or more of the merchant houses specializing in the import and distribution of commodities from China. Such companies have had many years of experience in importing from China and their trading staff visit China frequently. Some of these houses specialize in a particular range of commodities. A list of the merchant houses involved may be obtained from government agencies and chambers of commerce in most Western countries. In 1978, the British Importers' Confederation arranged a visit to China for a 16-strong group, mostly representing companies new to trade with China, with highly successful results.

Most of the merchant houses involved in trade with China work closely together on matters of common interest and will invariably advise a new buyer of the name of another merchant house, if they do not handle the commodity in which he is interested. Some established firms specializing in particular commodities are often able to offer goods of Chinese origin from stocks afloat or held in the importing country.

Banking, shipping, and insurance

The Bank of China, with its head office in Peking, is the only bank authorized to execute banking business with foreign banks and companies. It has branches throughout the main cities of China and in Hongkong, London, and Singapore. An office in Luxembourg was opened during 1979.

Companies which place orders with China normally make payment by opening a documentary irrevocable Letter of Credit in favour of the supplying corporation, either through their bankers or directly with the Bank of China, by arrangement. Newcomers are recommended to discuss procedure with their bankers or with the Bank of China.

Normal contract terms provide for payment to be made under the credit against delivery of shipping documents in China. Established companies may be able to arrange with the Bank of China for documents to be held by the bank and handed over against payment on arrival of the steamer in the Western port. This, however, is a matter of particular arrangement with the Bank of China.

Shipping arrangements for goods purchased in China are made by the trading corporations through the China National Foreign Trade Transportation Corporation. The importer has little option therefore but to buy on c.i.f.

or c.f. terms, unless he is buying products involving chartering, which he can initiate through his own shipping agents, the latter working in conjunction with the China National Foreign Trade Transportation Corporation and other shipping organizations. At present there are no ports in China able to handle containers.

Import restrictions

Before the entry of the UK into the European Economic Community, some restrictions by way of quota limitations existed for certain 'sensitive' items, but imports from China were generally exempt from restrictions and import duties on goods from China were not at a level which seriously restricted trade. Joining the EEC, however, involved changes in the quota system, which is now administered from Brussels, and an increase in the scale of import duties, some of which are at a level which has prohibited Britain from importing certain lines established over many years.

At the present time there are restrictive quotas on imports from China into the UK on the following items (similar restrictions on these items also apply to other countries within the EEC):

Matches
Gloves
Silk yarn
Silk fabrics
Wool and hair fabrics
Cotton and man-made fibre yarn and fabrics
Knitwear
Textile manufactures (household and apparel)
Footwear
Headgear
Household china and earthenware.

In the past, import restrictions in the USA operated largely through high import tariffs, e.g., for sugar confectionery from most countries the import duty was 7 per cent and from China a massive 40 per cent. When the proposed trade agreement between the two countries comes into force, Chinese imports into the USA will get Most Favoured Nation (MFN) treatment and attract much lower tariffs. At the time of writing (April 1979), China does not benefit from the EEC Generalized System of Preferences (GSP) accorded to certain developing countries, but this is at present under active discussion.

The quotas for sensitive items are also, at present, under review and there is strong pressure from traders to extend or eliminate quotas to help Britain and the EEC generally to increase their import trade with China. Quotas are allocated by the Commission to EEC countries and administered by governments under their own system. At present, in Britain, import licences for

Chinese goods under quota limitation are based mainly on past performances. It is normal, however, that when a quota is increased some
provision is made for newcomers.

The creation of new import lines
If the wish of the Chinese Foreign Trade Ministry to increase Western–
Chinese business is to be fulfilled, it is essential that, not only should the
volume of traditional imports of Chinese commodities be stepped up, but
also that strenuous efforts be made by both sides to identify and develop
new and improved lines, both based on agricultural and manufactured
products. This means more 'buy-back' arrangements and joint ventures
within China.

The new policy in support of increased exports provides for the following:

1. China will buy capital goods and technology to create new exports on
   suitable medium deferred-payment terms
2. China will sell a range of goods on consignment or deferred-payment
   terms to selected Western companies
3. China will enter into agreement with suitable companies to purchase
   plant and technology, and even some materials to manufacture goods to
   suppliers' specifications, on the basis that the cost is reimbursed to the
   supplier in the form of export of the end-product.
4. China will consider development of an export industry involving foreign
   investment with profit-sharing, payable in Western currencies and/or by
   export of the products.

These proposals are worthy of the most careful consideration by manufacturers in the U.K., using raw materials in their production which are
wholly or mostly available in China.

A number of merchant houses handling both export to and import from
China are already involved in negotiations for the development of new
export commodities, in conjunction with Western manufacturers. In 1979,
companies were visiting China to discuss new products for export.

The Chinese trading corporations are well aware of the reluctance of
western manufacturers to provide technology and plant which could create
competition for them by China in third countries. It is considered possible,
in such cases, to enter into agreements satisfactory to the manufacturers,
and the Chinese trading corporations will invariably honour trademarks
and registered designs incorporated in such arrangements in respect of their
exports to third countries—or agree to limit export to the West except under
licence.

Quality control and arbitration
The quality of China's export commodities is normally specified in the
export contract and is checked prior to export by an independent body,

known as the China Commodities Testing and Inspection Bureau (CCTIB), which issues certificates. Without such certificates the goods may not be exported. The effect of this is that quality complaints on Chinese commodities are minimal. The CCTIB will not 'carry the can' for any factory producing export commodities which do not meet the contract specifications. It is important therefore that orders placed with the trading corporations specify clearly the qualities purchased and the reference number or identification of the Chinese samples, where goods are purchased on sample.

Where disputes arise, a clause in the contract normally provides that such disputes should be settled 'by friendly negotiation between the parties.' Where no agreement is reached in this manner, arbitration is provided for by the China Council for Promotion of International Trades or by independent arbitration in Switzerland. In 25 years of importing from China, I have not yet needed recourse to arbitration, but I believe it important that export contracts are carefully examined and any areas of possible misunderstanding clearly set out, by agreement between the parties, before signature.

The export contract

This contract is almost invariably prepared by the Chinese side and forms the legal document on which the trading corporation prepares and ships the goods purchased. It specifies the usual detail—description of item, quantity, price, quality, shipment, payment terms, and arbitration. There is a certain amount of 'small print' on some of the contracts which varies from corporation to corporation. A specimen of a typical contract is included at the end of this chapter.

Negotiation of import contracts

Negotiation in China is usually carried out in the offices of the corporation at the Canton Fair or at the branches of the corporation in main cities. The Peking head offices can also negotiate contracts on behalf of their branches.

Negotiation outside China is usually carried out by telex or cable exchange and cable confirmation of orders booked can be relied on entirely, as long as full contractual details are specified and agreed in the exchange of cables. It is normal in specifying shipping dates to allow a two-months' spread, e.g., June/July, and also prudent to allow a little longer when selling on to home buyers.

Prices are normally fixed by the Chinese corporations on their own market information as to the world price applicable. Needless to say, some degree of bidding and counter-offering is normal in price negotiation. If the Chinese price is unreasonably high, some documentary proof that one can buy elsewhere at a lower price is helpful but not always accepted, since China has many markets for disposing of its export products.

Negotiations on all points of a contract are usually carried out in an amicable way but the negotiators are shrewd, experienced, and knowledgeable. They do not respond gladly to inept or inexperienced negotiators. It is important, therefore, for companies to keep their negotiators fully briefed by cable on all matters relating to the negotiation, and to allow their home offices to have the final say before completing a purchase, even if the negotiator has discretion.

Telex and cable facilities exist in most hotels and at the Canton Fair.

A TYPICAL EXPORT CONTRACT

CHINA NATIONAL TEXTILES IMPORT & EXPORT CORPORATION

No:

SHANGHAI SILK BRANCH

SALES CONFIRMATION

Date: To Messrs.

The undersigned Sellers and Buyers have agreed to close
the following transactions according to the terms and
conditions stipulated below:

by Buyers cable/letter dated

Sellers cable/letter dated

Quality No. Name of Commodity & Specification	Quantity	Unit Price	Amount	Time of Shipment

Packing: As per Sellers usual export packing.

Both Amount and Quantity 10% More or Less Allowed	Total Amount:

Loading Port and Destination

Term of Payment: by 100% value confirmed irrevocable letter of credit available by draft at sight with transhipment and partial shipments allowed, to reach the Sellers   days before the month of shipment, with shipment validity arranged till the 15th day after the month of shipment, and to remain valid for negotiation in the loading port until the 10th day after the shipment validity. A   % more or less should be allowed in the quantity and amount of the credit, and the word "ABOUT" should be mentioned before the quantity and amount. The terms and conditions in the L/C should be strictly in accordance with those in this contract.

Insurance: To be effected by Sellers covering All Risks and War Risks at 110% of invoice value as per Ocean Marine Cargo Clauses and War Risks Clauses (1/4/1972) of the People's Insurance Company of China (abbreviated as C.I.C. All Risks & War Risks).

Remarks

The Buyers   The Sellers   CHINA NATIONAL TEXTILES IMPORT &
                                                  EXPORT CORPORATION
                                                  SHANGHAI SILK BRANCH

. . . .

Please sign and return one copy of this Confirmation

10. Setting up a joint venture

MICHAEL L. EMMONS

NELLIE K. M. FONG

A crucial factor in the new long march by the People's Republic of China to modernize its economy is how it will finance the needed capital and technology from abroad. The use of compensation trading arrangements as a method of financing certain sectors of the economy was first discussed by the Chinese in early 1978. In November 1978, the New China News Agency officially recognized the use of compensation trading arrangements and indicated that approximately 100 had been entered into in the Canton, Shanghai, and Peking areas. The use of equity ventures was first discussed by the Chinese in late 1978. Even though there has been considerable discussion in the press about equity ventures, to the best of our knowledge by June 1979 the Chinese had not yet entered into any equity ventures with foreign businessmen. Before discussing the nature of compensation trading arrangements and equity ventures that have been negotiated and/or executed, it is necessary to review some of the changes that are occurring in China which affect these types of financing arrangements. The major changes are:

1. *Provincial authority:* the important shift of authority from the central government to the local provinces and municipalities to deal directly with foreigners. The executed compensation trading arrangements have been with local authorities. The recent creation of the Fujian Provincial Investment Enterprise Co., in the province of Fujian is an example of the expanded activity of provincial authorities dealing directly with foreigners. Decentralization has created confusion in this area because of the lack of overall policy guidelines and consistence in types of agreements that have been executed. It means that those provinces with large

159

population centres and easier transportation access will be much more active. This would mainly include the areas around Canton, Shanghai, and Peking. The foreigner must take into consideration when he is dealing with local authorities the limits of that body to control or provide services or support beyond its jurisdiction. This could involve the need to include the Bank of China, if the foreigner was attempting to receive a guarantee from the Bank, or ascertain the availability of electrical power, adequate transportation services, etc.

2. *Foreign investment code:* At present, China does not have a commercial legal infrastructure nor a direct tax system. This lack of commercial laws and the uncertainities as to a tax system has created difficulties for foreigners who are contemplating equity ventures or compensation trading arrangements. Recognizing this, the Chinese, during late 1978, began to consider the drafting of a foreign investment code and supporting body of law. There has been a great deal of speculation as to when it will be forthcoming and what it will encompass. The Chinese have indicated they are having considerable difficulty in drafting an all-encompassing foreign investment code. Further meetings on the foreign investment code were to be held by the Chinese during the middle of June 1979. The speculation was that the general policy guidelines of the foreign investment code would be announced during the summer of 1979 and the completed code released in 1980.

3. *Economic and political direction:* There have been numerous indications that the Chinese have shifted economic and political directions during the first six months of 1979. The mood of late 1978 was best represented by Mr Li Qiang, Minister of Foreign Trade, during his visit to Hongkong in December 1978. He publicly invited much greater participation by foreigners in China's effort to modernize its economy. During this period numerous foreign companies announced they had signed letters of intent for major projects throughout China. The feeling of trading euphoria began to change in 1979.

In February 1979, China announced a freezing of 22 contracts with various Japanese companies, due to foreign currency shortages, and a rearrangement of economic priorities. Subsequent announcements have been made of shifts in economic priorities, with agricultural development being most important, and less emphasis placed on heavy industry, except for oil, from which they are hoping to receive needed foreign currency. Incentive compensation was introduced to workers in certain industries in early 1979. The poster incidents in the major cities, and the sit-down strikes by students returning to Shanghai, have caused renewed concern in opening China up to foreigners. All of these factors have led to a slow down in the number of contracts being executed, and an increasing concern by foreigners as to the political and economic stability of China over the long term.

Compensation trading

It has been estimated that, as of the spring of 1979, approximately 400 compensation trading arrangements have been executed. The majority of the arrangements have been made with Chinese resident abroad, mainly from Hongkong, who are able and willing to accept the relatively loose terms under which the Chinese are now operating. Japanese companies, often through Chinese living abroad, have also executed numerous arrangements. Relatively few European companies have entered into compensation trading arrangements with the Chinese. Wallace Harper & Co. Ltd, a Hongkong-based British motor company, recently entered into a compensation trading arrangement to assemble motor vehicles just across the border from Hongkong in Shumchun (Shenzhen). Two American textile companies have executed compensation trading arrangements involving garments, and a United Kingdom company is operating a glass plant near Peking under a compensation trading arrangement.

The typical compensation trading arrangement involves the Chinese providing the land, labour, and, in some cases, the materials, and the foreigner providing the capital, machinery, and equipment, technology, training, and all or part of the materials and agreeing to purchase the entire output of the factory. Title to all equipment and material passes to China when it crosses the border. The foreigner receives his compensation through a percentage discount of the price for which the end-product is sold to him by the Chinese. The foreigner looks to the discounted price to recoup his investment and the ability to sell the product in China or outside to make his profit.

For example, if a United Kingdom corporation entered into a compensation trading arrangement to assemble electronic parts in China, it would incur the complete cost of obtaining and transporting the materials and equipment to construct and equip the factory, training the Chinese how to use it, and importing the parts to be assembled. Title would pass to the Chinese upon crossing the border. Assume it cost £1 million to construct the factory and that the units to be assembled by the factory were to be sold for £1000 each to the UK corporation; the Chinese would discount the selling price by 8 per cent until the UK corporation was able to recover its original investment of £1 million, plus a reasonable rate of return (compensation element). The ability of the UK corporation to sell the assembled items in the open market, or to use them in other equipment, would determine its profit.

There are numerous problems that could arise from the uncertainties that seem to be integral to compensation trading arrangements. Some of the more difficult questions that would need to be considered are:

1. What is the overall cost of the investment in terms of training, equipment, spare parts, etc?
2. What is a reasonable rate of return on the investment?
3. What is a reasonable selling price of the end-product to the foreigner?

4. What will the Chinese provide, beyond land and labour, in the way of utilities, transportation facilities, etc?
5. What will be the estimated rate and quality of production in order to determine the amount of discount and timing of recovery of investment?
6. What type of recourse is available to the foreigner in case of difficulties under the contract?

Attempting to identify, define and resolve these uncertainties through the contracting process without an existing legal structure is one of the main reasons why there have been so few agreements concluded with Europeans. The Chinese living overseas, with his personal connections, seems to be more capable of entering into compensation trading arrangements without the contractual formality required by the European.

Situations that seem to lend themselves to compensation trading arrangements are:

1. *Source of product:* If a foreigner wants to obtain a source of supply of a product manufactured in China, a compensation trading arrangement to process the product, with a right to the output of the factory, makes economic sense. The best example of this is a compensation trading arrangement that has been entered into with China to process cashmere. The foreigner imported the material and equipment to build and equip the factory and received the right to all of the output from the factory until his investment is recouped, plus the right to purchase output for a fixed period after recoupment of his investment.

2. *Intensity of labour:* With a relatively inexpensive and unlimited workforce in China, compensation trading would seem to be attractive to an industry that is labour-intensive. An additional prerequisite would be minimal cost to build and equip the factory. The best example is seen in the numerous compensation trading arrangements entered into with China in the garment industry which is labour-intensive and relatively inexpensive to equip. Availability of cheaper land is also an extremely attractive part of this package.

3. *China market:* Compensation-trading might involve arrangements whereby the end-product is sold within China, or whereby it is exported elsewhere even though a market exists or could exist in China. The Harper motor assembly arrangement discussed earlier is a good example in which the company might have positioned itself for a future market in China.

The types of compensation trading arrangements being discussed or executed in some of the different industries are as follows:

1. *Hotels:* The heady announcements of late 1978 by some of the major

hotel chains have not led to executed contracts in 1979. The concept is simple; the particulars have proved to be very difficult. There has been speculation that a few Chinese overseas have actually executed contracts to build hotels. One Chinese from Australia has concluded a deal for motel units. The terms being discussed are that the foreigners will import all necessary materials, down to the doorknobs, to build the hotel and train the Chinese to operate it, and the Chinese will provide the labour and land. The foreigners will receive the right to send a certain number of tourists to China and a fixed amount per each paying person who stays in the hotel, or a percentage of the profits from the hotel in return. Because of the uncertainties of how profits will be determined for an hotel, most foreigners are discussing the option of a fixed fee per occupant as compensation. The size of the investment will make these compensation-trading arrangements difficult to negotiate and conclude, especially until some type of foreign investment code is concluded by the Chinese.

2. *Automobiles:* Many of the major automobile companies have held discussions with the Chinese but only the local Hongkong motor car company of Wallace Harper & Co. Ltd, has signed a compensation trading arrangement with the Chinese. Construction has begun on the plant in the Shumchun (Shenzhen) area just across the border from Hongkong. Harper's agreement represents one of the major non-overseas Chinese compensation-trading arrangements. Harper will provide the materials, equipment, and technology to build the factory. They will ship the automotive parts to Shumchun and provide training and assistance to the management in assembling the vehicles. Title to all materials, equipment, and inventory parts will pass to the Chinese when it crosses the border. The Chinese will provide the land and labour. They will determine the selling price of the assembled vehicles to Harper and Harper will receive a discount on its sales price as compensation. Harper is scheduled to export all the assembled vehicles to Hongkong.

3. *Oil:* The oil industry continues to receive top priority in China, for obvious reasons. It is contemplated that the major oil companies will negotiate compensation-trading arrangements, whereby they would recover their investments through rights to receive a percentage of the crude at a discounted price. As to offshore oil fields, the Chinese have signed seismic-exploration contracts with major foreign oil companies. It is contemplated that the Chinese will accumulate information from the large-scale geophysical surveys over the next year, make the findings public and allow foreign companies to bid with equal knowledge on different areas. The terms of the compensation-trading arrangements with regard to cost of investment and technology, selling price relating to

market price, desire to develop Chinese refinery capacity, etc., coupled with the present lack of a commercial legal infrastructure and uncertainties as to the existence or non-existence of a tax system, will make it extremely difficult to conclude the compensation-trading arrangements in the oil industry.

4. *Light industry:* The majority of the executed compensation-trading arrangements involve the assembling and processing of garments, handbags, shoes, watches, electrical machinery, etc. The compensation-trading arrangement readily lends itself to this type of activity because of the limited economic risk by the foreign investor. It is an area that is very attractive to the Chinese abroad.

Equity ventures
The Chinese first began to discuss the concept of equity ventures in the fall of 1978. The fact the Chinese were even ready to discuss the possibility of equity ventures represents a dramatic shift from their stated policy, that there will be no foreign ownership in China. Even though the equity-venture arrangements being discussed are different in many ways from how foreigners normally view them, it is still important that they are being discussed. The completion of a foreign-investment code will be necessary before equity ventures can become a viable alternative. Any political shift from the present liberalized relations with foreigners would directly affect the possibility of equity ventures.

To our knowledge, there have not been any equity ventures consummated as of 1 June 1979. There has been a great deal of speculation about certain transactions with the normal resulting publicity, but none that we have been able to confirm. The latest speculation is that a European corporation was entering into a 49/51 equity venture with China. The payout would be over five years, with the European corporation being able to take out 25 per cent of its 49 per cent share of the profits with the remaining 75 per cent being reinvested in China. The European corporation would have limited representation in management. If the above is not speculation and has been executed, it seems clear that the reason for entering into it has to be more than economic.

Some of the features of the equity ventures being discussed and reported in the press are as follows:

1. *Foreign percentage of ownership:* Different sources have reported from 100 per cent to 49/50 percent, or the possibility of the Chinese having less than 50 per cent if two or more unrelated foreign parties have more than 50 per cent in total but each less than the Chinese portion. The 100 per cent equity ownership seems unrealistic in view of the requirement by the Chinese of control of the management.

2. *Management:* Chinese would have, at minimum, control of the directors and officers. The foreigners might have representation but the Chinese would clearly control management.

3. *Payout:* The feature of the retirement of the equity of the foreigner, through a payout over a stated number of years, is one of the aspects of the Chinese concept of equity ventures that is different from the European concept. The majority of the possible equity ventures being discussed have a fixed payout over five to ten years. Some have reported longer payouts when there is a continuing influx of needed technology or enhancement to the product.

4. *Taxes and repatriation:* This is a question mark. The introduction of a direct tax system has been discussed by the Chinese over the last five months, but nothing has been finalized. Obviously, the ability to repatriate profits will be crucial.

With a payout over a fixed period and limited management, the differences between compensation-trading arrangements and equity ventures seem to diminish.

Conclusion

There seem to be as many problems as there are opportunities with equity ventures and compensation-trading arrangements with China. If the foreigner is trying to obtain a source of supply of products peculiar to China or limited in availability, his alternatives are limited and equity ventures or compensation-trading arrangements might become a necessity. The foreigner seeking to market certain products in China might be faced with a similar situation. If the foreigner is seeking inexpensive labour and land, the opportunities and problems in China must be compared with other countries in the Asian area.

In the foreseeable future, the Chinese abroad, usually from Hongkong, with their understanding of China and personal contacts, will continue to dominate the compensation-trading activity. The European businessman will continue to approach compensation trading on a conservative and speculative basis. The introduction of a foreign investment code should help in this area. The introduction of policy guidelines only would be helpful. A detailed foreign-investment code, with its necessary rigidity, could be detrimental as well as helpful if it cannot keep pace with the changing China scene. The productivity of labour, inability to control or provide incentives to workers and lack of management and accounting systems are some of the important unknowns. All of these uncertainties cannot be covered in the contract and the foreigner must be willing to accept the economic risks if he wants to enter into compensation-trading arrangements with China.

The future of equity ventures in China is at best uncertain. A foreign-investment code must be introduced before they can be of major concern. It would seem that something more similar to compensation-trading arrangements, rather than joint ventures as they are understood in the Western world, will emerge.

China's law on joint ventures

Beijing, July 8 (Xinhua)—Following is an unofficial translation of the full text of the law of the People's Republic of China on joint ventures using Chinese and foreign investment, which was adopted on July 1 at the second session of the Fifth National People's Congress and became effective on July 8 on the order of Ye Jianying, Chairman of the standing committee of the National People's Congress:

Article 1. With a view to expanding international economic co-operation and technological exchange, the People's Republic of China permits foreign companies, enterprises, other economic entities or individuals (hereinafter referred to as foreign participants) to incorporate themselves, within the territory of the People's Republic of China, into joint ventures with Chinese companies, enterprises or other economic entities (hereinafter referred to as Chinese participants) on the principle of equality and mutual benefit and subject to authorization by the Chinese government.

Article 2. The Chinese government protects, by the legislation in force, the resources invested by a foreign participant in a joint venture and the profits due him pursuant to the agreements, contracts and articles of association authorized by the Chinese government as well as his other lawful rights and interests.

All the activities of a joint venture shall be governed by the laws, decrees and pertinent rules and regulations of the People's Republic of China.

Article 3. A joint venture shall apply to the foreign investment commission of the People's Republic of China for authorization of the agreements and contracts concluded between the parties to the venture and the articles of association of the venture formulated by them, and the commission shall authorize or reject these documents within three months. When authorized, the joint venture shall register with the general administration for industry and commerce of the People's Republic of China and start operations under license.

Capital

Article 4. A joint venture shall take the form of a limited liability company.

In the registered capital of a joint venture, the proportion of the investment contributed by the foreign participant(s) shall in general not be less than 25 per cent.

The profits, risks and losses of a joint venture shall be shared by the parties to the venture in proportion to their contributions to the registered capital.

The transfer of one party's share in the registered capital shall be effected only with the consent of the other parties to the venture.

Article 5. Each party to a joint venture may contribute cash, capital goods, industrial property rights, etc. as its investment in the venture.

The technology or equipment contributed by any foreign participant as investment shall be truly advanced and appropriate to China's needs. In cases of losses caused by deception through the intentional provision of outdated equipment or technology, compensation shall be paid for the losses.

The investment contributed by a Chinese participant may include the right to the use of a site provided for the joint venture during the period of its operation. In case such a contribution does not constitute a part of the investment from the Chinese participant, the joint venture shall pay the Chinese government for its use.

The various contributions referred to in the present article shall be specified in the contracts concerning the joint venture or in its articles of association, and the value of each contribution (excluding that of the site) shall be ascertained by the parties to the venture through joint assessment.

Board of directors

Article 6. A joint venture shall have a board of directors with a composition stipulated in the contracts and the articles of association after consultation between the parties to the venture, and each director shall be appointed or removed by his own side. The board of directors shall have a chairman appointed by the Chinese participant and one or two vice-chairmen appointed by the foreign participant(s). In handling an important problem, the board of directors shall reach decision through consultation by the participants on the principle of equality and mutual benefit.

The board of directors is empowered to discuss and take action on, pursuant to the provisions of the articles of association of the joint venture, all fundamental issues concerning the venture, namely, expansion projects, production and business programs, the budget, distribution of profits, plans concerning manpower and pay scales, the termination of business, the appointment or hiring of the president, the vice-president(s), the chief engineer, the treasurer and the auditors as well as their functions and powers and their remuneration, etc.

The president and vice-president(s) (or the general manager and assistant general manager(s) in a factory) shall be chosen from the various parties to the joint venture.

Procedures covering the employment and discharge of the workers and staff members of a joint venture shall be stipulated according to law in the agreement or contract concluded between the parties to the venture.

Profit

Article 7. The net profit of a joint venture shall be distributed between the parties to the venture in proportion to their respective shares in the registered capital after the payment of a joint venture income tax on its gross profit pursuant to the tax laws of the People's Republic of China and after the deductions therefrom as stipulated in the articles of association of the venture for the reserve funds, the bonus and welfare funds for the workers and staff members and the expansion funds of the venture.

A joint venture equipped with up-to-date technology by world standards may apply for a reduction of or exemption from income tax for the first two to three profit making years.

A foreign participant who re-invests any part of his share of the net profit within Chinese territory may apply for the restitution of a part of the income taxes paid.

Article 8. A joint venture shall open an account with the Bank of China or a bank approved by the Bank of China.

A joint venture shall conduct its foreign exchange transactions in accordance with the foreign exchange regulations of the People's Republic of China.

A joint venture may, in its business operations, obtain funds from foreign banks directly.

The insurances appropriate to a joint venture shall be furnished by Chinese insurance companies.

Production

Article 9. The production and business programs of a joint venture shall be filed with the authorities concerned and shall be implemented through business contracts.

In its purchase of required raw and semi-processed materials, fuels, auxiliary equipment, etc., a joint venture should give first priority to Chinese sources, but may also acquire them directly from the world market with its own foreign exchange funds.

A joint venture is encouraged to market its products outside China. It may distribute its export products on foreign markets through direct channels or its associated agencies or China's foreign trade establishments. Its products may also be distributed on the Chinese market.

Wherever necessary, a joint venture may set up affiliated agencies outside China.

Profit, wages may be remitted abroad

Article 10. The net profit which a foreign participant receives as his share after executing his obligations under the pertinent laws and agreements and contracts, the funds he receives at the time when the joint venture terminates or winds up its operations, and his other funds may be remitted abroad through the Bank of China in accordance with the foreign exchange regulations and in the currency or currencies specified in the contracts concerning the joint venture.

A foreign participant shall receive encouragements for depositing in the Bank of China any part of the foreign exchange which he is entitled to remit abroad.

Article 11. The wages, salaries or other legitimate income earned by a foreign worker or staff member of a joint venture, after payment of the personal income tax under the tax laws of the People's Republic of China, may be remitted abroad through the Bank of China in accordance with the foreign exchange regulations.

Article 12. The contract period of a joint venture may be agreed upon between the parties to the venture according to its particular line of business and circumstances. The period may be extended upon expiration through agreement between the parties, subject to authorization by the foreign investment commission of the People's Republic of China. Any application for such extension shall be made six months before the expiration of the contract.

In case of losses

Article 13. In cases of heavy losses, the failure of any party to a joint venture to execute its obligations under the contracts or the articles of association of the venture, force majeure, etc., prior to the expiration of the contract period of a joint venture, the contract may be terminated before the date of expiration by consultation and agreement between the parties and through authorization by the foreign investment commission of the People's Republic of China and registration with the general administration for industry and commerce. In cases of losses caused by breach of the contract(s) by a party to the venture, the financial responsibility shall be borne by the said party.

Article 14. Disputes arising between the parties to a joint venture which the board of directors fails to settle through consultation may be settled through conciliation or arbitration by an arbitral body of China or through arbitration by an arbitral body agreed upon by the parties.

Article 15. The present law comes into force on the date of its promulgation. The power of amendment is vested in the National People's Congress.

11. Japan and China

CHARLES SMITH

Sino-Japanese trade today

Japan's trade with China dates back to the earliest period of Japanese history for which written records survive—indeed Japan's system of writing was itself one of the earliest imports from China. The complementary economic relationship on which present-day Sino-Japanese trade is based dates, however, from the early decades of the twentieth century. The nature of this relationship has been, and remains, China's need for Japanese-manufactured goods (including semi-processed industrial raw materials) and its ability to supply Japan with food products, agricultural raw materials, minerals, and fuels.

Significance of the trade to the Chinese and Japanese economies
Japan's share of China's total foreign trade has been larger than of any other nation (communist or non-communist) since the mid-sixties and would appear to be destined for still further growth—although during 1978 some western European countries increased their sales to China even more rapidly than Japan. Estimates based on a collation of trade statistics published by China's trade partners, in the absence of any figures published by China itself, give Japan a 25 per cent average share of the total during the first half of the seventies, with the figure rising to 26.2 per cent in 1976. Some Japanese forecasters believe that, by 1981, Japan may account for between 31 and 36 per cent of China's trade. This forecast is based on the assumption that the annual growth rate of China's total foreign trade will average no more than 15 per cent during the three-year period from 1978–80 inclusive. A faster growth for China's total trade would presumably reduce the rate of increase in Japan's share of the total.

By contrast with the dominant position occupied by Japan in the foreign trade of China, China's share of Japan's trade remains relatively modest. It

169

Table 11.1 Highs and lows in Japan–China trade 1950–70

$ million	Japanese exports	Japanese imports	Total	% of China's trade
1950	19.6	39.3	59.9	4.8
1952	0.6	14.9	15.5	0.8
1956	67.3	83.6	150.9	4.5
1959	3.6	18.9	22.5	0.5
1966	315.2	306.2	621.4	14.1
1969	390.8	234.5	625.3	16.2

represented a mere 2.3 per cent of the total in 1977 and had shown no increase since 1965 (when the ratio was 2.8 per cent). It might appear from these statistics that Sino–Japanese trade is of far more importance to China than it is to Japan. This, however, begins to appear questionable if one takes into account other factors involved in the relationship. One highly significant point is that Japan's global foreign trade is of overwhelming importance to its overall prosperity, whereas foreign trade is, or has been, a statistically marginal component of China's GNP (trade accounts for 12 per cent of the Japanese GNP but only 5 per cent of that of China).

A second set of considerations relates to the products involved in China–Japan trade and the extent to which either country is dependent on the other as a market or source of supply in each case. China is a market of prime importance to the Japanese steel industry, accounting for 16.2 per cent of total steel exports in the first half of 1978 and for a possible 20 per cent in 1979 (which would mean that steel exports to China would, for the first time, exceed those to the USA). It is more important still to the Japanese chemical fertilizer industry, having absorbed 64.5 per cent of the industry's total exports in 1977.

Table 11.2 Japan–China trade 1970 to 1978 (in units of $ million)

	Japanese exports	Japanese imports	Total	% of China's trade
1970	568.9	253.8	822.7	20.1
1971	578.2	323.2	901.4	19.3
1972	608.9	491.1	1100.0	22.0
1973	1039.5	974.0	2013.5	19.5
1974	1984.5	1304.8	3289.3	23.4
1975	2258.6	1531.1	3789.7	26.2
1976	1662.6	1370.9	3033.5	23.0
1977	1938.6	1547.3	3485.9	24.6
1978	3049.1	2032.1		

Source: Japanese customs clearance statistics.

The third major category of Japanese exports to China, industrial plant, has fluctuated sharply in recent years but regained importance in 1978 and could become more significant still during the early eighties (depending on Chinese economic policies). The importance of the Chinese market to plant exporters in 1978 can be gauged by the fact that plant exports to other markets (mainly the Middle East) were tending to fall during the year. The value of contracts under discussion with China during the second half of 1978 is believed to have exceeded $10 billion, substantially greater than the total value of plant orders expected from all other markets during fiscal year 1978.

The dependence of China on Japan as a source of supply for the major items just mentioned is very high indeed. Japan appears in some recent years to have supplied over 90 per cent of China's steel imports (which in turn account for an estimated 20 per cent of total steel consumption). Japan is also dominant as a supplier of chemical fertilizers—in 1977 fertilizer imports from Japan amounted to 1.9 million tons compared with imports of 500 000 tons from western Europe and 17 000 tons from the USA. Finally, Japan appears to have secured about half of the orders for complete industrial plants which China placed with non-communist suppliers between 1972 and 1974.

These high levels of Chinese dependence on Japanese supplies should not necessarily be regarded as permanent or unchangeable. What appears much more likely is that China has bought heavily from Japan in the past because Japanese prices (including freight costs) were attractive compared with those available from other suppliers. Increases in Japanese prices resulting from yen revaluation were reflected, during the first nine months of 1978, in a decline in the quantity of Japanese chemical fertilizer shipments to China, which coincided with a sharp rise in imports from western European suppliers such as France and Norway. (The *value* of Japanese fertilizer exports during the first nine months of the year, however, still showed an increase of 15.1 per cent.) In the case of steel, a similar trend appeared to have set in by mid-1978. Japanese exports increased by 6.1 per cent, in terms of volume during the first nine months of the year, but China increased its steel purchases more sharply from European suppliers, including West Germany, Britain, France, and the Netherlands.

The prices at which Japanese steel is exported to China have for many years remained a closely guarded secret within the industry itself. They appear, however, to be set at levels about 20 per cent below average world market prices, presumably in consideration of the fact that China negotiates bulk purchases which are much larger than those available in other markets. Steel export negotiations are conducted twice a year between the six major Japanese integrated steel producers and the Chinese trading corporation handling steel imports. Negotiations are invariably tough, with the Japanese side holding out for higher prices and the Chinese buyers offering (at least from 1978 onwards) to step up their purchases significantly, in return for the

Table 11.3 Japan's steel exports to China and the USA (in units of 1000 tons)

	To China	% of total exports	To USA	% of total exports
1966	646	6.5	4696	47.5
1967	610	6.7	4349	47.6
1968	1005	7.6	6916	52.6
1969	1258	7.9	5651	35.3
1970	1569	8.7	5922	32.9
1971	1948	8.1	6268	25.9
1972	1716	7.8	6258	28.5
1973	2661	10.4	5287	20.7
1974	2887	8.7	6510	19.7
1975	2836	9.5	5724	19.1
1976	3518	9.5	7444	20.1
1977	4533	13.0	7596	21.7
1978	2493	16.2	2897	18.8
(Jan.–June)				

Source: Daiwa Securities Co.

maintenance of a low price level. The importance of the biennial negotiations to the Japanese steel industry has grown sharply in the last two years during which China has caught up with the USA as the main overseas market for Japanese steel.

As a supplier to the Japanese market, China inevitably looms less large than Japan does as a supplier to the Chinese market. Its exports centred traditionally, i.e., up to about 1972, on animal and vegetable products, including some items, such as chestnuts, redbeans, and prawns, for which demand in Japan is strong and usually exceeds available supplies. Since the beginning of the seventies, China has rapidly increased its textile exports to Japan, thereby duplicating the experience of other newly industrialized Asian nations which have sold more textiles to Japan, as the Japanese textile industry has gone into rapid decline. The largest single Chinese export item, however, and the one which holds out most promise for future growth is crude oil.

China made its first shipments of oil to Japan in 1973 (the year after the normalization of Sino-Japanese diplomatic relations) and by 1977 had stepped up exports to 6.6 million tons (accounting for slightly less than 3 per cent of Japan's total crude oil imports in that year). Under the 1978 two-way trade agreement (see below), its exports were scheduled to reach 7 million tons in 1976 and then to rise steadily to 15 million tons by 1982. Crude oil accounted for 38 per cent of China's total export earnings in the first nine months of 1978, as against a 25 per cent share for textiles.

Its position at the top of the list of Chinese exports to Japan, however, does not necessarily imply that this is the Chinese product which finds the readiest market in Japan, or is most popular with consuming industries. Despite Japan's overwhelming dependence on imported oil as an energy source (approximately 73 per cent), and despite its urgent need to decrease its reliance on the Middle East, Chinese oil has not proved easy to fit into the pattern of Japanese energy consumption.

The major problem is that Chinese oil, or rather the oil at present exported to Japan from the Taching field in north-east China, has a high specific gravity and yields a relatively low ratio of kerosene and other light oil products, for which demand exists in Japan. The absorption of greater quantities of Chinese oil will require changes in the structure of the Japanese refining industry, which is at the moment geared to refining light Middle-East oil. These changes, including major investments in new refinery equipment, are expected to be made eventually but the costs will be high and the time scale may be a matter of several years.

The determination of Japan to continue buying Chinese oil, and in fact to step up purchases sharply in the near future, thus relates, not so much to demand for oil from Japanese users, as to the need to buy *something* from China so as to balance Japan's exports of manufactured products. This need exists because China's foreign exchange reserves and bilateral surpluses with other trading partners are too small to support a large and continuing deficit with its biggest trading partner.

How trade is conducted

Like all other nations, Japan conducts its Chinese trade by means of business negotiations with the state trading corporations which handle different groups of products exported or imported by the Peoples' Republic of China. Japanese companies also frequently make use of the Canton Trade Fair (twice-yearly in April–May and October–November) to conduct routine business negotiations with their Chinese opposite numbers. The Japanese business presence at Canton is usually larger than that of any other national group with the exception of Chinese from abroad. The number of Japanese businessmen attending the fair exceeded 1000 for the first time in

Table 11.4 Japan's oil imports from China

	Units of 1 million kilolitres	% of imports from China (by value)
1973	1.5	3.3
1974	4.6	31.4
1975	9.2	48.2
1976	7.0	41.0
1977	7.7	42.3
1978	8.7	37.3

Source: Japan External Trade Organization.

the spring of 1970 and passed the 2500 mark in the autumn of 1972 (immediately after the normalization of diplomatic relations). Japanese businessmen at Canton are allocated a different hotel from that reserved for visitors from Western nations. An agreement exists under which individual Japanese trading companies are entitled to a pre-determined number of hotel beds for the duration of the Fair, the number being related to each company's normal share of total Sino-Japanese trade.

Japan also resembles Western countries in its methods of trade promotion in the China market. General exhibitions of Japanese industry have been held in Peking and Shanghai at irregular intervals since 1956 (most recently in 1975). Exhibitions devoted to individual industries began to be held from 1967 onwards and have tended to assume a more important role than general industrial fairs. Among the industries so far covered by specialized exhibitions are: scientific instruments, machine tools, earth-moving equipment, printing and packing machinery, environmental protection, and agricultural and fishing technology.

China has held a series of exhibitions in Japan since the mid-fifties, varying greatly in size (and in commercial success). The last exhibition, held in four Japanese cities during the spring and summer of 1977, included some 11 000 articles and claimed spot sales of just over 3 billion yen ($15 million) during a six-month period. Exchanges of trade missions between China and Japan, a comparative rarity in the early post-war period, began to increase rapidly from late 1977 onwards. In the first nine months of 1978, Japan dispatched 127 missions to China and received 70 missions in return. The missions covered a wide range of products and sectors including oil development (a mission to China from the Japan National Oil Company) and finance (a mission from the Japan Bankers' Association).

From late 1978 onwards, China began to show interest in studying Japanese methods of economic planning and management through the exchange of economic study missions. A mission composed of members of the State Planning Commission spent one month in Japan in autumn 1978, immediately after the official visit to Tokyo by Vice-Premier Deng Xiaoping. China then invited a mission of Japanese economists to visit Peking in order to study, and comment on, China's methods of economic planning. The Japanese mission, which went to China in early 1979, was headed by Dr Saburo Okita, a former president of the Japan Economic Research Centre (a well-known independent economic research agency).

Japanese private companies, in common with western European companies, have traditionally been denied permission to establish branch offices in Peking or other Chinese cities (although China appeared to be on the point of yielding to pressure on this matter at the end of 1978). Despite the ban on branch offices, all of Japan's major general trading companies have maintained *de facto* permanent presences in Peking since the early seventies. This has been done by rotating staff members on short-term business visas, usually valid for a maximum of one or two months, in such a way as to ensure that a minimum of three or four executives (in the case of one major trading concern) are in China all the time.

The big Japanese trading companies hold permanent reservations of Peking hotel rooms which they have equipped with telex facilities. Up to the end of 1978, China declined to allow Japanese trading company personnel stationed in Peking to employ Chinese staff as drivers or telex operators, and insisted on regarding such people as temporary guests in Peking hotels. Plans were afoot, however, to accommodate Japanese trading companies (as well as other Japanese and non-Japanese companies) in a new 40-storey trade-centre building. The construction contract for this project was expected to be awarded to Japan.

Japanese general trading companies constitute a large proportion of the Japanese business presence at the Canton Fair, and are frequently called upon to dispatch executives to China as advisory members of missions representing specific industries. In order to back up these activities, most of the major trading concerns maintain departments in their head offices, specializing in trade with China. This represents an exception to the general pattern of trading company organization which is based on product or industry divisions not on departments dealing with different geographical areas. The necessity for operating specialized trade departments is explained by the 'special circumstances' of trading with China, i.e., by the distinctive approach of the People's Republic of China to such matters as finance, insurance, patents, etc.

One major trading concern which boasts a long-term trading relationship with China employs around 40 Chinese-language graduates in its China Trade Promotion Department, but also has other Chinese specialists on secondment to product divisions or at overseas branches. The company concerned says that the need for specialist advice on trade with China is tending to diminish, as China's trading corporations themselves become more familiar with international trading practices. Any diminution of the number of staff employed in the Chinese department at the company's head office in Tokyo will, however, be more than compensated by the numbers needed to open a branch in Peking (if and when China gives its consent).

Japanese banks were relatively slow to establish direct relations with the Bank of China after the establishment of the People's Republic of China. From 1953 (when trade was resumed after the interruption caused by the Korean War) until 1963, trade accounts between the two countries were settled mainly in sterling, through the London offices of the Bank of Tokyo (Japan's specialist foreign exchange bank) and the Bank of China. The two banks entered into direct-correspondent relations in 1963 but continued to use the pound as the main settlement currency, supplemented by the French franc and the Deutschmark after the 1967 devaluation of the pound.

In 1969, Japan began to seek an agreement with China on a system of settlement, using the Japanese yen and the Chinese yuan, but China withheld its consent until the summer of 1972, a few months before the normalization of Sino-Japanese diplomatic relations (and some years after most of China's West European trading partners had negotiated direct settlement arrangements with the People's Republic of China.

The floating of the yen and other major currencies in early 1973 produced new problems for the financing of Japan–China trade and created a need for a futures market in yen and yuan (to which China finally agreed in early 1975). By 1975, 26 Japanese banks (including the 13 major city banks) had entered into correspondent relations with the Bank of China. Trade was conducted mainly in yuan and yen for a time, but a shift back towards dollar-denominated trade began after China agreed, in 1976, to accept the standard international system of pricing its oil exports in dollars. The currency denomination of deferred-payment credits on Japanese plant exports to China became a major issue from mid-1978 onwards (see below).

The Long-Term Trade Agreement and the future of Sino-Japanese trade

Negotiation and signing of the agreement
In February 1978, Japan and China signed a long-term trade agreement providing for an equal exchange of $20 billion worth of goods over an 8-year period (1978–85). The products to be exchanged are crude oil and coal (to be exported by China) and industrial plants, construction materials, construction machinery and equipment (to be shipped by Japan). The agreement includes figures for the tonnages of coal and oil to be supplied by China up to 1982, and calls for discussions to be held before the end of 1981 on coal and oil shipments during the remaining three years of the eight-year period. It also states that shipment levels set for the final three years must increase annually from the levels attained in 1982. (The 1982 shipment levels are: 15 million tons for oil, 2 million tons for coking coal, and 1.5 million to 1.7 million tons for steam coal.)

The value of industrial plant to be purchased by China from Japan is set at $7–8 billion during the first five years of the agreement period, while the value of construction materials, machinery, and equipment to be supplied is set at $2–3 billion. Further purchases of industrial plant and construction materials may be made by China during the final three years of the agreement period (depending, presumably, on how much oil and coal Japan buys from China during the same three years).

The Long-Term Trade Agreement was signed in Peking by two 'private-level' bodies established for the purpose (The Japan–China Long-Term Trade Consultation Committee, under the chairmanship of Mr Yoshihiro Inayama and the China–Japan Long-Term Trade Consultation Committee, under the chairmanship of Mr Liu Xiwan.) It represents the fruit of five years of intermittent discussions between businessmen and officials of the two nations. A proposal to exchange Japanese exports of industrial plant for imports of Chinese crude oil was first made to the late Premier Zhou Enlai by the president of the Nippon Steel Corporation, Mr Yoshihiro Inayama, in the autumn of 1972, immediately after the normalization of Sino-Japanese diplomatic relations. The idea was well received on the Chinese side but discussions on a formal trade agreement were delayed by two sets of obstacles.

On the Japanese side, difficulties arose over the absorption of the large amounts of oil which it was proposed that China should supply to Japan. Mr Inayama originally suggested a target figure of 100 million tons but this was progressively and drastically scaled down during the four years following the original proposal. On China's side, the rising influence of 'radicals' (Chairman Mao's wife and her colleagues from Shanghai) on national economic policy between 1974 and 1976, meant that the basic principle of the exchange of Chinese fuels and raw materials for Japanese manufactured goods was called into question.

Japan began to show a renewed interest in negotiating an oil-for-plant trade agreement with Japan in the spring of 1977 (after the radical 'Gang of Four' had been arrested in Peking). From this time until the winter of 1977–78, negotiations were held on the details of the agreement, with the toughest bargaining centring on the amounts of crude oil to be absorbed by Japan. The Japanese side at first offered to import 9.32 million tons of Chinese oil by 1982 (a figure arrived at by coordinating the demand projections of major industries such as steel, electricity, and oil) but later revised its offer to 11.3 million tons. Finally, a political decision was taken to accept China's demand that oil shipments should reach 15 million tons by 1982.

The decision was 'political' in the sense that the Japanese negotiating team agreed to China's demand without any corresponding commitment by Japanese oil-consuming industries to buy the additional oil. The problem of bridging the gap between Japan's estimated industrial requirements of 11.3 million tons and the obligation to buy 15 million tons is one that has to be solved by the Japanese sponsors of the Trade Agreement before 1982. Because the agreement is a private one, responsibility rests theoretically with the Long-Term Trade Consultation Committee presided over by Mr Inayama. In reality, however, responsibility rests with the Japanese government and specifically the Ministry of International Trade and Industry, which actively supported the negotiations from the outset.

Although the Long-Term Agreement calls for the balancing of trade over an eight-year period, it does not require that trade should be balanced annually. The annual balancing of trade during the early years of the eight-year period is in fact regarded as unlikely, given that China will concentrate its orders for Japanese plant during the first few years of the agreement period, whereas Japanese purchases of Chinese oil will reach their maximum levels during the final years (1983–85). The agreement provides for the imbalance in Japan's favour to be covered by the use of a deferred-payment formula for Chinese plant purchases. It does not specify the terms on which such payments will be made, i.e., there is nothing in the text of the agreement about currencies or interest rates.

The Long-Term Agreement does not cover all Sino-Japanese trade. Amongst Japanese exports, steel (other than structural steel) and chemical fertilizers are excluded. Among Chinese exports, food products and agricultural raw materials are excluded. An important loophole is the provision that China may decide whether specific plant imports from Japan should, or should not, be regarded as forming part of the $7–8 billion worth of plant to be bought under the terms of the agreement. Plant import contracts which are considered to be outside the terms of the agreement would count as part of China's 'ordinary' trade with Japan and would be over and above the total of $7–8 billion.

In the spring of 1979, China and Japan extended the agreement by five years to 1990 and increased its value to $60 billion. The deal included a plan for joint consultations in 1981 on shipments to Japan of coal and crude oil after 1983. But uncertainty was hanging over all future trade plans because Peking had announced in February that it was readjusting its economy. This involved freezing contracts worth $2.8 billion for purchases from Japan. In May, it began to negotiate to switch these contracts from a cash to a deferred-payments basis.

Significance of the Long-Term Trade Agreement for the growth of trade between China and Japan

The agreement was regarded as a milestone in Sino-Japanese trade relations when it was signed in 1978. This was because it was the first trade pact between China and Japan (or between China and any other country) to incorporate the principle of a long-term supply of fuels and other raw materials, in return for the supply of capital goods. In terms of its impact on trade values, the agreement is expected to contribute the doubling of Japan's exports to China over a three to four-year period, (i.e., from less than $3 billion in 1977 to over $6 billion by 1981). China's exports to Japan will rise more slowly, perhaps hitting $4–5 billion in the early eighties. (These figures include estimates for both 'agreement' and 'non-agreement' trade.)

The agreement appears to have been of some value to China in creating a model or precedent for trade pacts with other advanced industrial nations. Its specific value to Japan, apart from promising a sharp increase in plant exports during the period up to 1981, was to secure for the Nippon Steel Corporation the virtually water-tight promise that it would be named chief contractor for the 6 million ton Shanghai integrated steel plant. This will be the first fully integrated steel plant to be built in China and is expected to cost up to $2 billion. It will, in other words, account for a significant portion of the plant orders to which China is committed under the Long-Term Agreement.

Despite its apparently concrete nature, the signing of the Long-Term Trade

Agreement left open a number of important questions about the future of Sino-Japanese trade, both within and beyond the eight-year period which it is designed to cover. Major areas of uncertainty include: the level and trend of Chinese plant orders after 1981, given that most of the orders to be made within the terms of the agreement are due to be placed during the next three years; the future of Japan's exports of products such as steel and fertilizers for which China's domestic production capacity will increase as a result of the plant import programme; the ability of Japan to absorb Chinese products other than oil and coal during the period up to 1985; and its ability to continue stepping up oil imports beyond the 1985 deadline.

China has indicated that it sees the $20 billion trade pact as the first stage in a series of two-way trade agreements with Japan, under which increasing shipments of Chinese oil and coal would be balanced by Japanese supplies of capital goods. Japan has no reason not to welcome the principle of an indefinite extension of the Trade Agreement. it does, however, face problems in negotiating an immediate extension or enlargement of the existing agreement. One of these is that the Japanese oil refining industry is not equipped to absorb larger quantities of Chinese heavy oil than are at present provided for under the agreement. Absorption of greatly increased quantities of Chinese crude oil would have to be balanced by a new round of investment in Japanese refining capacity. But Japan is unwilling to make such investments until China provides some indication as to whether future oil shipments are likely to consist mainly of heavy oil, similar to that from the Daqing field in north-east China, or of oil from yet-to-be developed offshore fields (which could be lighter in quality).

A final problem which stands in the way of rapid increases in Sino-Japanese trade, beyond the targets set by the Long-Term Agreement, is that of finance. China's ability to pay was seen as the central issue in all discussions about the viability of its industrial modernization programme. As far as Japan was concerned, however, there was also the more specific problem of China's ability or willingness to accept a foreign-debt burden, denominated largely or even partially in yen. China took the view that the yen is certain to continue appreciating against the US dollar and against softer European currencies, such as the pound and the lire over the long as well as the short term. It would have preferred to finance its plant imports from Japan with low-interest-rate, dollar-denominated loans extended by the Japanese Export-Import Bank which was, technically, in a position to fund such loans by borrowing from Japan's large foreign currency reserves (amounting to $33 billion at the time of writing).

No precedent existed, however, for the extension of dollar-denominated loans by the Exim Bank to foreign borrowers and the creation of such a precedent would, almost certainly, have proved embarrassing. It could have led to requests for dollar loans from other Japanese trading partners, including probably the Soviet Union which remains interested in involving Japan in the joint development of Siberian natural resources. This, in turn, could attract accusations from Japan's Western competitors, including the USA, that Japan was using soft currency loans as an unfair method of subsidizing its exports.

In mid-May 1979, however, a Bank of China delegation signed a $2 billion yen-denominated loan agreement with the Japanese Export–Import Bank (at exceptionally low interest rates) and agreed with a 31-strong Japanese banking syndicate on basic conditions for a $2 billion loan and $6 billion refinance facility. These two non-government loans were to be used to finance Sino-Japanese trade under the Long-Term Trade Agreement.

Differences over the currencies (and to lesser extent interest rates), to be used in deferred-payment credits on Japanese exports to China, are not expected to affect the implementation of the Long-Term Agreement itself, given China's concrete commitment to buy a fixed value of plant orders from Japan over the eight-year period. Orders over and above the limit set in the agreement could, however, be diverted elsewhere if China remains dissatisfied with Japanese credit terms; indeed, Japanese exporters cited currency problems as the reasons why orders for two medium-sized plants— a 7 billion yen synthetic-alcohol plant and a 15 billion yen high-pressure polyethylene plant—were diverted to West Germany in the summer of 1978, after negotiations with Japanese suppliers had reached an advanced stage.

Summary of future prospects
Most Japanese analysts believed up to the summer of 1978 that Japan's share of China's total foreign trade would continue to grow rapidly into the early eighties, perhaps reaching as much as 35 per cent of the total by 1985. These forecasts are now being reconsidered in the light of price and currency problems and in the light of China's evident interest in diversifying its trade relations. (Competition for traditional Japanese exports such as steel seems likely to become increasingly fierce from new industrial countries such as Brazil and Spain and conceivably even from South Korea during the next few years—to say nothing of the emergence of the USA as a competitor for plant orders.) Japan's dominant position in the Chinese market would face a still more serious challenge if a major new market for China's oil were to emerge. For the present, however, this appears unlikely, although oil exports to other Asian markets are being actively promoted by China.

A plus factor for the future of Sino-Japanese trade is the probability that China will increasingly seek technology exchanges and production—sharing agreements, in addition to straightforward two-way trade relations, and that Japan will be well placed to participate in these kinds of relationships. Japanese textile manufacturers have already sold plant and equipment to China, in return for the long-term supply of finished products (the products covered were pyjamas and ladies' underwear). More substantive production-sharing agreements could eventually emerge in the electronics or motor industries.

A final advantage enjoyed by Japan in trading with China derives from its closeness to both China and Russia and its position of official neutrality in the Sino-Soviet dispute.

Despite the signature (in August 1978) of the China–Japan Treaty of Peace and Friendship (with its inclusion of an 'anti-hegemony clause', which is understood both in Peking and Moscow to be directed against the Soviet Union), Japan retains the option of strengthening its relations with the Soviet Union by means of investment in the development of Siberian natural resources. China has every reason to try to prevent the formation or strengthening of a Soviet-Japanese economic partnership. For this reason, it will continue to ensure that Japan remains a principal trading partner.

12. Europe and China

STEPHEN BILLER AND MARGARET VAN HATTEM

Part 1. The role of the EEC
by Stephen Biller

The nascent relationship between the European Community and the People's Republic of China will require nurturing and organization if the physical problems of distance and communications are to be solved. Such problems must be overcome by creating the confidence and trust which can lead to a more profound understanding of one another by European and Chinese peoples. These aims are apparently shared by Japan and the United States of America, signified by the Japan–China Trade Agreement and Sino–Japan Treaty of Peace and Friendship in 1978, and the opening of diplomatic relations at ambassadorial level between the USA and China on 1 January 1979.

In commercial terms, the firms of the European Community find themselves in fierce competition with their Japanese and American counterparts, firms whose technological, managerial, and financial strengths represent a challenge to European firms in industrial sectors of major importance to China's economy. But China and Europe possess unique mutual interests on which both could capitalize in the casting of all aspects of their relationship.

China and the European Community

Since the late sixties, numerous European political leaders have visited China to be told of the importance which China attaches to the growing unity of Europe manifested in the European Community. After its inception in 1958 the European Community was viewed by China as a 'capitalist machination.' The withdrawal from China of Soviet technical and financial aid in 1960 torpedoed economic development and injured the pride of a people schooled in self-reliance by their leader, Chairman Mao. Since then, apart from the hiatus of the 1966–69 Cultural Revolution, the Chinese have increasingly fostered their relations with the West.

The European Community has occupied a special place in China's foreign policy, a policy based on Chairman Mao's 'Theory of the Differentiation of the Three Worlds', the nations of the European Community, Japan, Canada, and Australia constituting key elements of the 'second world', the 'first world' being represented by the superpowers, and the 'third world' comprising the developing nations, including China. Chairman Mao regarded the second-world countries as a force with which to unite in the struggle against superpower hegemony. In October 1970 he said, 'We should win over these countries, such as Britain, France, and West Germany.' At the National People's Congress in Peking in January 1975, Prime Minister Zhou Enlai declared, 'We are helping the countries of western Europe in their efforts to achieve unity.'

China has followed with interest the development of the European Community, reporting the decisions of the meetings of the European Council in the New China News Agency and supporting the unique partnership which is evolving in the Lomé Convention, binding the European Community and the developing countries of Africa, the Pacific, and the Caribbean. The interest of China in the European Community was reflected in the diplomatic contacts between the Chinese Embassy in Brussels and the European Commission, beginning with informal contacts between Chinese diplomats accredited to the Belgium and European Commission officials, followed by the accreditation of a New China News Agency correspondent in October 1973.

Apart from the political importance which China attaches to the European Community, technical matters contributed to a strengthening of contacts. Bilateral trade agreements between member states and China expired at the end of 1974, in accordance with previous decisions on the creation of a common trade policy in the European Community. In November 1974, the European Commission sent a memorandum to China, and to other state trading countries, together with an outline agreement setting down the broad guidelines which might serve as a basis for the negotiation of a subsequent trade agreement between China and the European Community.

Early in 1975, the Chinese government announced its decision to establish diplomatic relations with the European Community at ambassadorial level. At the same time, Chinese ministers stated their intention of considering favourably the proposal to negotiate a trade agreement, suitable to both parties, which would replace the expired or expiring bilateral agreements. In September 1975, Mr Li Lien-pi presented his credentials to the President of the Council of Ministers, and to the President of the European Commission, as the first Ambassador of the People's Republic of China to the European Community. However, by the spring of 1979, the European Community had still not reciprocated by appointing a European Community delegation to Peking.

In February 1977, the second Chinese ambassador to the European Community, Mr Huan Hsiang, said that China was ready to continue exploratory talks concerning the conclusion of a trade agreement. Discussions then took place in Brussels. In March 1977, China invited European Commission officials to pursue the discussions in July, in Peking, with officials of the Ministry of Foreign Trade. During their meetings, Chinese officials stressed the importance to China of a strong European Community and their determination to continue negotiations with a view to concluding an agreement. This was eventually signed in April 1978, and came into force on 1 June 1978. It took the form of a non-preferential trade agreement lasting five years.

The role of European firms

Since Chairman Mao's death in 1976 and the accession of a pragmatic leadership bent on modernization, the Chinese people have been asked to attain a degree of industrialization by the third millenium which took the nations of Europe more than 100 years. In a country endowed with over 900 million souls, such industrialization will only be achieved by the most methodical organization. Industrialization of this magnitude by the Chinese people, within their chosen timescale, will require unique working and financial arrangements by commercial enterprises and other institutions of the European Community, if these enterprises are to prosper while helping the Chinese people to prosper.

Some large firms, particularly those possessing a unique technology, are capable of meeting China's needs by direct negotiation with Chinese enterprises and appropriate officials. Other large firms and nationalized undertakings, particularly those which possess competitive technologies or products, can approach Chinese enterprises individually, possibly seeking advantageous financial arrangements supported by their national government. Such firms are likely to find themselves embattled with US and Japanese firms, a competitive situation which is obviously attractive to the buyer. How very much more satisfactory it would be for such European Community firms if they formed working parties, together with their Chinese counterparts, under the sympathetic political umbrella of one of the Community's institutions, to gain a larger share of the Chinese market.

Chinese officials have pointed out privately that if an offer by a European firm is commercially and technically similar to that offered by non-European competitors, the European firm will be favoured for political reasons. How many business leaders in the European Community are aware of this potential additional strength hidden in their bargaining locker? How many Japanese and US firms are contemplating the establishment of associate enterprises with Community firms, based in the European Community, for the purpose of entering the China market through the European door? If the final commercial decision by Chinese enterprises proves to be political, then special working relationships are required by business leaders and the highest operating levels, in say, the European Commission.

Small and medium firms are potential future commercial giants, firms which often possess home-grown technologies or other specialities, and managerially and financially are often insufficiently strong to approach the Chinese market. There is a need to provide a China Bureau for such firms, housed possibly in the European Commission, so that their Chinese market potential might be given the right support, circulation to appropriate Chinese enterprises and financial backing if necessary.

But most importantly, China must be capable of selling to the European Community. Europeans should consider what Europe needs and how to aid China in marketing and selling.

Evolution of the European Community—China Trade Agreement
In order to prepare the European Commission for the Trade Agreement, the European Parliament's Committee on External Relations drafted a report on economic and trade relations between the European Community and the People's Republic of China. The report and motion for resolution were debated and unanimously approved by the European Parliament in July 1977, more than two months before the Commission sought a negotiating mandate from the Council of Ministers.

The agreement to be concluded with China, it said, should be used not only to settle the technical trade and customs problems contained in the outline agreement, but also to provide a framework for a progressive and pragmatic development of economic relations between the parties. It recommended setting up a highly flexible structure for contacts between the signatories, so that a regular assessment could be made of the working of the agreement and the prospects for the cooperation of European technology in China's development. It suggested that, for this purpose, the agreement could be based on the accord concluded by the Community with Canada in 1976, which gives a joint cooperation committee wider powers to facilitate economic and trade cooperation between the parties.

During the debate on the report by Members of the European Parliament, new proposals were discussed. These included:

1. A European investment bank, commercial, and merchant banks to raise jointly the finance needed to implement substantial projects.
2. European capital to be allowed to play a part in assisting the development of the Chinese economy.
3. Reciprocity in the acknowledgement and use of intellectual property such as royalties.
4. Arrangements to enable Chinese enterprises to meet the needs of Community firms for strategic raw materials.
5. A standing conference on the development of the economic and commercial relationship, comprising Chinese ministerial and official representa-

tives, the chairmen and overseas directors of large companies, financial experts, Commission and Council representatives, and possibly nominees of the European Parliament and of the Economic and Social Committee, with subordinate industrial sectoral conferences.
6. The establishment of a Community delegation in Peking (there is already a Community delegation in Washington).

Contributions by Members of the European Parliament are often based on consultations with interested bodies and individuals. However, only much later did the fact emerge that, when drawing up its agreement with China, the Commission had not consulted industry and those specialized organizations concerned with fostering trade with the People's Republic. It was hardly surprising that the final text of the agreement was of little practical value to businessmen and contained few of the European Parliament's suggestions. However, there are some redeeming features in the agreement, for example:

–Article 6 calls for economic and industrial exchanges and visits.
–Article 8 of the agreement specifies that payment for transactions shall be made in the currencies of member states, in renminbi or any convertible currency accepted by the two parties. The acceptance of the renminbi as an international trading currency introduces an additional currency to the international money markets, one which will play a greater role as China's economy gathers strength.
–Article 9 envisages the establishment of a Joint Committee for Trade, comprising representatives of the European Community and of China, meeting annually to monitor the implementation of the agreement, and among other things to make recommendations 'that may help the objectives of this agreement', that is to say, the creation of conditions favouring trade. It also laid down the establishment of working parties to assist it in its work.

Implementing a trade agreement with China

Consideration of the right mechanisms to implement a trade agreement requires some familiarity with the 'nuts and bolts' of overseas marketing and selling. Businesses are concerned with cash flow and profit within an identifiable timescale. For many firms, large and small, China has represented a market with longer-term potential, but always a market in which they wanted a share. But they were unlikely to put a greater proportion of their commercial nest eggs in the Chinese basket, without a clearly under stood method for winning a place in it. The Trade Agreement should have enabled effective use of the political advantage—their Europeanness. European firms look jealously at the very efficient instrument for fostering trade with China that the Japanese have achieved (see Chapter 11, on China's trade with Japan). The Japan–China Long-Term Trade Agreement, was signed in February 1978, although negotiations appear to have been in progress between March and November 1977, at the same time as the Community's negotiations. When the two agreements are compared, it is not surprising that Chinese officials were privately expressing disappointment with the outcome of their negotiations with the Community.

However, it was still clear, as was pointed out in the European Parliament's second debate on the Trade Agreement, that there were opportunities for community firms in raw material exploration, exploitation, plants for chemical fertilizer, insecticides and petrochemicals, modern technology for heavy automotive equipment, railway technology, aircraft, defence equipment, deep-sea drilling equipment, coal-mining equipment, computers and electronic components. Although in the spring of 1979 the Chinese began to reconsider their industrial priorities, they continued to emphasize their long-term interest in trade.

In September 1978, Community firms were reported to be allowed to open a liaison office in Peking. It was hoped that the European Commission would sponsor a European Community Delegation office in Peking which might also house the offices of leading European firms.

The European Community must compete

In January 1979, the European organizations for the promotion of trade with China convened a conference to determine their strategy in the China market. It was essential that the European Community's industrial strengths and weaknesses should be analyzed and matched to China's needs. The responsibility for capturing markets in a free-enterprise system clearly rests with commercial enterprises. They should use the political institutions which can help to catalyze business if they are taken into the confidence of business leaders.

The European Community institutions and firms need raw materials, particularly the ores of those metals used in high technology industry. China is currently a net importer of these materials, yet claims to possess untapped commercially exploitable resources in south-western China and Tibet. Europe and China have a clear prospective mutual dependence in minerals which ought to be developed, a potential source of export earnings from European countries during the last years of this century and thereafter. The USA and Canada, on the other hand, are rich in raw materials so that it is doubtful whether a relationship could grow out of a mutual dependency in this sector.

If raw materials are fundamental to industrial Europe, agriculture is clearly fundamental to China's ability to feed a population of 900 million people. The Community's agricultural research institutes, seed specialists, animal breeders, and fishery farmers have developed plant and stock of great importance to an increasingly hungry world. Some of these institutes have particular experience of farming in difficult climates. Irrigation, fertilizer and insecticide application are all important techniques in improved agricultural productivity.

There is a highly productive farming society in the European Community which offers proof of the efficiency of the machinery and chemicals which Community firms have developed. However, US firms clearly offer strong competition in this area. Agriculture also happens to be one of those unexplored areas for cooperation with China in the context of the Lomé Convention. Success in the creation of such a triangular relationship will require more Community solidarity than exists at present, and considerable imagination and political drive on the part of the European Commission, Council, and Parliament.

Many business leaders, parliamentarians, and officials in Europe and Japan will be contemplating the entry of the USA into the China market in terms of dominance in the electronics, computer, telecommunications, space and aerospace sectors. Such dominance is not a foregone conclusion. China is well aware of the size and significance of its market, and equally well aware of the dangers inherent in a commercial marriage with one particular technology or product system. China will probably protect itself by acquiring systems based on at least two different design and/or production philosophies, for it has well learnt the lesson of dependence on one source of technology in the sudden withdrawal of Soviet aid in the sixties. For example, Europeans and Japanese can challenge US firms in the Chinese market for the supply of technology to manufacture large-scale integrated circuits. In these sectors firms need only their desire for a new market, aided by an element of political guidance in establishing a commercial relationship with Chinese enterprises. Railway dieselization and electrification are other high priorities in China's modernization plan.

In addition, China is examining the possibility of investing in nuclear power stations. China may wish to gain operating experience of reactors based on US technology, or to make a technological jump in choosing the fast-breeder reactor, European development of which is more advanced than in any other industrialized country. China may wish to associate its research institutes in the research and development of novel energy sources, activities which are well advanced in Community firms with energy interests and in the European Community's Joint Research Centres.

China's leaders are seeking the modernization of their country with rapidity. It is important to their success that their modernization plans should be achieved without social, political, or economic stresses. The European Community therefore needs to consider the establishment of a standing conference with Chinese leaders, possibly within the terms of existing political cooperation in the European Community. An early go-ahead is required for the Joint Committee on Trade and working groups. These might take the form of consultative bodies operating in the sectors previously described, that is, raw materials, all aspects of agriculture, electronics and applications, aerospace, land transport, energy, steel and coal, finance. A European export bank could play a key role in operating and monitoring the financial mechanisms and rules of trade. It is fundamental to the success of the relationship with China that the European Community should play a more dynamic role.

Part 2. Countries, companies, and deals
by Margaret van Hattem

The fall of the 'Gang of Four' in 1976, and the subsequent announcement by China's leaders of ambitious modernization and development plans, inspired the same sort of gold-rush atmosphere in Europe as was experienced in Japan and the USA. As China's new leaders made public pronouncements and even foreign trips, which indicated a growing interest in foreign trade, investment, and finance, some of Europe's biggest companies tripped over each other in the rush to secure lucrative contracts, while leading businessmen scrambled to get a place on the many official or semi-official trade delegations to China.

For a short period in 1978, announcements, often premature, of billion-dollar deals with China appeared in the press almost every other day. The new preoccupation went so far that even some investment portfolio managers began assessing stock in the light of companies' chances in the Chinese trade. Obviously this could not last. In the spring of 1979, European entrepreneurs, like China's leaders, began to take a more realistic look at the prospects for trade and development. However, although China was cutting back its shopping list and its leaders demonstrating an unexpectedly flexible attitude to what some foreign companies had regarded as firm contracts, Europeans appeared confident in general that the prospects for investing in Chinese development over the next decade at least were good.

That is to say the prospects were good for large companies. The Chinese, according to European bankers and businessmen already involved in trade with China, had about as much knowledge of Western business as could be expected from a country that had shut itself off from the rest of the world for three decades. Hence, came their preference for a package deal, their reliance on a tried and trusted industrial giant to form a consortium to cover all aspects of a particular contract... feasibility studies, construction of plant, supplies of equipment, finance and so forth. At that stage, there was little room and less encouragement for the small European operator wishing to get into the Chinese market under his own steam. If he could not get in under a big consortium umbrella, he would find the going very tough.

This also applied to those wishing to buy from China. Small-scale importers of Chinese textiles, for example, reported intensely frustrating struggles over many months to make contact with Chinese suppliers, to arouse interest in European trade promotion efforts for Chinese products, to get help or even information from Chinese trade organizations. While much of the importing into Europe from China appeared to be in the hands of giant trading companies like East Asiatic, some is still dealt with by overseas Chinese with family ties. For the small or medium-scale non-Chinese operator, there were few trade, finance, or information organizations specifically geared to Chinese trade. The few importers who were doing well, in carpets and objets d'art, for example, tended to be those who got a foot in the door before 1949.

In selling to the West, as in buying from it, the Chinese appeared increasingly interested in the big package deal, such as the use of Chinese coal in part-payment for the construction and equipping of coal mines in China by European companies. Although some European companies complained about this growing practice, especially when certain German firms were exempted, many appeared so keen to get established in China that they were seriously considering the terms.

Most large deals between China and European companies appear to be initiated during trade missions. There does not seem to be much constant contact. This has meant that the Chinese tend, on their successive shopping trips, to go back to old and proven partners for specific needs. European observers have noted, for example, that iron and steel contracts go to the German giants, aircraft contracts to the British, agricultural machinery to the Italians; electric power to the French, and so forth. It also means that contact with the Chinese tends to be on a national, rather than on a multinational or European basis.

Although the recent EEC-China Trade Framework Agreement made a move towards approaching China on a European footing, it was seen from the start as a political rather than an economic gesture. Trade between the PRC and EEC members bypasses the Community institutions completely, except in 'sensitive' sectors such as textiles where import curbs (which the Chinese find difficult to accept since the EEC has a huge surplus in trade with China) are involved. The consortiums formed to tender for Chinese contracts tend to be strictly national; Europeans must eliminate each other, as well as their American and Japanese competitors, before securing a deal.

Whether this will, in the long term, weaken European vis-á-vis the others is a question beginning to concern some traders and bankers in the EEC. But the lobby for a united EEC front for a European China Trade and Information Centre, for European consortia including companies of different nationalities, not to mention Euro–Japanese or Euro–American consortia, is a weak one which those companies with strong links with the PRC see little immediate interest in supporting.

Statistics outlining the development of trade between EEC countries and the PRC show, above all, how far ahead of its EEC partners West Germany is, and how rapidly it is increasing this lead (see Table 12.1). Why are the Germans so successful? Partly because the Chinese like to deal with them, partly because they try harder.

The Germans share with the Japanese an excellent record on price,

Table 12.1 EEC—China trade (in US$ millions)

| | 1973 | | 1974 | | 1975 | |
	Export	Import	Export	Import	Export	Import
EEC 9	610	550	811	707	1422	810
GERMANY	250	120	320	165	523	223
FRANCE	74	120	137	156	373	174
BRITAIN	170	96	144	133	178	132
ITALY	62	105	90	98	145	129
BENELUX	51	86	84	122	181	126

| | 1976 | | 1977 | | 1978 | |
	Export	Import	Export	Import	Export	Import
EEC 9	1318	951	908	994	1900	1212
GERMANY	622	272	501	288	995	367
FRANCE	355	195	95	194	197	227
BRITAIN	126	156	109	183	175	212
ITALY	127	155	86	161	188	200
BENELUX	79	141	99	134	338	170

technical quality, thoroughness, and ability to deliver on time, the last being of particular importance to a planned economy like China's where production targets are supposed to be met. Moreover, the Germans, like the Japanese, are faster than most of their competitors in putting together a consortium offering a complete package deal, from feasibility study through construction to delivery of supplementary equipment.

There are also strong political overtones. China is believed anxious to strengthen ties with Germany as a counter to any rapprochement between Bonn and the Eastern Bloc. It is also interested in securing German, as well as British, French, and Italian arms supplies and it is suggested that civilian contracts could, from time to time, be used as levers for military ones.

The Germans have consolidated on their long-standing ties with China. Many German firms have been dealing with China, albeit on a small scale, since well before 1949. The German banks, the Deutschebank and the Dresdner Bank in particular, have built up a level of expertise in commercial relations with China which, apart from the British banks, is probably the highest in Europe. These banks have highly specialized China sections which make a point of being well briefed on the latest developments in Chinese trade. They offer relatively generous credit to the smaller and medium-sized exporters and, should China's leaders relax their attitude to Western credit along the lines already indicated, can be expected to play a major role in supplying finance for Chinese development projects.

The German government, for its part, has played an active role in the development of commercial relations. Its Economics Ministry has a large and highly specialized China section. Many of the larger German firms deal directly with the Chinese authorities, needing no intermediaries, but those not-so-well established in the China trade, or operating on a smaller scale, are believed to depend heavily on the government for information, contacts, finance, and so forth.

Building up a composite picture of the major Sino–German deals is complicated by the fact that many 'contracts' reported in the press during 1978 turned out to be only declarations of intent, which could take years to realize. However, the major deals and near-deals included the following:

Iron and steel: Schloeman Siemag, which in 1974 headed an 18-member consortium of German companies to build a $325 million addition to the Wuhan Iron and Steel Works (the second largest in China), was invited in 1978 to tender for what was, to date, the biggest contract available to foreigners: a $14 billion iron and steel plant in Hebei Province. Negotiations were expected to be finalized before the end of 1979. Originally, the Germans were optimistic, but the Chinese 'readjustment' of priorities in the spring of 1979 downgraded all new steel plants. Dresdner Bank is reported to have declared itself ready to form a consortium and arrange finance.

Coal: A consortium of German firms including Krupp, Orenstein and Koppel signed a protocol with the Chinese for a $4.2 billion contract covering: the building of five deep mines and the extension of a sixth in Hebei and Anhui provinces; the extension of two open-cast mines in north-eastern China; the construction of a new factory to produce mining equipment; and the modernization of seven existing factories. The deal was believed to include a 5 to 10-year bank credit to the Bank of China.

Non-ferrous metals: Metalgesellschaft of Frankfurt and its heavy engineering subsidiary Lurgi signed a contract to supply 22 plants for processing non-ferrous metals, to be built in several Chinese provinces. The deal was comprehensive, covering all stages from exploration to marketing, and covered many years of cooperation. The value was said to be several billion Deutschmarks.

Petrochemicals: Lurgi had orders totalling $850 million to build six plants, all placed with its coal and oil technology subsidiary, Lurgi Kohle and Mineraloeltechnik. They included a coal-based ammonia synthesis plant due for completion in 1982, two aromatic complexes, and two terephthalic acid plants.

Uhde of Dortmund (part of the Hoechst Group) secured a $100 million order for five petrochemical plants, including an acetaldehyde plant, an ethanol plant and a high-pressure polythene plant for the Daqing complex. In addition, it contracted for two other acetaldehyde plants in Jilin and Peking.

Space and aviation: Messerschmidt–Bolkow–Blohm signed three cooperation agreements with China covering space technology, medicine, and aviation. The total value was unknown but the Space-Technology Agreement, reported to be worth $300 million, covered supply of German technology to build television satellite systems. (The other agreements covered the manufacture and use of medical equipment such as lasers, and supply of German technology in the manufacture and use of helicopters.)

Seen in context of the enormous shopping lists put out by the Chinese in their most optimistic moments, or of contracts won by or under negotiation with the Japanese, the German performance looked less startling. However, within Europe, Germany already accounted for nearly 40 per cent of the EEC's trade with China and looked likely to increase its lead during the next few years.

Following a sharp slide in its exports to China, France was making determined efforts to recover lost ground. Over the past six years, French imports from China have fluctuated between $120 million and $195 million. Exports, however, fell in 1977 to $95 million from $373 million two years previously, recovering only part of the way in 1978. This was due to the completion of shipments of machinery under the huge Technip–Speichim deal, signed in 1973, for a petrochemicals and synthetics complex, and the lack of other contracts to replace it. However, there appeared to be strong political overtones as well. When the French Prime Minister, M. Raymond Barre, visited Peking in January 1978, his hosts left him in no doubt as to their disapproval of détente between western Europe and the USSR, and, specifically, of Franco–Soviet détente. But although M. Barre informed them that France would continue its policy of détente, the Chinese did not hide their appreciation of France's anti-Soviet policy in Africa, nor of France's extension of its own nuclear and conventional forces.

The year 1978 concluded with the signing of a seven-year $13.6 billion trade and cooperation agreement between France and China, which envisaged an eight-fold expansion of bilateral trade. Included in the deal was a $2.5 billion contract for Framatome, Creusots–Loire's nuclear subsidiary, to build two 900 mega-watt pressurized water nuclear reactors (under Westinghouse Licence), but the Chinese cancelled the deal in July 1979. Chinese officials were reported to remain interested in France's Mirage 2000 supersonic fighter planes and in missiles. Presumably, if the French wished to realize the prospects for a share in China's defence development, so tantalizingly held out to them, they would have to balance the conflicting relationship with China and the USSR very carefully indeed.

That the Chinese would not have it all their own way was, however, demonstrated by the terms of credit extended to them in the cooperation agreement. This provided for a 10-year credit line (for the purchase of French capital equipment), extended by a consortium of 18 French banks, and of around 30 billion French francs, guaranteed by Coface (the official French export credit guarantee organization). Interest was fixed at 7.25 per cent to 7.5 per cent, depending on the duration of the loan, in line with the going OECD rate for the poorest nations. The Chinese had, however, been pressing hard for 5.75 per cent, the rate the French were offering to the USSR. It was not all clear how, when, or to what extent this credit was to be used up. Future orders were expected to depend, in part, on the overall pace of Chinese development but it was also clear that the Chinese would be watching closely for any unwelcome developments in Franco–Soviet relations.

Although the Italians were wistfully pointing out that Marco Polo went to China before Henry Kissinger discovered it, Italy had been left on the fringes of the Chinese shopping spree and was anxious to get into the act.

Unfortunately, the signing of big contracts for farm machinery and oil equipment which the Italians were seeking was likely to be influenced by Rome's willingness to supply arms, something at which the Italian Communist Party was expected to balk. In mid 1978, China had sent three military missions to Italy, the first two mainly exploratory, the third making specific enquiries. They were reported to have asked for sophisticated electronic guidance systems from Aer Italia, Elettronica San Giorgio, Selenia and Sit–Siemens, and for highly accurate rapid-fire cannon from the Oto–Melaria Artillery Works at La Spezia. Little was known of how the negotiations were developing.

Meanwhile, other deals were hanging in the air. Fiat was understood to be in the process of concluding a deal to sell a tractor plant, a process begun four years ago, and despite several trade missions to Peking by Confindustria, and a turn-out of 35 Italian companies at last October's farm machinery exhibition in Peking, the orders were slow in coming.

As an exporter to China, Britain has lagged some way behind West Germany and France, and last year even fell behind Italy. This was in spite of long ties with China and numerous knowledgeable and well-established trading firms (who nevertheless helped to boost British imports from China substantially). The major problem was that in China's previous buying round in 1972–73 the British were almost entirely left out. While Peking looked to Britain for mining machinery and aircraft, the contracts for complete steel and chemical plant which the Chinese were seeking at the time went to Japan, West Germany, France, and the USA.

After Mao's death, the Chinese looked like buying heavily again from the West and trade promotion officials in London made a concentrated effort to interest the Chinese in British steel and chemical plant, railway technology, power generation, shipbuilding, and oil-exploration gear, as well as the traditional stand-bys. In late 1977 and throughout 1978 the traffic in ministers and delegations between Britain and China was intense. The Chinese expressed interest in all these sectors but it was clear that competition with other countries was fierce and it was only in defence equipment—notably the Harrier jump jet fighter—that Britain had the edge.

When one of China's top decision makers, Vice-Premier Wang Zhen, visited Britain in November 1978 and made a firm offer to buy the Harrier, James Callaghan, the then Prime Minister, replied that arms deals could only take place as part of a general trade package which would include civilian technology. This was clearly going to take time to work out, but detailed commercial negotiations on the Harrier continued.

Despite this rebuff, the Chinese remained seriously interested in Britain's steel modernization programme and to a lesser extent in other sectors, but despite a British ministerial delegation to Peking in February 1979 and the signing of a £7 billion 1979–85 trade pact, the 'readjustment' by the Chinese of their economic priorities in the spring of 1979 delayed possible large contracts further.

Deals actually signed during the 1978–79 exploratory period included the following: a $76 million contract with Davy Powergas for two chemical plants, a deal for $140 million with the Dowty Group for mining equipment and for $20 million with Gullick Dobson, a request to British Steel for a study on updating the Shoutou Steel Works in Peking, and an agreement with British Petroleum to survey part of the Yellow Sea for offshore oil.

Trade between China and the other EEC members was growing but was small compared with the big contracts under discussion with the Germans, French, and British. The state-owned China Ocean Shipping Corporation (COSCO) took on the East Asiatic Company of Copenhagen as a consultant in the modernization of shipping and port facilities, and the company was believed to be negotiating a contract to rebuild the Tianjin and Shanghai port areas, with container facilities. The Dutch government was involved in negotiations to build a $2 billion coal port at Lianyungang, and the major Dutch dredging companies are believed to be well placed for contracts under China's 23-year plant to link its five major waterways, by way of a Peking–Hangzhou canal, and to expand its major ports. These negotiations were all delayed, however, in China's 'readjustment' policy.

The smaller EEC member states, the Benelux, Danish and Irish, lag well behind when it comes to making contact with the Chinese, and in the general availability of information. Banque Bruxelles Lambert has some expertise in Chinese trade, but cannot be compared with, for example, the main German banks; nor are its credit terms anything like as generous. The only non-government organization dealing with China on a European, rather than a strictly national basis is the Europe–China Association (see Appendix III) based in Brussels.

13. The USA and China

COLINA MacDOUGALL

China's commerce with the United States has mirrored its political attitudes almost more than any of its other trading relationships has done. It has been sensitive, not only to China's general foreign policy stance, but even to its domestic political struggles. This was because of the controversial nature of relations with the USA within the Chinese leadership, at least while the 'Gang of Four', Chairman Mao's wife and her colleagues, were influential. Attitudes to the USA, whether there should be any relationship at all and, if so, how far it should go, were important and divisive issues.

Since former President Nixon's visit to Peking in 1972 and the accompanying Sino-American thaw, trade has taken place, but with remarkable ups and downs. These have reflected not only economic pressures and the changing circumstances of world trade but also the variances of attitude towards the USA in particular and foreign trade in general. While these swings were evident in China's trade with other Western countries during the seventies, the tendency was the most marked in the case of the USA.

The normalization of relations between Peking and Washington in January 1979, which involved the transfer of recognition from Taiwan to Peking and the abrogation of the defence treaty between the US and the Taiwan governments, should have eased these conflicts. Yet, the immense importance and superpower status of the USA inevitably means that China's trade with it will continue to be influenced by politics. In 1978, there was much talk of the USA playing the 'China card', putting pressure on the Soviet Union by threatening a Washington–Peking rapprochement. It continues to remain possible—although not very likely, simply because of Peking's need for trade—for China to play the US, or even the USSR, card in its foreign policy and commercial relations, by fostering or cutting back trade as appropriate to its objectives.

That said, however, the establishment of full diplomatic relations in 1979, and the gradual elimination of the remaining obstacles to trade, were expected to lead on to larger and more consistent exchanges. By the late seventies, China's need for sophisticated equipment, to update the fifties basis of its industry which had been supplied by the Soviet Union, was strongly apparent. The requirement to modernize was recognized in China, even though in the spring of 1979 it appeared that the Chinese leadership was reconsidering the ambitious plans and targets it had announced in 1978. The advanced nature of US industry was attractive to the Chinese, who had been seeking the most up-to-date technology, and in certain fields like oil exploration, petroleum processing and strip mining, the USA was probably the world leader. Chinese exports to the USA had crept steadily upwards since trade began in 1972 (though some of the apparent increase was due to· inflation), and the size of the market and increasing experience of US importers in dealing with China's state trading corporations seemed to assure future expansion.

The history of the recent trade between the two countries, short though it was even by 1979, contained some useful lessons for exporters and importers everywhere. One was the difficulty for both Americans and Chinese of understanding each other's systems well enough to do business satisfactorily. US importers sometimes suffered badly from, for instance, Chinese incomprehension of the need to get a shipment to the US in time for the pre-Christmas shopping season.[1] US exporters and would-be exporters devoted hours, days, and weeks to expounding the finer points of technology or discussing details of supplies of spare parts, sometimes without ever making a sale. Both political and economic factors caused much slower growth of trade in the early and mid-seventies than was originally expected, and a cautious view would suggest that this might be carried over into the eighties.

The erratic nature of the trade showed up both in the rise and fall of quantities and in the commodities traded. In the first two years after the Nixon visit, two-way trade soared upwards to over $920 million in 1974, fell away to only $337 million in 1976, to rocket again in 1978 when it reached over $1.1 billion. In the years of heavy trade, the USA had a very substantial surplus.

During 1973 and 1974 the Chinese bought large quantities of grain, soya beans, and cotton, then dropped the grain in 1975 and the cotton in 1976. In the first year (1973), the Chinese bought iron and steel scrap, but that too faded (the result, in part, of US restrictions). Aluminium made a brief and spectacular appearance, at $40 million-worth in 1975 and $26 million in 1976. In 1977, cotton and soya beans made a substantial comeback and polyester staple at $19 million made a new and useful appearance, as did urea fertilizer. Then, in 1978 the figures rocketed again with wheat and corn

---

1. This and other experiences of US importers are described more fully in various issues of the *China Business Review*.

Table 13.1 US trade with China (in US$ millions)

	1978	1977	1976	1975	1974	1973
US exports	818	171	135	207	820	664
US imports	324	203	201	158	115	64

together reaching $360 million, cotton $157 million, and polyester, soya beans, and fertilizer all beating their previous totals.

On the equipment side, the picture was just as variable. In 1972, the Chinese signed up for ten Boeing 707s worth $125 million. In the following year they bought eight ammonia plants from M. W. Kellogg for a total of $200 million. At the time these were seen as harbingers of enormous contracts to come, but the early promise was never fulfilled and complete plant sales languished.

Chinese exports to the USA were less inconsistent but still sometimes showed unexpected surges and retreats. Textile shipments, for instance, in late 1975 increased so much that they raised calls for quotas, but in 1976 they fell off again. In 1978 they rose once more, and the USA, to try to control the flow, began quota negotiations. Tin sales bumped up and down, hitting $40 million in 1975, dropping back to $4 million in 1977, and bouncing up to $16 million in 1978.

These apart, the backbone of the trade—mainly traditional Chinese exports such as silk, handicrafts, antiques, feathers and down, bristles, fireworks, tungsten, and antimony— has expanded at a fairly steady pace. However, the need for China to increase its sales, to earn foreign exchange to pay for its technology purchases, will probably require greater effort on the part of both governments to see that this happens in an orderly fashion. To maintain a market, importers need assurance of reasonably firm Chinese supplies and prices. These have certainly not existed in the past, either for American or other foreign buyers. For instance, in the Canton Fair of spring 1978, the price of down—for which the USA provides a major market— rose by a massive 53 per cent. In addition, to avoid disruption of its domestic industries, the US needs to regulate the erratic inflow of foreign goods such as shoes or textiles.

The events of 1979

This historic year saw at last the establishment of full diplomatic relations between China and the United States on 1 January and the exchange of ambassadors on 1 March. It also saw the dramatic visit by Vice-Premier Deng Xiaoping to the USA at the end of January, which revealed him as a master politician capable of reassuring Congress as to China's peaceful intentions towards Taiwan, for which even liberal Congressmen retained a feeling of responsibility, despite their acknowledgement that full diplomatic relations with Peking were long overdue. In addition, he came across as a showman able to charm Texas crowds and millions of television viewers by donning a ten-gallon hat.

Outside Washington, during his tour of Atlanta, Houston, and Seattle, Deng met powerful American businessmen, including leaders of the automotive, oil, and aircraft industries, attracting attention to the size of the Chinese market for technology. During his visit, three agreements indirectly connected with trade were signed, on scientific and technical cooperation, on consular relations, and on cultural relations. The understanding on cooperation in space technology included the intention by the Chinese government to purchase a satellite ground station. This was the sequel to a trip to China in autumn 1978 by the President's scientific and technical adviser.

Deng's visit laid the foundations for the resolution of the claims/frozen assets question, which had long bedevilled trade relations, and the signature of a trade agreement through which China could obtain Most-Favoured Nation (MFN) tariff treatment for its exports to the USA and, if required, Export-Import (Exim) Bank financing (government credit at subsidized rates). In the talks during Deng's visit between the Chinese and US delegations, it was agreed in principle that these questions should be settled and the then American Treasury Secretary, Michael Blumenthal, and Commerce Secretary, Mrs Juanita Kreps, scheduled visits to China for later in the spring. For the US government, the timetable was: first, the settlement of the claims/assets question, then the trade agreement with the granting of MFN.

American trade with China had been considerably inhibited by the problem of claims and frozen assets. The claims were those of US citizens and organizations who had held property in China, for which they had not been compensated when it was expropriated by the communist government. The assets in question were those of the Chinese government held in the USA and frozen on the outbreak of the Korean war.

While this problem remained unresolved, as it had been for nearly 30 years, any Chinese funds or property on US soil were liable to attachment by claimants, which meant that for fear of litigation there could be no direct bank dealings, no Chinese air or shipping services to the USA, and no Chinese trade exhibitions. While it was possible to carry on trade without, there seemed little doubt that direct (and therefore cheaper) banking services, more trade promotion, and more frequent and efficient shipping would facilitate it. In the meantime, traders dealt with the Bank of China through third-country banks in the USA and goods were carried on non-Chinese ships.

As to MFN, burdened with heavy tariffs, Chinese goods had to compete in the USA with those from other countries which attracted much lower rates. While it has been argued that in fact MFN would not have made a vast difference, the Chinese resented the very high tariff barrier. It averaged about 24 per cent compared with about 8 per cent for goods receiving MFN, and was in some cases much higher.

The question of Exim Bank financing became an important, even an urgent, one at the end of 1978 when Europe and Japan were organizing their government lending facilities for China, so as to provide cheap credit if required. It was felt in the USA that if the Chinese opted to buy turnkey plant on credit (which seemed logical in view of the vast costs involved and China's limited foreign currency reserves), they would certainly go to countries where government-subsidized credit, like Britain's ECGD deposit facility (see Chapter 6 on finance), was available, which would cut out US suppliers.

Under US legislation, the Trade Act of 1974 empowered the President to extend MFN and Exim Bank financing as part of a trade agreement to non-market countries, provided certain conditions were met. The trade agreement and extension of MFN were subject to a resolution of approval by Congress. For some years, a stumbling block to a Sino-US trade agreement appeared to be an amendment to the Act by Senators Jackson and Vanik which provided that no country should be eligible to receive MFN, US government credits, credit guarantees, or investment guarantees if the President determined that the country in question prevented its citizens from emigrating. This was qualified in the Act by a compromise allowing the President to waive the emigration requirement for 18 months, if this were thought to promote the free emigration objectives, and a further amendment proposed in 1978 made the conditions of the waiver less demanding.

However, Peking's more liberal policies on human rights and emigration at the end of 1978 seemed to have satisfied many Congressmen on this score; indeed, its relaxed attitude to people leaving the country had become a positive embarrassment to Hongkong by mid-1979. In any case, the presidential waiver was available if required, although there would have been some difficulty in using it unless it were applied also to the Soviet Union, as the administration wished to be even-handed in its treatment of both communist giants.

The 1974 Trade Act laid down that only countries which entered into a specified form of trade agreement with the USA could receive MFN. The important provisions were that the agreement should include safeguard arrangements for talks if imports were threatening market disruption, should provide copyright, patent and trademark protection, make arrangements for settlement of disputes, and promote trade by encouraging exhibitions and ready travel for businessmen. These practical stipulations explain why a Sino-US agreement was expected to be more helpful than the EEC-China pact, and while it would not specify values of trade or commodities involved, as did the Sino-Japanese one, it would usefully formalize some of the trading mechanisms.

The intractable claims/assets question appeared finally settled during the visit to Peking in May 1979 of Commerce Secretary Juanita Kreps, who signed the agreement under which China was to pay $80.5 million in settlement of the $197 million claim, a proportion of 41 cents in the dollar.

At the same time, the USA agreed to unblock all Chinese-related assets, worth approximately the same amount. Although China's chances of collecting this money were fraught with uncertainty because of legal issues and other problems, the settlement was amicable and the Chinese apparently anxious to put the issue aside and get on with trade.

Mrs Kreps and the Chinese Foreign Trade Minister, Li Qiang, initialled the draft trade agreement during her visit to China. This degree of progress was unexpected as the requirements of the 1974 Trade Act had faced the Chinese with provisions they had never before encountered in a commercial pact. However, Mrs Kreps said that before the signed trade agreement was submitted to Congress for approval, the administration also wanted the conclusion of an agreement restricting Chinese textile exports to the USA.

At the time of Mrs Kreps' visit, the US government was also reported to have sent draft shipping and aviation agreements to the Chinese. As to shipping, its unreliability had been a constant matter of complaint by American importers to Chinese agencies. In any case, American shipowners wanted a share in the carrying trade which they did not have previously as, in common with Chinese practice everywhere, in the US trade Peking insisted on handling the shipping in both directions, as a measure of economy.

With no regular shipping service, on the Chinese import side where the commodities were mainly bulk items like grain, Peking-chartered ships largely carried the goods. As to China's export trade, 90 per cent (according to 1976 figures) was transhipped through Kobe or Hongkong, picked up in small lots by feeder vessels from Chinese coastal ports and packed into containers for transport on non-Chinese liner services (mainly American and Japanese) to the USA. But delays were notorious—sometimes as long as a year. Direct shipment in Chinese-chartered ships, which by the mid-seventies were calling at US ports about once a month, was nearly as slow, sometimes delivering goods bought at the previous Canton Fair in the course of the current one. It was hoped that a shipping agreement would iron out some of these problems, though fears were expressed that American freight charges were so high that the Chinese might be driven to other markets, particularly for grain.

The beginnings of trade: 1972–74

When trade resumed between China and the USA (on a tiny scale in 1972 but moving rapidly into hundreds of millions of dollars in 1973), the two countries had been cut off from one another for over 20 years. The USA had no long-standing well-established China trading firms, as did Britain and the countries of continental Europe, who were so accustomed to going twice-yearly to the Canton Fair that their hotel rooms were booked for them on a semi-permanent basis.

Nor, at this stage, was there much government expertise to assist would-be traders, except at a second-hand level. China experts in the State Department had mostly been purged in the McCarthy era of the fifties and, although a new generation came up through the sixties, at that time they were observers rather than practitioners of relations with China. Thus, trade in this very specialized field began from zero, accompanied by all the difficulties one would expect to attend commerce between a rigidly bureaucratic society untrained in the habits of making money, and a highly individualistic, quick-thinking, market-oriented group of traders.

Where the USA excelled was in its political and economic China-watching capability, originally intended to keep Washington informed, for policy reasons, as to the state of play within China. Chinese studies in the USA had for many years been taken seriously both in the academic world and in government. Even in the sixties, and still more in the seventies, the pool of experts on China was large enough to generate widely differing types of research and vastly different views, thereby stimulating continual exchanges of opinion between scholars and government officials. Immensely thorough research work beyond the resources of other countries was done on the Chinese economy.

In 1973, the USA and China each opened a Liaison Office in one anothers' capitals and in Washington a trade promotion body, the National Council for US–China Trade, was established. In due course the China desk in the Department of Commerce, together with the National Council, set about channeling the economic information available on China in the direction of would-be traders. During the middle and late seventies, an impressive amount of detail was collected, in various market surveys, to assist the businessman and, while this was scanty compared to what was available on other more accessible countries, it was still the best in the Western world.

There was enormous enthusiasm for the new trade. Numerous American businessmen wished to travel to China and to do business with the Chinese, without the remotest conception of what this was likely to entail. They flocked to the Canton Fair, some more as tourists and others in search of a quick profit. The resumption of relations released in the USA a pent-up nostalgia and demand for things Chinese which had become over-romanticized during the years of the freeze, and there was no shortage of people to supply it.

However, in the early years lack of experience hampered trade. At the beginning it did not affect US exports greatly because these consisted mainly of huge shipments of wheat, corn, cotton, aircraft, and machinery for the Kellogg plants, the sale of which was relatively straightforward as the Chinese had decided swiftly upon them. The import trade was a different matter. Shipping delays caused serious losses as the Chinese simply did not understand, for instance, that a consignment of fashion goods had to arrive at the appropriate season or would be unsaleable. Nor had they realized that food products sent late through the Panama Canal were likely to spoil if the weather was hot. Packaging was a severe problem as the wrong can sizes, badly designed wrappers, unsuitable brand names (White Elephant and similar) made Chinese goods less attractive than their competitors on supermarket shelves.

A Chinese textile delegation to the USA in early 1975 was confronted with a formidable list of problems by American importers. Chinese fabric widths were too narrow, samples too short, finishes like easy-care and permanent press were insufficient, there was too much shrinkage, shipments were late, invitations to the Canton Fair arrived at the last minute, while the Chinese failed to realize the importance of making a price differential between wholesale and retail buyers, or putting in private labels or of US government regulations.

Many US companies complained that they ordered one thing and received another, for example a 10-inch plate instead of a 9-inch one, or a white lining for a bag instead of a red one. One US company was landed with $37 000 worth of smashed glasses broken, not because they were badly packed, but because the stems were weak. Porcelain often arrived dirty, sometimes with the dirt in the glaze. Too many expensive goods came packed in brown paper, indistinguishable from cheaper items. Silk flowers were packed too close and arrived so crushed as to be unusable.

Inadequate labelling led to much trouble. Chinese stick-on labels did not satisfy US customs. Sometimes the Chinese did not label inner cases with style numbers as specified in the contracts, so that the retailer had to return them to the wholesaler for repacking, thus wasting time and money. Contrary to standard procedure, some Chinese invoices did not show the number, weight, and size of cartons expected. Sometimes different samples arrived in one box with one reference number, making it impossible to order accurately from the sample.

Food items probably represented the greatest problem. In the early years the Chinese had great difficulty in complying with the rigorous US food import regulations, partly because they were unfamiliar with them, but also no doubt because the principle of self-reliance which operated during the middle seventies when the 'Gang of Four' was in the ascendant, must have made cooperation with foreign agencies politically difficult. Under US regulations, foreign producers of low-acid canned foods were obliged to register with the US Food and Drug Administration (FDA), describing the canning process. Not until the late seventies did these registrations begin to materialize in significant numbers.

In the early years, food shipments from China were frequently detained by the US customs. Shrimp was a particularly troublesome commodity and in 1974 insurance against shrimp detention (for excessive decomposition) became increasingly expensive. Even in 1976, the *China Business Review* reported that typically, during one week in June, commodities detained included peanuts, sugar candy, canned lotus root, shrimp, chillies, honey, drugs, white rabbit roll, canned apple, and preserved vegetable. Reasons given included inadequate labelling, decomposition, and 'the presence of insect fragments.'

The years of slump: 1975–76

Trade fell off badly in 1975 owing to the huge drop in US exports. This was the result of the events of 1974, during which a coolness had begun to settle on the Sino-US honeymoon. After the restoration of semi-diplomatic relations and soaring trade in 1973, attacks on all foreigners in the leftist 'anti-Lin anti-Confucius' compaign of 1974 threatened Americans as well, particularly as there was no movement on the American transfer of full diplomatic relations from Taiwan to Peking.

In 1974 there had also been Chinese dissatisfaction with US wheat which, on arrival at Chinese ports, was found to be infected with a fungus, TCK (tilletia controversa kuehn), or wheat smut, which was common in the USA and regarded as harmless but did not exist in China. From early 1974 wheat shipments fell behind schedule and by the end of the year the Chinese were asking for postponements. In January 1975 further wheat contracts were cancelled and not until 1977 did the Chinese resume agricultural purchases. While the Chinese clearly had good practical reasons for not wanting US wheat, the timings of both cancellation and resumption suggest that the decisions contained strong political elements. On the US side, shippers became wary of involvement with the Chinese, resenting the Chinese right of rejection at the Chinese port. In 1976 a senior executive of a leading American grain-dealing firm said it cost $1 million to place a rejected shipment elsewhere.

Although the trade figures were lower in 1975 owing to the events of 1974, in fact the climate of relations improved. Several important trade delegations took place, from the CCPIT (China Council for the Promotion of International Trade) and the state trading corporations to the USA, and the first technical seminar trade groups—the harbingers of many more in later years—went to China. President Ford visited Peking in November 1975, though there was no immediate development on the political side.

Yet, simply the passage of time and increased contact began to ease the problems. Imports from China rose steadily as buyers learned gradually about negotiating with the Chinese and the pitfalls of US regulations. In October 1975 the first US bank, the Bank of America, established correspondent relations with the Bank of China and in the ensuing months several more followed suit. Many more Americans travelled to China, including engineers who were building the Kellogg chemical plants, and Chinese engineers visited the USA for training. Some American exporters had frustrating experiences; one machine-tool company negotiated for over a year, only to walk away finally because the Chinese kept hammering down the price.

The nadir of the trade came in 1976, to no one's surprise despite the better climate in 1975. In 1976 China reduced its imports world wide because of the political turmoil that followed the death in January of Premier Zhou Enlai, and, in September, of Mao Zedong. Exports were severely hampered because of the catastrophic earthquake at Tangshan in north China which destroyed many of the trading corporations' offices in Tianjin and disrupted railway services and supplies of raw materials. Indirectly this eased an awkward problem: the growth of Chinese textile shipments at the end of 1975, which raised calls in the USA for the imposition of quotas. Since the shipments dropped anyway in 1976, there was no need at that time for US action.

An important trend became discernible in 1976, though it did not immediately bear fruit: the growing number of American technical seminars held in China at the invitation of the Chinese, and of American visitors calling at Peking in response to a request to present a seminar, or to discuss terms of an unsolicited proposal they had previously submitted. The accession of a new Chinese leadership at the end of 1976 looked like stimulating new efforts to break the logjam over the Taiwan question, and the fresh emphasis on pragmatism in Peking seemed likely to give the USA more chance in trade. After the death of Chairman Mao and arrest of the 'Gang of Four', the USA appeared to encourage the new leadership by granting permission to the Control Data Corporation to sell two computers to China. These had been delayed for 18 months as sensitive items.

Some of the difficulties US importers faced in 1976 were almost certainly due to the earthquake and disturbed political situation in China. Importers complained, for instance, of lack of advice from shippers in China: 'Sometimes the goods arrive at the dock and we haven't received a single document, let alone notice of arrival.' But in other respects the Chinese trading corporations seemed to be getting the US message at last, for the Light Industry Mission to the USA that year agreed to sell jewellery only to importers, not to retailers who, because of their direct dealings with the Chinese, had previously been able to sell to the customer at a lower price.

Trade takes off again: 1977–78

The year 1977 began with a burst of 'minifairs', the small specialized fairs that China had started holding to sell individual products like carpets or furs. US buyers were particularly active. By mid-1977, US sellers of industrial equipment were back in the market with sales of trucks and oilfield equipment, bulldozers, and machine tools. In the summer, Amoco sold a chemical process for use in plant the West German firm of Lurgi were to build at the Peking chemical works, and the number of groups travelling to China to make technical presentations increased. Six Chinese delegations came to the USA, including an important second one from the CCPIT.

The Chinese were beginning to understand a great deal more about the US market. They started to give exclusives to importers, to speed up registration with the FDA, and they came to a number of helpful understandings with a visiting importers' group about such matters as pharmaceutical labelling and inspection of US-bound textiles.

At the end of 1977 a new threat to the smooth expansion of trade appeared. The US Work Gloves Manufacturers' Association complained to the International Trade Commission that the import of Chinese cotton work gloves was disrupting the market. After hearing evidence, however, the complaint was dismissed as the Chinese were not the predominant suppliers in the market.

In the autumn of 1977 the Chinese resumed buying American agricultural goods. They purchased cotton, soya beans, and soya-bean oil and, in due course, wheat for shipment in 1978. This turned the tide for the volume of export trade which, in spite of the new activity in the year, would have come well below that of 1976 without it. China was still recovering from the effects of the previous year's political struggles and had only just begun to look seriously at the world's technology, so was hardly ready to buy complete plant. The agricultural purchases were taken to mean that the Chinese wished again to encourage the USA though it was also clear that poor harvests in China in previous years had made agricultural imports necessary.

The announcement of China's modernization plans in spring 1978 and the much more flexible attitude to trade on the part of Chinese officials set off a new 'China fever'. Already the Chinese had indicated much more interest in US technology by inviting as many as 30 US technical seminars in 1977, but the process speeded up rapidly. Instead of taking years, Chinese responses to proposals came back in a few months, and by the middle of the year the number of seminars held already equalled the 1977 total.

The Chinese showed renewed interest in US petroleum equipment, and by mid-summer two firms, Marathon LeTourneur and Bethlehem Singapore—the latter 70 per cent US owned—had sold three offshore platforms. In the second half of the year no less than five US firms were discussing offshore oil exploration with the Chinese, and in early 1979 a contract was awarded to Atlantic Richfield. Other US oil interests were involved in similar deals with British Petroleum, Shell, and Elf-Aquitaine.

Towards the end of the year the pace speeded up further. Kayser Engineers signed a preliminary agreement for $100 million in August 1978 to develop two iron mines. In December Fluor Corporation signed a similar agreement to develop a copper mine. Agriculture Secretary Robert Bergland, visited China in the autumn, a visit which was followed up unofficially by the news that China would buy 6 million tons of grain annually from the USA for the next three years, and Energy Secretary James Schlesinger, toured China for a month looking at fuel resources.

The pause of 1979

Like suppliers of complete plant elsewhere in the world, some American firms went as far as preliminary agreements with the Chinese for sales, only to find in early 1979 that Peking was having second thoughts. This appeared to be the case with Bethlehem Steel and US Steel, both of which had negotiated contracts for iron mining and processing facilities which might have run into hundreds of millions of dollars. Chinese plans for hotel chains supplied by foreign companies also hit problems, apparently suspending negotiations which had already progressed some way with (among numerous others) Intercontinental (a Panam subsidiary) and Hyatt.

Smaller deals seemed to go ahead with less difficulty. For instance, the Coca-Cola agreement, signed in December 1978 for the drink itself initially, to be followed by a bottling plant, got under way, and contracts for computers were signed with IBM, Sperry Univac, and Control Data.

On the banking side contacts became closer. In the spring of 1978 the First National Bank of Chicago announced that it had expanded its correspondent relations with the Bank of China, and could handle Letters of Credit, payments, etc., without risks of claims/assets litigation. In this, they were followed by the Chase Manhattan Bank, Manufacturers' Hanover, and Morgan Guaranty.

The first US bank to claim full banking relations was the Bank of America, in January 1979. It was clear that US banks were deeply anxious in case European and Japanese banks should secure any loan business that might develop to finance China's ambitious import schemes, and US bankers stepped up their visits to Peking. In the spring of 1979, however, despite the increase in official contacts and the signing of the claims/assets agreement, the Chinese cancelled a $30 million loan offered by the Chase Manhattan Bank to finance the initial stages of the proposed trade centre in Peking. This the Chinese had awarded to American interests in early 1979, despite tough competition from the Japanese.

In 1978, and particularly in 1979, realization dawned on the Chinese of the need for bigger exports. In April 1978, an importers' delegation sponsored by the National Council went to China and found a new readiness to accept foreign orders, designs and materials. Discussion of China's willingness to include private foreign labels on its exports broke new ground, as did suggestions of importing foreign equipment and raw materials for processing into export goods. The Chinese side showed a much greater willingness to comply with US government regulations on imports and there was a much greater exchange of information. At the Canton Fair that spring there was considerable discussion of buy-back and barter deals, and contracts for linked purchases were signed.

By the end of 1978 US firms were showing interest in the new Chinese proposals for joint ventures, which the Chinese were clearly viewing as a less expensive way of raising the technical level in China and of speeding up the output of export goods. But Peking was still working on a commercial code to satisfy foreign investors, and by mid-1979 only the basic principles seemed to have been decided.

Joint ventures looked likely to be an important feature of the future development of Sino-US trade, along with greater consideration on the Chinese side of the needs of US buyers. While Peking had become more cautious about its expenditure on foreign technology during 1979, a proportion of projects seemed certain to go ahead, and for them foreign exchange would be required. Even with credits, which the Chinese accepted although by mid-1979 they had not drawn on them, China would still need to boost exports to pay off the loans in due course. But the expansion of sales abroad was not easy for a country whose main products were textiles and other light industry goods, plus minerals, the development of which still needed much investment.

Thus, while the future looked promising from the point of view of increased contacts and better government-to-government relations, it seemed that it would need both ingenuity and goodwill on both sides to push up trade substantially. With a world-wide choice of eager potential suppliers for industrial goods, the Chinese were under no compulsion to buy from the USA. A friendly political attitude and readiness to buy on the part of the USA seemed likely to be influential factors in the future successful development of trade.

Appendix I
Going to China[1]

Travel

The PRC may be reached by the following international air services: Japan Air Lines, Pakistan International, Ethiopian, and Iran Air, each twice weekly to Peking, and Swissair, Aeroflot, Tarom, and Air France, once a week; Swissair, Pakistan International, and Japan Air Lines, once a week to Shanghai. The Chinese airline, CAAC, serves Tokyo, Moscow, Paris, Tehran, Karachi, and Bucharest. Regular CAAC flights from Hongkong to Guangzhou (Canton) began during the Fall 1978 Fair, thus ending the necessity of travelling by train to reach the Fair. In addition, in November 1978 a hovercraft service from Hongkong to Canton was initiated.

Visas

Visa applications may be made through the nearest Chinese Embassy (normally allow 3 days for receipt) or through the China Travel Service (CTS) in Hongkong or Kowloon (normally allow 4 days for receipt). Two copies of the visa form and four passport-sized photos are required.

To obtain a visa for a business visit, an invitation from a corporation or other government entity is usually required. Persons who have applied for visas and have not received them prior to arrival in Hongkong should produce evidence that their visit has the concurrence of an official organization in China. Without such evidence, an invitation from the appropriate Chinese authorities must be negotiated, a process that could take considerable time.

1. Much of the information in these appendices is based on *Doing Business with China*, published by the US Department of Commerce, 1978, and is reproduced by permission.

Currency regulations

The China Travel Service in Hongkong or the inbound airline provide forms for declaring personal effects such as calculators, watches, jewellery, and other items of value, in addition to the amounts of foreign currency (including traveller's cheques) taken into China. This declaration is necessary for the exchange of traveller's cheques or cash into Chinese currency.

Foreign currency may be changed by the People's Bank of China located in the customs building at the border, in hotels, or on the Hongkong-to-Canton train. Receipts for these transactions must be kept and turned in upon departure.

Personal and prohibited items

Personal items essential to the visitor during the trip may be brought into China in reasonable quantity. Small amounts of medicines, up to four bottles of foreign spirits, and up to 600 cigarettes may be brought in for personal consumption. Visitors may also receive medicines, spirits, or cigarettes through the mail, but the total value each time should not exceed 50 RMB; for visitors from Hongkong and Macao the amount should not exceed 20 RMB.

Visitors may bring in a typewriter, a tape recorder, a film projector, a copying machine, and similar items necessary for conducting business in China. Such items will be exempt from customs duties if taken out of China on departure.

Certain items are prohibited entry into China including Chinese national currency, lottery or raffle tickets, and any books, journals, films, and tapes, which would be harmful to or cast aspersion on Chinese politics, culture and morals. Such items are subject to confiscation before entry.

Travel facilities

Domestic air service consists of regular CAAC air flights within China. Trains are comfortable and efficient, although long distances may be involved. It takes 24 hours from Canton to Shanghai, and 36 hours from Canton to Peking. Within the cities, taxis are available. The fare is usually 60 fen per kilometer but can vary. There is a minimum charge for 2 kilometers. Since it is impossible to hail a taxi from the street, it is advisable to keep one's taxi for short shopping trips, or arrange with the hotel to be met by one after meetings. In Canton and Peking restaurants will call taxis for their patrons.

Accommodation

Reservations can be made through Luxingshe (China International Travel Service), but frequently the host organization in China selects one's hotel.

Hotels are the Xin Chiao and the Peking Hotel in Peking; the Peace Hotel, Qing Chiang, and Shanghai Mansions in Shanghai; and the Dong Fang Hotel in Canton. Most offer rooms with bath or shower.

Hotels in Peking cost approximately 50 RMB per day, and those outside Peking 20–25 RMB daily.

Restaurants

All hotels for foreigners offer both Western and Chinese food. There are many fine restaurants in Peking including: the Large Beijing Duck, the Small Beijing Duck, the Capital, the Minorities, and a Mongolian restaurant in the Bei Hai Park (see Appendix 4). In Canton there are the North Garden (Pei Yuan), South Garden (Nan Yuan), Riverside (Pang Qi), Moslem (Hui Min), and Floating Restaurant. When taking a party to a restaurant, some meals may need to be ordered 12 to 24 hours in advance to allow for proper preparation. Hotels and Luxingshe can recommend good restaurants.

Sightseeing and entertainment

Enquiries may be made of the host organization, the sponsoring trade corporation, or Luxingshe concerning visits to places of historical interest. Some of the more popular are:

Peking   The Forbidden City, Temple of Heaven, the Summer Palace, the Valley of the Ming Tombs, and the Great Wall.

Canton   Cultural Park, Island of Sha Mien, Cung Hua Hot Springs, and Martyrs Memorial Park.

There are frequent performances of the Chinese national opera, ballets, and theatre groups, as well as sporting demonstrations. In addition, trips to nearby communes and factories can be arranged. Cars with drivers and guides may be hired through Luxingshe.

Generally, the initiative for entertainment should be left to the Chinese officials. Business visitors normally find it difficult to reciprocate. However, when one is entertained at a banquet, it is acceptable and often desirable to host a 'return' banquet before departing for home. Normally the Chinese will provide assistance in arranging for the return banquet.

Social customs

In China, the family name is always mentioned first. Thus, Wang Fuming should be addressed as Mr Wang.

Normally a visitor will be invited to dinner at a restaurant during his stay, most often by the organization that is sponsoring his visit. Dinner usually begins about 6.30 or 7 p.m. The guest should arrive on time or a little early. The host normally toasts his guest at an early stage in the meal with the guest reciprocating after a short interval. The usual procedure is to leave shortly after the meal is finished. The guest makes the first move to depart.

Tipping is forbidden. However, it is appropriate to thank the hotel staff and other service people for their efforts on your behalf. Generally, gifts should be of nominal value and presented to the host group; individual gifts are not necessary although little mementos of the occasion may be appreciated.

It is customary to present business cards, and it is helpful if one side is printed in Chinese. Presentation of cards may not be reciprocated. Cards may easily be printed in Chinese in Hongkong.

Visitors should conduct themselves with restraint and refrain from loud boisterous actions.

Photography

Generally photographs are allowed although the Chinese may exhibit sensitivity to shots of airports, bridges, ports and the like, or anything of military significance. If there is doubt as to the suitability of the subject, consult your tourist guide or a Chinese official before taking the picture. The Chinese generally allow undeveloped film to be taken out of the PRC, but reserve the right to make exceptions, and occasionally do.

Only certain brands of film can be processed in China: Kodacolor (negative), Agfa Color and Sakura (both positive and negative). Fuji Color (negative only), and Ektachrome (positive only).

Dress

It is cold in Peking from December to March and visitors are advised to dress warmly. Since offices are not heated to levels most Westerners are accustomed to, sweaters may provide real comfort. In the summer in north China and during the greater part of the year in the south, tropical or lightweight clothing may be worn. Visitors to the Canton Fair dress informally in open-necked sports shirts and lightweight trousers. Women will probably feel most comfortable wearing trousersuits or slacks. A lightweight pullover may be useful in the evening. It is also advisable to take cool, comfortable footwear, a lightweight hat, and mosquito repellent.

Climate

In north China the temperature ranges from 5°F in January to 104° in July and August. Exceedingly dry and dusty for most of the year, Peking becomes rather humid during the rainy season of July and August. South China is subtropical and fairly hot until the end of October. The climate around Shanghai in east China is very similar to south China with much higher rainfall than Peking. Spring and autumn are the best times to visit

China, from the point of view of temperature. Dust storms can be expected in north China during April and May.

Language
Chinese (also called Mandarin, Guo Yu, and Pu Tung Hua—common speech) is the national language, although several other dialects are frequently used, especially Cantonese in the south. The written language is uniform. Business visitors will find that the people with whom they negotiate either speak English or will have interpreters available. Luxingshe can advise business visitors on reliable translation services.

Time
All of China including Hongkong is on Peking time.

Public holidays
Official public holidays are 1 January—New Year, 1 May—Labour Day, 1, 2 October—National Days. The 3-day Spring Festival (Chinese New Year) occurs in January or February, varying from year to year.

Hours of business
Government offices and corporations are open from 8 a.m. to noon and from 2 to 6 p.m. Monday through Saturday (with minor variations during the cold and hot seasons). Sunday is treated as a holiday. Appointments are rarely made before 9 a.m., and it is not advisable to seek a Friday afternoon appointment. The Chinese negotiate both in the morning and the afternoon. Business discussions tend to last longer than in the West.

Shops are open from 9 a.m. to 7 p.m. everyday including Sunday. 'Friendship Stores,' for foreigners only, are located in major cities and carry a wide variety of Chinese goods, especially arts and crafts.

Weights and measures
Most of the PRC's foreign trade is conducted in the metric system but domestic Chinese weights and measures should be understood:

$$1 \text{ jin (catty)} = 0.5 \text{ kilograms } (1.102 \text{ lb})$$
$$1 \text{ dan (picul)} = 0.0492 \text{ tonnes}$$
$$1 \text{ mou} = 0.0668 \text{ ha } (0.1647 \text{ acres})$$

The domestic Chinese measuring system is limited to agricultural accounting and shops dealing in agricultural produce.

Electricity

Both single phase, 220 V AC, 50 cycle and 3-phase 380 V AC, 50 cycle power are in use. Plugs are normally 2 or 3 pin flat (5 amp), but in hotel rooms there is usually one connection for a 2-pin round continental-type plug. The bathrooms in the Peking Hotel have 110 V outlets.

Communication facilities

Telephone, telex, and cable can be used for communication with China's foreign trade corporations and with visitors to China. Telex and cable facilities at the Canton Trade Fair may involve considerable delays due to the large number of business people at the Fair. Telephone services to Hongkong have been excellent since the installation of a new coaxial cable. International telecommunications facilities in Peking are easier to use because fewer foreign business visitors are trying to use them.

Telephone charges for a 3-minute call to China are $12 plus tax (early 1979). Telex facilities cost $3 per minute and there is a 3-minute minimum usage. Cable charges are 34 cents per word for the full rate and 17 cents per word for the night rate. (Charges from China to the United States appear to be similar.)

Head offices of foreign trade corporations have both cable and telex facilities. Branch offices can be reached by cable. International cable credit cards are accepted.

Visitors to China can utilize public telex facilities in Peking and Canton but must punch their own tape. However, there is no provision for two-way telex service unless the receiving party is able to send a telex back immediately upon receipt of the incoming message before the direct circuit is closed.

The telephone system in Peking and other cities is automatic. Domestic telecommunications charges are relatively inexpensive. In some cases, a domestic cable to a Chinese foreign trade corporation from a business person in China may facilitate communications.

Emergency contact of visitors

If it is necessary to contact a traveller in China on an emergency basis, it is best to notify the China Travel Service in Hongkong or the appropriate embassy in Peking. (See Appendix 3 for phone numbers.)

Exit procedures

Before leaving the country, the traveller should exchange Chinese yuan for foreign currencies, since Chinese money may not be taken out of China.

Before exit, the traveller's declarations of personal belongings will again be checked. Valuable items such as watches, cameras, pens, and radios registered at the customs house at entry must be brought out again on the visitor's return trip. Items which may not be taken out of the PRC will be confiscated. These include: Chinese national money; gold, platinum, silver, and other precious metals such as personal ornaments (unless they have been declared at entry), any books, photos, tapes, or other media which pertain to Chinese national secrets; items of artistic value pertaining to the Chinese Revolution, history, or culture. Permission of the Chinese Cultural Agency is necessary to export any ancient artistic items or books.

After clearing customs, the visitor must walk from the Chinese side of the border to the Hongkong side if travelling by rail. If leaving via CAAC, the traveller will clear Chinese customs at Bai Yun airport in Canton and must clear Hongkong customs upon arrival at Kaitak Airport.

Appendix II
The spelling of Chinese names

In *pinyin*, Mao Tsetung becomes Mao Zedong, Chou En-lai – Zhou Enlai, Lin Piao – Lin Biao, and Chiang Ching – Jian Qing. Below are listed new and old spellings of the names of current Chinese leaders, new and old spellings of the names of the provincial-level administrative units of China and their centres, and the names of 20 additional ports which may be useful. The *pinyin* for placenames in minority regions reflects pronunciation in the local language, not Chinese. The book uses the conventional forms of Peking, Canton, Inner Mongolia, and Tibet. (Where no equivalent is given, the spelling is unchanged.) The leadership list was correct up to June 1979.

| Chinese Communist Party | Chinese Leaders | |
	New	Old
Chairman:	HUA Guofeng	HUA Kuo-feng
Vice-Chairmen:	DENG Xiaoping	TENG Hsiao-ping
	LI Xiannian	LI Hsien-nien
	CHEN Yun	CHEN Yun
	WANG Dongxing	WANG Tung-hsing
	YE Jianying	YEH Chien-ying

Other members of the Political Bureau.

	CHEN Xilian	CHEN Hsi-lien
	CHEN Yonggui	CHEN Yung-kuei
	DENG Yingchao	TENG Yingchao
	FANG Yi	
	GENG Biao	KENG Piao

Continued

| Chinese Communist Party | Chinese Leaders | |
	New	Old
	HU Yaobang	HU Yao pang
	JI Dengkui	CHI Teng-kuei
	LI Desheng	LI Teh-sheng
	LIU Bocheng	LIU Po-cheng
	NI Zhifu	NI Chih-fu
	NIE Rongzhen	NIEH Jung-chen
	PENG Chong	PENG Chung
	ULANHU	ULANFU
	WANG Zhen	WANG Chen
	WEI Guoqing	WEI Kuo-ching
	WU De	WU Teh
	XU Shiyou	HSU Shih-yu
	XU Xiangqian	HSU Hsiang-chien
	YU Qiuli	YU Chiu-li
	ZHANG Tingfa	CHANG Ting-fa
Alternate members:	CHEN Muhua	CHEN Mu-hua
	SEIPIDIN	SAIFUDIN
	ZHAO Ziyang	CHAO Tzu-yang
State Council		
Premier:	HUA Guofeng	HUA Kuo-feng
Vice-Premiers:	CHEN Muhua	CHEN Mu-hua
	CHEN Xilian	CHEN Hsi-lien
	CHEN Yonggui	CHEN Yung-kuei
	DENG Xiaoping	TENG Hsiao-ping
	FANG Yi	
	GENG Biao	KENG Piao
	GU Mu	KU Mu
	JI Denggui	CHI Teng-kuei
	KANG Shien	KANG Shih-en
	LI Xiannian	LI Hsien-nien
	WANG Zhen	WANG Chen
	XU Xiangqian	HSU Hsiang-chien
	YU Qiuli	YU Chiu-li
	WANG Renchung	WANG Jen-chung

| Administrative units | | | |
| Province/region/special municipality | | Centre | |
New	Old	New	Old
Anhui	Anhwei	Hefei	Hofei
Fujian	Fukien	Fuzhou	Foochow
Gaungdong	Kwangtung	Canton (Gaungzhou)	
Gansu	Kansu	Lanzhou	Lanchow
Guangxi	Kwangsi	Nanning	
Guizhou	Kweichow	Guiyang	Kweiyang
Hebei	Hopei	Shijiazhuang	Shihchiachuang
Heilongjiang	Heilungkiang	Harbin	
Henan	Honan	Zhengzhou	Chengchow
Hubei	Hupeh	Wuhan	
Hunan		Changsha	
Inner Mongolia (Nei Monggol)		Hohhot	Huhehot
Jiangsu	Kiangsu	Nanjing	Nanking
Jiangxi	Kiangsi	Nanchang	
Jilin	Kirin	Changchun	
Liaoning		Shenyang	
Ningxia	Ningshia	Yinchuan	
Peking (Beijing)			
Qinghai	Chinghai (Tsinghai)	Xining	Sining
Shaanxi	Shensi	Xi'an	Sian
Shandong	Shantung	Jinan	Tsinan
Shanghai			
Shanxi	Shansi	Taiyuan	
Sichuan	Szechwan	Chengdu	Chengtu
Tianjin	Tientsin		
Tibet (Xizang)		Lhasa	
Xinjiang	Sinkiang	Urumqi	Urumchi
Yunnan		Kunming	
Zhejiang	Chekiang	Hangzhou	Hangchow

Additional ports			
Xingang	Hsinkang	Qinhuangdao	Chinwangtao
Qingdao	Tsingtao	Dalian	Dairen
Shantou	Swatow	Zhanjiang	Tsamkong
Xiamen	Amoy	Huangpu	Whampoa
		Lianyungang	Lienyunkang

Appendix III
Useful addresses

1. China's state trading corporations

Against each corporation is listed the main items which it offers for export; not all branches of the same corporation deal in the same list of items since each is concerned with the regional products which come under its general control. Any importer who is in doubt as to which branch of the corporation handles the items in which he is interested should write, in the first instance, to the Peking head office of the corporation concerned.

China National Cereals, Oils and Foodstuffs Import and Export Corporation

82 Donganmen Street,
Peking, People's Republic of China.
Cable: ARTCHINA PEKING
Telex: 22105 CNART CN PEKING

Principal imports and exports:
Cereals, edible vegetable oils and vegetable oils for industrial use, oil seeds, seeds, oil cakes and other feeding stuffs, salt, livestock and poultry, meat and meat products, animal fats, eggs and egg products, fresh and quick-frozen fruits and fruit products, fresh, dried and quick-frozen vegetables, salted and preserved vegetables, aquatic and marine products, canned goods, sugar and sweets, wines and spirits, beverages, dairy products, rice-made products, condiments, etc.

China National Native Produce and Animal By-Products Import and Export Corporation

82 Donganmen Street,
Peking, People's Republic of China.
Cable: CHINATU HS PEKING
Telex: 22283 TUSHU CN PEKING

Principal imports and exports:	Tea, coffee, cocoa, tobacco, bast fibre, timber, rosin, feeding stuffs, forestry produce, firecracks and fireworks, spices, essential oils, nuts and nut products, dried vegetables, dehydrated vegetables, salted vegetables, patent drugs and medicinal herbs, as well as other native produce.
	Bristles, tail-hairs, casings, hides, leathers, fur-mattresses, fur products, bristle brushes, carpets, wool, goat hair, goat wool, camel wool, rabbit hair, feathers and feather products, and other animal by-products.

China National Textiles Import and Export Corporation

82 Donganmen Street,
Peking, People's Republic of China.
Cable: CHINATEX PEKING
Telex: 22280 CNTEX CN PEKING

Principal imports and exports:	Raw silk, spun silk yarn, tussah silk, tussah spun silk yarn, raw cotton, cotton yarn, wool, man-made fibres, spun rayon yarn, sewing threads, woollen knitting yarns, blended knitting yarns, grey cloth, bleached, dyed, printed and yarn-dyed cotton fabrics, blended fabrics, linen, worsted and woollen fabrics, plush, interlining woollens, silk piece goods, tussah silk piece goods, man-made fibre piece goods, mixed silk-rayon piece goods, boiled-off silk piece goods, dyed, printed, yarn-dyed and jacquard silk piece goods, velours, garments for men, women and children, pure-silk knitwear, cotton knitwear, woollen knitwear, man-made fibre knitwear, blended fibre knitwear, cotton manufactured goods, various blankets, silk ready-made goods, silk-woven and silk-embroidered articles for household use, and their works of art.

China National Light Industrial Products Import and Export Corporation

82 Donganmen Street,
Peking, People's Republic of China.
Cable: INDUSTRY PEKING
Telex: 22282 LIGHT CN PEKING

Principal imports
and exports:

General merchandise, paper and paper boards, building materials, electrical appliances, radio and TV sets, photographic and cinematographic equipment and supplies, stationery, musical instruments, sports goods, toys, leather shoes and other leather goods, etc.

China National Arts and Crafts Import and Export Corporation

82 Donganmen Street,
Peking, People's Republic of China.
Cable: ARTCHINA PEKING
Telex: 22165 CNART CN PEKING

Principal imports
and exports:

Pottery and porcelain, drawn-work and embroidered articles, ivory carvings, jade and semi-precious stone carvings, pearls and gems, jewellery, lacquer wares, cloisonne wares, chinese paintings and calligraphy, antiques and imitation, straw, wicker, bamboo and rattan-plaited articles, furniture, artistic handicrafts, and other handicrafts for daily use.

China National Chemicals Import and Export Corporation

Erligou, Xijiao,
Peking, People's Republic of China.
Cable: SINOCHEM PEKING
Telex: 22243 CHEMI CN PEKING

Principal imports
and exports:

Chemicals, rubber, rubber tyres and other rubber products, petroleum and petroleum products, chemical fertilizers, agricultural chemicals and insecticides, pharmaceuticals and medicines, chemical reagents, medical instruments and supplies, surgical dressings, dyestuffs, pigments, paints, printing inks, etc.

China National Machinery Import and Export Corporation

Erligou, Xijiao,
Peking, People's Republic of China.
Cable: MACHIMPEX PEKING
Telex: 22242 CMIEC PEKING

Principal imports
and exports:

Mechanical processing equipment, metallurgical machinery, petrochemical plants, mining equipment, transportation equipment, building machinery, agricultural machinery and implements, hoisting equipment, tools, ball and roller bearings, machinery for light industry, electrical equipment and materials, various kinds of measuring and testing instruments and meters, and other industrial equipment and supplies.

China National Machinery and Equipment Export Corporation

12 Fu Xing Men Wai Street,
Peking, People's Republic of China.
Cable: EQUIPEX PEKING

This is predominantly an exporting corporation, but the inclusion of the list of exports hereunder will give an indication to intending importers of the areas open to them for the type of project referred to on pages 5 and 6.

Principal exports:

Machine tools, forging and pressing equipment, woodworking machinery, tools, heavy-duty machinery, mining machinery, machinery for petroleum and chemical industry, general-utility machinery, agricultural machinery, power generating machinery, electric generating set, automobiles, rolling bearings, hoisting equipment, building machinery, machinery for the printing industry, electric motors, electric devices and equipment, electric instruments and meters, physical instruments, optical instruments, complete equipment for hydro-electric power stations, refrigerating works, ice-making equipment, standard fasteners, and woodscrew making, etc.

China National Metals and Minerals Import and Export Corporation

Erligou Xijiao,
Peking, People's Republic of China.
Cable: MINMETALS PEKING

Principal imports
and exports:

Steel plates, steel tubes, section steel, wire rod, steel sheets, railway material, quality steel, silicon steel sheet, steel wire, steel strips, steel wire rope, welding electrodes, wolfram ore, antimony regulus, antimony sulphide (crude antimony), antimony trioxide (antimony white), antimony ore, ferro tungsten, zinc ingots, tin, mercury, non-ferrous metals products and semi-products, pig iron, steel scrap, iron ore, cement, coal, etc.

China National Instruments Import and Export Corporation

Erligou, Xijiao,
Peking, People's Republic of China.
Cable: INSTRIMPEX PEKING
Telex: 22242 CMIEC CN

> Telecommunication equipment, electronic computers,
> TV centre equipment,
> radio broadcasting equipment,
> radio positioning and ranging equipment,
> electronic components,
> electronic instruments,
> nuclear instruments,
> electrical instruments,
> physical-optical instruments,
> electron-optical instruments,
> optical metrological instruments,
> geodesic and aerophotogrametric surveying instruments,
> electron-magnetic analysis instruments, material testing machines
> and equipment,
> geophysical surveying instruments,
> pollution testing equipment,
> laboratory instruments and appliances,
> industrial processing instruments.

China National Complete Plant Export Corporation
An Ding Men Wai,
Peking, People's Republic of China.
Cable: COMPLANT, PEKING

Exporters only of complete factories, works and production units, usually,
but now exclusively, as part of an economic aid agreement.

2. Other Chinese trade-related organizations
Bank of China (BOC)
17 Xijiaominxiang,
Peking, People's Republic of China.
Cable: HOCHUNGHUO PEKING
Cable for all branches CHUNGKUO

China Council for the Promotion of International Trade (CCPIT)
4 Taipingqiao Street,
Peking, People's Republic of China.
Cable: COMTRADE PEKING

China National Chartering Corporation
Erligou, Xijiao,
Peking, People's Republic of China.
Cable: ZHONGZU PEKING
Telex: 22153 TRANS CN; 22154 TRANS
CN; 22265 TRANS CN

China National Export Commodities Packaging Corporation
2 Chang'an Street,
Peking, People's Republic of China.
Cable: CHINAPACK PEKING

It supplies packing materials for export commodities.

China National Foreign Trade Transportation Corporation
Erligou, Xijiao,
Peking, People's Republic of China.
Cable: ZHONGWAIYUN PEKING
Telex: 22153 TRANS CN; 22154 TRANS
CN; 22265 TRANS CN

This corporation arranges customs clearance and delivery of all import/export cargoes by land, sea, and air, or by post. It may act as authorized agent clearing and delivering goods in transit through Chinese ports. In addition, it arranges marine and other insurance and institutes claims on behalf of cargo owners on request.

China Ocean Shipping Corporation
6 Dongchang'an Street,
Peking, People's Republic of China.
Cable: COSCO PEKING
Telex: 22264 CPC PK CN

China National Publications Import Corporation
P.O. Box 88,
Peking, People's Republic of China.
Cable: PUBLIM PEKING

China's importer of books and periodicals.

Guozi Shudian
P.O. Box 399,
Peking, People's Republic of China.
Cable: GUOZI PEKING

Guozi Shudian exports China's books and periodicals and arranges subscriptions to Chinese newspapers and periodicals on behalf of foreign readers.

People's Insurance Company of China
108 Xijiaominxiang,
P.O. Box 2149,
Peking, People's Republic of China.
Cable: 42001 PEKING

Scientific and Technical Association
31 Ganmianhutong,
Peking, People's Republic of China.

With the CCPIT, this organization plays a role in and may be consulted on
arranging scientific and technical symposia in China. It is responsible for
planning scientific research and development and plays a leading role in
organizing and controlling the professional societies, such as the Society of
Automation, Society of Electronics, and many others.

Some of the trade organizations have agents in Hongkong. These agents,
their addresses, and the FTCs they represent are as follows:

China Resources Company (CRC)
Bank of China Building,
Des Voeux Road Central,
Hongkong.
Cable: CIRECO HONG KONG

CRC represents China National Machinery Import and Export Corporation,
China National Chemicals Import and Export Corporation, China National
Metals and Minerals Import and Export Corporation, and China National
Textiles Import and Export Corporation.

Far East Enterprises Corporation (FARENCO)
Bank of China Bldg.,
Des Voeux Road Central,
Hongkong.

FARENCO represents the China Foreign Trade Transportation Corporation and arranges transhipment of goods to and from the PRC through
Hongkong.

Hua Yuan Company
37–39 Connaught Road West,
Hongkong.
Cable: HYCOMP HONG KONG

Hua Yuan represents China National Light Industrial Products Import and
Export Corporation, and China National Native Produce and Animal By-
Products Import and Export Corporation.

Ng Fung Hong
Bank of China Building,
Des Voeux Road Central,
Hongkong.
Cable: NGFUNG HONG KONG

Ng Fung Hong represents China National Cereals, Oils, and Foodstuffs
Import and Export Corp.

Teck Soon Hong Ltd
37–39 Connaught Road West,
Hongkong.
Cable: STILLON HONG KONG

Teck Soon Hong represents China National Native Produce and Animal
By-Products Import and Export Corporation, China National Light Indus-
trial Products Import and Export Corporation, and China National Textiles
Import and Export Corporation.

3. Trade promotion bodies and government agencies

Europe

Director General for External Relations,
Directorate General I,
Commission of the European Communities,
200 rue de la Loi,
1049 Brussels, Belgium.
Tel: 735 0040/735 8040
Telex: 21877 Comeu B

Sino–British Trade Council,
Third Floor,
25 Queen Anne's Gate,
London SW1H 9BU, UK.
Tel: 01–930 9545/930 9600

Commercial Relations & Export Division (4),
Department of Trade,
1 Victoria Street,
London SW1, UK.
Tel: 01–215 7877

The 48 Group,
c/o Monitor Consultants,
25 Bedford Row,
London WC1R 4HD, UK.
Tel: 01–405 2963

Irish Export Board,
Lansdowne House 4,
Dublin, Republic of Ireland.
Tel: 6 58 81

Dr Barbara Findorff,
Secretary General,
The Europe–China Association,
Square de la Quiétude 7,
1150 Brussels, Belgium.
Tel: 771 6977

Camera di Commercio Italiana per la Cina,
18 via Corducci,
Milan, Italy.
Tel: 86 27 65

Association Belgique–Chine asbl,
Commission-Economique,
rue Meridien 13,
Brussels, Belgium.
Tel: 219 22 35

Mrs M Monod-Broca,
Secretary General,
Comité France–Chine
31 Avenue Pierre Premier de Serbie,
75/84 Paris Cedex 16, France.
Tel: 723 6196/6161/6158

USA

The National Council for US China Trade,
Suite 350,
1050 17th Street, NW,
Washington, DC 20036, USA.

Japan

Japan External Trade Organization,
(JETRO),
2 Akasaka Aoi-cho,
Minato-ku,
Tokyo, Japan.

US Department of Commerce,
Industry and Trade Administration,
Office of East–West Country Affairs,
PRC Affairs Division, Room 4044,
Washington, DC 20230, USA.

Japan Association for the Promotion
of International Trade,
Nihon Building,
Otemachi 2–6–2,
Chiyoda-ku,
Tokyo, Japan.

Appendix IV

Peking addresses and telephone numbers

Aeroflot	522 181
Ma Shao Hu-T'ung	
Tung-chih Men Nei	
Air France	556 531
Room 4036	
Peking Hotel	
Airport	
Arrival/Departure Enquiries	552 515
CAAC Freight Office (City)	552 945
Bookings—Internal	553 245
Bookings—International	557 878
Customs	550 054
Bank of China	330 887
Hsi Chiao Min Hsiang	
Capital Hospital	553 731
(Medical and Dental)	
Shuai-fu Yuan	
Cereals, Oils & Foodstuffs Corp.	528 831
Tung An Men 82	
Chemicals Corporation	891 289
Erh Li Kou, Hsi Chiao	
Ch'eng-tu Restaurant	336 356
Jung-hsien Hu T'ung	
Ch'ienmen Hotel	338 731
Hu Fang Ch'iao	

China Council for the Promotion of	
International Trade (CCPIT)	557 809
Tung An Men 82	
China Travel Service	553 509
Chu Shih Ta-chieh	
Ts'inghai Restaurant	442 846
Tung Szu Pei Ta-chieh	
Chin Yang Restaurant	331 661
Hsi Chu Shih K'ou Lu	
off Ch'ien-men Wai	
Ch'uan Chu Te Restaurant	751 379
(Big Duck Restaurant)	
Ch'ien-men Wai Ta-chieh	
Ch'u Yuan Restaurant	
(See Hsing Chiang Restaurant)	
Civil Aviation Administration	
of China (CAAC)	
Airport Office	552 515
City Office	555 531
Domestic Ticketing	554 415
International Ticketing	557 878
Cargo Office (City)	552 945
Chu Shih Ta-chieh	
Feng Tse Yuan Restaurant	332 828
Hsi Chu Shih K'ou Lu	
off Ch'ien-men Wai	
Fire Brigade (Emergency Number)	119
Foreign Languages Bookstore	554 783
235 Wang-fu Ching	
Foreign Languages Printing House	893 218
Erh Li Kou	
Foreign Ministry	
Main Switchboard	553 831
Consular Dep't	554 687
Information Dep't	555 505
Protocol Dep't	552 642
Foreign Trade, Ministry of	550 257
Tung Ch'and-an Chieh	
Friendship Hotel	890 621
Wei Kung Ts'un	
Friendship Store	593 531
Chien-huo Men Wai	
Hsiang Chiang Restaurant	661 414
(Formerly Ch'u Yuan Restaurant)	
Opposite Covered Market	
Hsi Tan Pei Ta-chieh	

Hsin Ch'iao Hotel	557 731
Ch'ung-wen Men Wai	
Huan Ch'iao Hotel	558 851
(Overseas Chinese Hotel)	
Chu Shih Ta-chieh	
Huai Yang Restaurant	660 521
Hsi Tan Pei Ta-chieh	
Hung Pin Lou Restaurant	336 461
Hsi Ch'ang-an Chieh	
(Near Hsi Tan)	
International Club	550 602
Chien-kuo Men Wai	
K'ao Jou Chi Restaurant	445 921
(Now Shou-tu Barbecue Restaurant)	
Shih Ch'a Hai	
Light Industrial Products Corp.	556 749
Tun An Men 82	
Machinery Corporation	891 243/974
Erh Li Kou, Hsi Chiao	
Metals & Minerals Corporation	892 376
Erh Li Kou, Hsi Chiao	
Mintzu Hotel	668 541
Hsi Ch'ang-an Chieh	
Mintzu Restaurant	550 069
(Formerly Tung Lai Shun Restaurant)	
North Entrance Tung Feng Market,	
Wang-fu Ching	
Native Produce & Animal By-Products	554 124
Corp.	
Tung An Men 82	
Omei Restaurant	660 085
Hsi Tan Market	
Hsi Tan Pei Ta-chieh	
Peace Hotel	553 310
Chin-yu Hu-t'ung	
Peking K'ao Ya Restaurant	750 668
Capital Hospital Road	
off Wang-fu Ching	
Peking Exhibition Center	893 417
Hsi Chih-men Wai Ta-chieh	
Peking Hotel	552 231/556 531
Tung Ch'ang-an Chieh	
Pien Yi Fang Restaurant	750 505
(Now Shou-tu K'ao ya Tien-	
Small Duck Restaurant)	
Hsien Yu-k'ou Hu-t'ung	

Post, Telephone, Telegraph Building	664 900
Hsi Ch'ang-an Chieh	
Railway Station	
Peking Central—Enquiries	554 866
Peking Central—Customs	556 242
Kuang An Men—Enquiries	330 031
Kuang An Men—Customs	331 973
Fang Chin Hsiang	
Shou-tu Restaurant	554 581
Jen-min Lu	
Shou-tu (Small) Restaurant	660 925
Hsi Szu Nan Chieh	
Sinkiang Restaurant	890 721
Erh Li Kou Road	
(Near Zoo)	
Swissair	556 531
Room 1735	
Peking Hotel	
Taxi Service	
International Club	593 888
Central	557 461
Textiles Corporation	550 258
Tung An Men 82	
Tungfang Hotel	30 690
Canton	

Appendix V

Commodities for export and import

The following is a list of some commodities that the Chinese are currently exporting.

Live animals
Meat and meat preparations
Fish and fish preparations
Rice
Fruit and vegetables
Tea
Hides and skins, undressed
Tung oil
Vegetable oils
Edible nuts
Pepper and other spices
Mineral waxes
Gum resin
Fireworks
Fluorite
Crude petroleum and refined products
Tin
Tungsten
Antimony
Glass, glassware, and pottery
Hog bristles
Bicycles

Feathers and down
Furs, dressed (except seven embargoed furs)
Handicrafts and works of art
Strawbaskets, hats, and other articles
Musical instruments
Raw silk, silk yarn, fabrics, and manufactures
Cotton cloth and manufactures
Carpets

The following is a list of commodities that the Chinese are currently importing or appear likely to import in the near future.

Wheat
Corn
Cotton
Soya beans and soya-bean oil
Tallow
Breeding stock
Iron and steel scrap
Steel structurals, plates and sheets
Steel tube and pipe, seamless
Aluminium and semimanufactures
Copper and semimanufactures
Nickel and semimanufactures
Synthetic yarns and fibres
Nitrogenous fertilizers, manufactured
Phosphate rock
Urea
Organic chemicals and dyestuffs
Rubber and rubber products
Plastic materials
Diamonds
Metalworking equipment, including transfer machines and numerically controlled machine tools
Pulp, paper, and papermaking equipment
Ball, needle, and roller bearings
Computers and calculating machines
Telecommunication equipment
Scientific instrumentation
Process control instrumentation
Nuclear power station equipment
Complete plants and technology for power generation, steel making and finishing; petroleum refineries; petrochemicals; synthetic fibers; ammonia, urea, and other nitrogenous fertilizers; phosphate fertilizers; and television tubes.

Pumps, centrifuges, and filtering equipment
Mining and construction machinery
Agricultural machinery
Commercial jet transport aircraft and helicopters
Airport ground support equipment, including aircraft landing systems
Trucks, on and off highway
Diesel locomotives and other railway rolling stock
Paper and paperboard equipment
Petroleum exploration, drilling and production equipment
Refinery and other high-pressure compressors
Offshore drilling equipment
Power generation equipment, including turbine peaking units

Appendix VI
Market profile—People's Republic of China

Foreign trade

Imports 1978, $10 billion; 1977, $7.1 billion. Principal suppliers: Japan, Federal Republic of Germany, Australia, Canada, Romania, United States, United Kingdom, and France. Principal imports: Machinery and equipment, grain, steel, textile fibres (natural and synthetic), non-ferrous metals and fertilizers.

Exports 1978, $10 billion; 1977, $8 billion. Principal buyers: Hongkong, Japan, Romania, Singapore, Federal Republic of Germany, and United States. Principal exports: Foodstuffs, textiles, crude oil, clothing, chemicals, and handicrafts.

Trade policy Foreign trade is a state monopoly conducted principally through 10 foreign trade organizations. Recent changes: central ministries playing greater role in trade negotiations, industrial corporations formed under ministries, greater flexibility in trading practices, ideological opposition to borrowing on international money markets dropped. Foreign trade gains importance in 1976–85 Ten Year Plan. Import of complete plants, equipment, and advanced technology needed for achieving ambitious plans targets. Major drive under way to expand export production and improve competitiveness of exports.

Trade prospects Direct trade with the United States resumed in 1972; potential for US exports appears good. Apparent best prospect categories: agricultural commodities; complete plants; machinery and equipment for the power, coal, petroleum, steel, non-ferrous metals, electronics, transport, and food-processing industries; agricultural machinery; and industrial raw materials.

Foreign investment

No direct investment has been allowed in China since 1950. A change in policy is under consideration, however.

Finance

Currency   Renminbi (RMB, the people's currency), basic unit, yuan (30 December, 1978: 1.58 Yuan = $1). Highly stable; not internationally convertible.

Banking system   Centrally controlled government monopoly. Bank of China conducts foreign transactions.

Balance of payments   Peking has excellent credit rating; foreign exchange reserves (not including gold) are roughly estimated at $2–$3 billion in early 1979. Trade surpluses in 1976 and 1977 appear to have improved the balance-of-payments position considerably.

Economy

Predominantly agricultural; characterized by centralized planning, administration, and control. GNP—1978 preliminary estimate of $407 billion in 1977 dollars; estimated annual rate of growth 1952–78, more than 6 per cent.

Agriculture   Characterized by intensive farming and high yields; irrigation is common, crop rotation practised; fruits grown in great variety. Principal crops: rice, wheat, potatoes, soyabeans, cotton, tea, silk, and tobacco. Present emphasis on increasing productivity.

Industry   Principal industries: iron and steel, coal, textiles, food processing, machine building, petroleum. Average annual rate of industrial growth 10 per cent.

Tourism   Major effort under way to expand tourist facilities. Negotiations are continuing with several foreign companies for the construction of hotels in Chinese cities.

Economic plan   In March 1978, China announced a new Ten Year Plan (1976–85) for modernization of agriculture, industry, national defence, and science and technology that would propel China into the front ranks of the industrialized nations of the world by the year 2000. Plan calls for agricultural production to increase 4 to 5 per cent annually. Industrial growth must average more than 10 per cent annually. Plan calls for 120 key projects, including: 10 new steel plants, 9 non-ferrous metal complexes, 10 new oil and gas fields, 8 coal bases, 30 electric power stations, 5 harbours, and 6 trunk railroads. Other major projects will include truck and diesel engine plants, colour television, and integrated circuit plants, and a domestic satellite communications system.

Basic economic facilities

Transportation   All major transportation facilities are state-owned: more than 880 000 km of highways, 52 000 km of railroads, and about 176 000 km of inland waterways, 25 per cent of which are navigable by steamer.

Communications   Well-developed telegraph service; nationwide radio network; limited telephone and TV systems.

Power   Generating capacity on 1 January 1978 about 40.5 million kW (62 per cent thermal, 38 per cent hydroelectric) and production about 136 billion kWh^{-1} in 1977.

Natural resources

Land   9.6 km^2, mostly mountainous or hilly, only about 10 per cent cultivated, 8 per cent forest.

Climate   Generally temperate in north and subtropical in south. Annual rainfall increases from north to south (635 mm in Peking, 1905 mm in Guangzhou).

Minerals   Coal, iron ore, oil, tin, antimony, tungsten, mercury, molybdenum, silver, lead, copper, zinc, and bauxite.

Population

Size   Estimated at 1 billion in mid-1978, 85 per cent rural. More than 8.5 million in Peking City, capital and most important commercial centre; other principal cities (in millions): Shanghai (12.5), Tianjin (7.5), Shenyang (4), Wuhan (3), and Guangzhou (3).

Language   National language is Chinese. Principal dialects: Peking (Mandarin—official), Cantonese, Shanghai, Fujianese, Hakka.

Education   A significant shift in educational policy has taken place since 1977. Current emphasis is on academic excellence and on scientific research.

A number of universities have been reopened, and 153 new specialized colleges will be established. Plans call for sending a large number of students to study abroad.

Labour Working age population estimated at 565 million, of which 406–452 million are in agriculture.

Appendix VII
Foreign trade organizations of

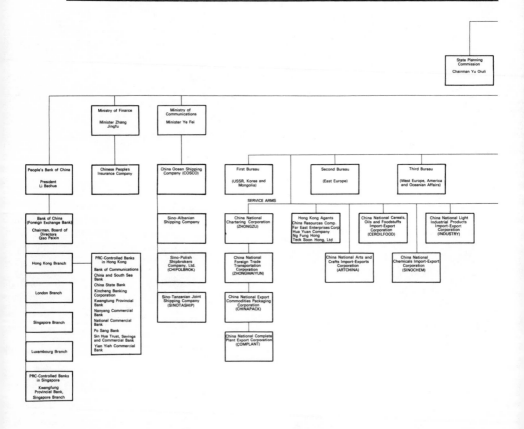

State Planning Commission

Chairman Yu Oiuli

Ministry of Finance

Minister Zhang Jingfu

Ministry of Communications

Minister Ye Fei

People's Bank of China

President Li Baohua

Chinese People's Insurance Company

China Ocean Shipping Company (COSCO)

First Bureau

(USSR, Korea and Mongolia)

Second Bureau

(East Europe)

Third Bureau

(West Europe, America and Oceanian Affairs)

Bank of China (Foreign Exchange Bank)

Chairman, Board of Directors Qiao Peixin

SERVICE ARMS

Sino-Albanian Shipping Company

China National Chartering Corporation (ZHONGZU)

Hong Kong Agents
China Resources Comp.
Far East Enterprises Corp
Hua Yuan Company
Ng Fung Hong
Teck Soon Hong, Ltd

China National Cereals, Oils and Foodstuffs Import-Export Corporation (CEROILFOOD)

China National Light Industrial Products Import-Export Corporation (INDUSTRY)

Hong Kong Branch

PRC-Controlled Banks in Hong Kong

Bank of Communications
China and South Sea Bank
China State Bank
Kincheng Banking Corporation
Kwangtung Provincial Bank
Nanyang Commercial Bank
National Commercial Bank
Po Sang Bank
Sin Hua Trust, Savings and Commercial Bank
Yien Yieh Commercial Bank

Sino-Polish Shipbrokers Company, Ltd. (CHIPOLBROK)

China National Foreign Trade Transportation Corporation (ZHONGWAIYUN)

China National Arts and Crafts Import-Exports Corporation (ARTCHINA)

China National Chemicals Import-Export Corporation (SINOCHEM)

London Branch

Singapore Branch

Sino-Tanzanian Joint Shipping Company (SINOTASHIP)

China National Export Commodities Packaging Corporation (CHINAPACK)

Luxembourg Branch

China National Complete Plant Export Corporation (COMPLANT)

PRC-Controlled Banks in Singapore

Kwangfung Provincial Bank, Singapore Branch

This chart does not include changes

the People's Republic of China

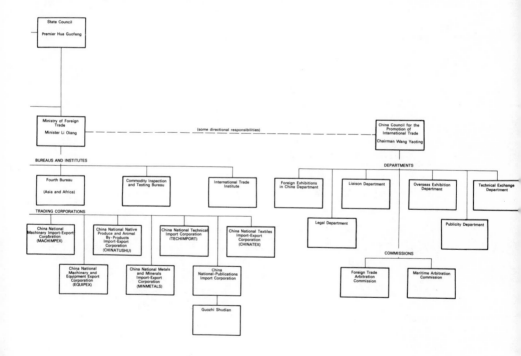

State Council
Premier Hua Guofeng

Ministry of Foreign Trade
Minister Li Qiang

(some directional responsibilities)

China Council for the Promotion of International Trade
Chairman Wang Yaoting

BUREAUS AND INSTITUTES

Fourth Bureau
(Asia and Africa)

Commodity Inspection and Testing Bureau

International Trade Institute

DEPARTMENTS

Foreign Exhibitions in China Department

Liaison Department

Overseas Exhibition Department

Technical Exchange Department

TRADING CORPORATIONS

China National Machinery Import-Export Corporation (MACHIMPEX)

China National Native Produce and Animal By-Products Import-Export Corporation (CHINATUSHU)

China National Technical Import Corporation (TECHIMPORT)

China National Textiles Import-Export Corporation (CHINATEX)

Legal Department

Publicity Department

China National Machinery and Equipment Export Corporation (EQUIPEX)

China National Metals and Minerals Import-Export Corporation (MINMETALS)

China National-Publications Import Corporation

COMMISSIONS

Foreign Trade Arbitration Commission

Maritime Arbitration Commission

Guozhi Shudian

after spring 1979

Bibliography

General

Aird, John S., *Chinese Economy Post-Mao*, Vol. 1: *Policy and Performance*, Joint Economic Committee of the US Congress, Washington, D.C., 1978

Barnett, A. Doak, *Uncertain Passage: China's Transition to a Post-Mao Era*, The Brookings Institution, Washington, D.C., 1974.

Eckstein, Alexander, *China's Economic Revolution*, Cambridge University Press, Cambridge, 1977.

Fairbank, John King, *The United States and China*, 4th rev. edn., Harvard University Press, Boston, Mass. 1979.

Galbraith, John Kenneth, *A China Passage*, Houghton Mifflin Company, Boston, 1973.

Hinton, William, *Fanshen: A Documentary of Revolution in a Chinese Village*, Random House, New York, 1968.

Lee, Chae-Jin, *Japan Faces China—Political and Economic Relations in the Post-War Era*, John Hopkins University Press, Baltimore, 1976.

MacLaine, Shirley, *You can get there from here*, Norton, 1975; Bantam Books, New York, 1976.

Solomon, Richard H. and Talbott Huey, *A revolution is not a Dinner Party*, Anchor Press-Doubleday, Garden City, New York, 1975.

Snow, Edgar, *Red Star over China*, Vintage Books, New York, 1971.

Terrill, Ross, 800,000,000: *The Real China*, Laurel Press, New York, 1972.

Terrill, Ross, *Flowers on an Iron Tree: Five Cities of China*, Little, Brown and Company, Boston, 1975.

Wilson, Dick, *Mao, the People's Emperor*, Hutchinson, London, 1979.

Travel guides

Felber, John E., *The American's Tourist Manual for The People's Republic of China*, International Intertrade Index, Newark, New Jersey, 1978.

de Keijzer, Arne J. and Fredric M. Kaplan, *JAL Guide to the People's Republic of China*, Eurasia Press, Fairlawn, New Jersey, 1978.
Nagel's Encyclopedia-Guide: China, Nagel Publishers, Geneva, 1975.

Fiction

Hsia Chih-yen, *The Coldest Winter in Peking*, Doubleday, Garden City, New York, 1978.

US Department of Commerce Publications

China's Economy and Foreign Trade, 1977–78, October, 1978.
Coal Mine Equipment: a Market Assessment for the People's Republic of China, March, 1977.
Construction Equipment: a Market Assessment for the People's Republic of China, March, 1976.
Electric Power Equipment: a Market Assessment for the People's Republic of China, February, 1975.
Motor Vehicle Industry of the People's Republic of China, by John Phipps, November 1978.
Prospects for People's Republic of China Hard Currency Trade through 1985, by Gary Teske, Hedija Kravalis, and Allen Lenz, February, 1979.
Telecommunications Equipment: a Market Assessment for the People's Republic of China, February, 1977.

CIA Publications

Various research papers published by the CIA have been microfilmed by the Library of Congress Photoduplication Service. Persons interested in purchasing either microfilms, unbound electrostatic positive prints, or more recent unfilmed publications should direct their enquiries to:

Photoduplication Service,
Library of Congress,
Department C-251,
10 First Street, SE,
Washington, DC, 20540,
USA.

Microfilm 1

People's Republic of China: International Trade Handbook, October 1973.
An Index of Construction Activity in China, March 1974.
China: Role of Small Plants in Economic Development, May 1974.
People's Republic of China: International Trade Handbook, September 1974.
People's Republic of China: Foreign Trade in Machinery and Equipment Since 1952, January 1975.

Production of Machinery and Equipment in the People's Republic of China, May 1975.
Prices of Machinery and Equipment in the People's Republic of China, May 1975.

Microfilm 2

People's Republic of China: Handbook of Economic Indicators, August 1975.
People's Republic of China: Chemical Fertilizer Supplies, 1949–74, August 1975.
People's Republic of China: International Trade Handbook, October 1975.
Value Added by Work Brigades in Railroad and Highway Construction in China, 1952–57, November 1975.
China: Energy Balance Projections, November 1975.
China: Agricultural Performance in 1975, March 1976.
China's Minerals and Metals Position in the World Market, March 1976.
Chinese Merchant Ship Production, March 1976.
People's Republic of China: Estimated Yuan Value of Foreign Trade in Machinery and Equipment, 1951–73, April 1976.

Microfilm 3

People's Republic of China: Handbook of Economic Indicators, August 1976.
People's Republic of China: Timber Production and End Uses, October 1976.
People's Republic of China: International Trade Handbook, October 1976.
China: The Coal Industry, November 1976.
China: Oil Production Prospects, June 1977.
China: Real Trends in Trade with Non-Communist Countries 1970, October 1977.
China: Economic Indicators, October 1977.
China: 1977 Midyear Grain Outlook, October 1977.
China: A Look at the 11th Central Committee, October 1977.
China's Cement Industry, November 1977.
China's Economy, November 1977.
China: International Trade 1976–1977, November 1977.

Other publications

China: The Nonferrous Metals Industry in the 1970s, May 1978.
China: Gross Value of Industrial Output, 1965–77, June 1978.
China: International Trade, 1977–78, December 1978.
China: Demand for Foreign Grain, January 1979.
Chinese Coal Industry: Prospects over the Next decade, February 1979.

Index

complied by K. G. B. Bakewell

The index records subjects, names of persons, and organizations mentioned in the text, authors of (or organizations responsible for) publications mentioned in the text or bibliography, and titles of journals. It is arranged 'word by word', so that 'Air transport' precedes 'Aircraft'. Initials and acronyms are filed as words, so that 'NCNA' follows 'Navigational'. References to footnotes are indicated by 'n' and the number of the note after the page reference.